The
Army Wife

☆

THE ARMY WIFE

POSTWAR EDITION

By

Nancy Shea

New York  London

HARPER & BROTHERS
PUBLISHERS

TO ARMY BRIDES

of

TODAY and TOMORROW

CONTENTS

FOREWORD

THIS book is not intended to be a handbook of etiquette. It is a book of common sense written for brides and newcomers into the Service.

It is written by an Army wife who has enjoyed to the fullest the pleasures of Service life and has tasted its disappointments, griefs and anxieties. Mrs. Shea was prompted, in writing this book, by her own experiences and by the experiences of others. In the Service many unnecessary pitfalls may be avoided by knowing the facts about Army life, and these facts have been given in this delightfully informative volume.

In my long life in the Army I have known numbers of Army wives whose own lives, and the lives of their families, would have been made happier and more successful had they had access to a book of this type. Knowing the important part the Army wife plays in her husband's military career, I feel that this book meets a real need in the National Defense Program of today and the future.

ELIZABETH A. HELMICK

ACKNOWLEDGMENTS

GRATEFUL acknowledgment of the author is extended to Lieutenant General Ira Eaker, whose encouragement and co-operation were largely responsible for this book.

I also wish to express my sincere appreciation to Dr. Willard Wilson of the Department of English at the University of Hawaii, who reviewed the original manuscript and offered many helpful suggestions.

I am greatly indebted to Mrs. Eli Helmick for stories and social customs of the old Army.

I am particularly grateful to Mrs. Marcia Lystad, former Official Cadet Hostess at the U. S. Military Academy, for reviewing the chapter on "The Cadet Girl at West Point."

I wish to thank Mrs. Robins, widow of the late General Augustine W. Robins, who is an authority on customs of the Service.

I am also indebted to a number of Public Relations officers of the War Department and the Air Forces, particularly to Major General Emmett O'Donnell and to his aide, Lieutenant Charles E. Trumbo, Jr.

Hundreds of Army wives, and many officers have been gracious and interested enough to contribute current information to help make this book a success. Acknowledgments are particularly extended to:

Ruth Spaatz, wife of General Carl Spaatz
Ruth Eaker, wife of Lieutenant General Ira Eaker
Catherine Waitt, wife of Major General Alden Waitt

Helen McAuliffe, wife of Major General Anthony McAuliffe
Ethel Wyman, wife of Major General Willard Wyman
Margery Haynes, wife of Major General C. V. Haynes
Charlotte Gates, wife of Brigadier General Byron Gates
Edith Lynch, wife of Brigadier General Edmund C. Lynch
Mildred Stearley, wife of Brigadier General Ralph Stearley
Alberta Snavely, wife of Brigadier General Ralph Snavely
Marjorie Fitzmaurice, wife of Brigadier General James M.
  Fitzmaurice
Peggy McGinley, wife of Brigadier General Eugene McGinley
Lucy Lewis, wife of Brigadier General Thomas H. Lewis
Irma Caldwell, wife of Brigadier General Charles Caldwell
Virginia Todd, wife of Brigadier General W. E. Todd
Polly Kessler, wife of Brigadier General A. A. Kessler, Jr.
Sue Mundy, wife of Brigadier General George W. Mundy
Lee Morgan, wife of Brigadier General William M. Morgan
Margaret Kurtz, wife of Colonel Maurice Kurtz
Emily Boyle, wife of Colonel George L. Boyle
Ruth Senter, wife of Colonel Oscar Senter
June Williamson, wife of Lieutenant Colonel W. H. Williamson
Nancy Pavick, wife of Colonel John Pavick
Jane McCall, wife of Major R. A. McCall
Lillian Weidner, wife of Captain J. J. Weidner
Barbara Ballard Naylor, wife of Lieutenant J. A. Naylor, U.S.N.
Lois Redmond, Air Force Hostess
Lillian Ballard, Air Force Hostess
Katherine Bobzien, Air Force Hostess

And last, I wish to thank my husband, Colonel Augustine Francis Shea, for his help and interest in assisting me in the writing of the original manuscript and whose love, loyalty and patience over a span of twenty years made this book possible.

N. B. S.

INTRODUCTION

TODAY, with the constantly changing conditions in the reorganization of our postwar Army, I feel that, were it possible, this edition of The Army Wife might best be presented in loose-leaf form because there will still be many changes in the next few years.

The average Army wife is versatile, however, and she will change as conditions demand. It is my intention to keep the book up to date with the current major changes as they occur in future years. The idea of the original volume grew out of the need that the author herself often felt for such a book. It is a feeling shared, but maybe not expressed, by many Army women.

What actually induced me to write the book was a transport trip on which I accompanied my husband to Hawaii in the late autumn of 1940. In the ship were 165 brides, most of whom were new to the Army and anxious to get off to a good start. These pretty young girls by whom I was surrounded were not so reticent as the brides of World War I. They asked eager questions: "What about all these Army customs? Who calls upon whom? How many calling cards should be left? How long should a social call last? How soon should a dinner obligation be returned?" They were anxious for knowledge, they wanted to do the correct thing socially . . . the way the Army does it! But how were they and how are the new brides of today to learn? Living on an Army post for the first time is definitely a new experience.

To the bride it may appear that Army people have a special language of their own. She wonders what G.I. really means and is surprised to learn that the initials stand for "government issue" and is not just the popular or war term for an enlisted man or a soldier with no rating. It may just as well apply to soap, coffee, barracks, beds or furniture. . . . Just what is a P.X. and the Com? . . . And in her sheltered life at home she never heard of a striker (meaning an officer's servant!). Neither have many Army wives for a long time!

This book is addressed to Army brides and to women young in the Service. I not only saw but felt the need for such a book, so I began writing during the voyage. I have tried to present the type of book I should have enjoyed having as a bride, and in addition, pretending that one of the brides of today might be my own daughter, I have attempted to give of the best of my experience, understanding and love for the Service to these young girls. The book is written in this spirit.

It is not intended for the seasoned Army woman, although there *is something new* and the experienced Army matron will be interested in reading about Army life in the occupied countries and stations of wartime where to date she has not lived. The seasoned Army woman has already learned the hard way, as I did, but perhaps she will be interested in agreeing or disagreeing with the author. I have chosen to write in an informal conversational style, and I have taken considerable rhetorical liberty; however, I hope that my efforts may in some way help young Army women to understand what is expected of them in the Service, and what an interesting life is theirs owing to their husbands' being in the Army.

There are undoubtedly mistakes in these pages, mistakes of various kinds, but in so far as the information is not official and is given to help the brides of today and tomorrow, perhaps the errors are not too serious. In matters of etiquette, it may be a question of opinion, and if you do not agree, then continue in the way you prefer. The author in no way wishes to set herself up as an authority. The purpose here is to offer simple, friendly advice.

ARMY LIFE FROM A WOMAN'S VIEWPOINT

Some twenty years ago, I had the pleasure of hearing a retiring general officer give a most interesting talk to a group of Army women. The subject was "The Unwritten Efficiency Report." He pointed out that as an officer chooses the military career as his profession, so does a young woman choose a career in the Service when she becomes engaged to an Army officer. And as an officer has an efficiency report filed in Washington, just so has his wife an "unwritten efficiency report," unfiled but known, labeled and catalogued throughout the Service. This unwritten efficiency report may be the means of bringing special assignments of honor to an officer or it may deprive him of an enviable detail for which he has worked faithfully. An officer junior in grade may receive the plum all because the senior officer's wife was not a suitable person for the particular post. For instance, the War Department considers an officer's qualifications, and also those of his wife, before making appointments of military attachés to foreign countries. An attaché's wife is expected to entertain, and to able to take her place in diplomatic circles. It is also well if she speaks one or more foreign languages, and an outside income is always helpful, though not exactly a requirement. She must be a woman of charm and tact, and well versed in all social requirements. There are a few sad examples of officers in the Army today (and also in the Navy) who should be holding key commands but who have been passed over. Sometimes the fault lies at the wife's door! If she is the stormy petrel type, or the too ambitious type, she may have hurt her husband's career permanently.

When a young woman finds herself carried away by the glamour of the Service and the charm and dazzle of the epaulets, she should combine practicality with youth and ask herself a few questions: Shall I like Army life? Shall we be poor, or fairly well off? Can we raise a family properly on Army pay? To what financial security can we look forward? What are the advantages and disadvantages of Army life?

Of course I realize that it is a foolish waste of time even to suggest such questions to romantic youth; yet they are highly important questions, and much unhappiness might be averted if a young officer and fiancée could bring themselves to face facts before the wedding day. It is far better to break engagement ties than to suffer and eventually break marriage bonds in a divorce court all because the Army wife could not adjust herself to life in the Service.

When a young woman asks herself, "Shall I like Army life?" the answer depends solely upon her individual tastes. If she is spoiled and cannot bear to be separated from her girlhood friends and home, then she won't like Army life. If she enjoys travel, a life in which one moves often and sometimes on a few hours' notice, if she is able to adjust herself to conditions and take whatever comes with a smile, then she will be happy!

"Shall we be poor or fairly well off?" You will be poor in this world's goods, my darling! A second lieutenant's base pay is the princely sum of $180 per month, and the highest salary that he may ever draw, if he rises to the exalted grade of lieutenant general, is $9,700 per year minus income tax. According to the present pay scale, the renumeration may not appear very attractive; however, Army people figure the rewards of service by other standards. There are liberal allowances for quarters when not furnished in kind, and medical attendance is free for members of the Army and their families. Since everyone knows to the penny exactly what an officer in each grade draws in the way of salary, there is no competitive spending or dressing. It isn't necessary to keep up with the Jones family, and show or pretense by officers and their families is definitely frowned upon in the Army. An officer's commission gives him and his family entree into the best society . . . something that no amount of money can buy, in some instances, in civil life. Don't expect your life as an officer's wife to be a bed of roses or sheltered ease, but with it all there is something mighty attractive about being a "camp follower"!

"Can we raise a family on Army pay?" It has been done, and is being done every day, though it takes good management and co-operation. "Statistics show that Army marriages stand next to bottom in divorce ratios." Judging by the great numbers of children on Army posts and those traveling on government transports, one might conclude that the Army is quite prolific.

"To what financial security can we look forward?" Everyone, even youth, is concerned today with old-age security. In the Army a retirement system is offered whereby an officer is retired for life upon three-quarters of his base pay, or the pay that he is drawing at the time of his retirement. In case of physical incapacity for active service, due to accident or ill health, he is retired at the above rate of pay. At the age of sixty-four he is similarly retired. After thirty years of service he may request retirement on his own application, and after forty years of service he can demand it. If an officer dies while on the active list, his widow will receive a small pension.

"What are the advantages and disadvantages of Army life?" Travel is considered one of its advantages. Interesting tours of duty in Alaska, Panama, Puerto Rico, Hawaii, Europe, Japan, the Philippines, and details to South American countries, with their attendant travel opportunities, are very broadening, and the average Army wife welcomes foreign-service orders. Social entree in foreign countries and association with cultured groups at home are definitely an asset. To some, the Service offers the attraction of a disciplined and orderly life. Old-age security in the form of retired pay is another attractive feature.

The disadvantages all seem to hinge on Army pay and the expenses and discomforts of frequent moves. However, the lot of the average Army wife appeared very attractive to a student officer at Fort Leavenworth one day as he looked up gloomily from a map problem over which he had been laboring. Over in the corral, he could see his wife and a group of Army women jumping their horses in preparation for a scheduled horse show. Looking out the front window, he enviously watched another group of Army wives starting a golf tournament, and from the tennis courts beneath his windows he could hear the score being called by feminine voices.

Mumbling in his beard, and settling down to the grind of studying, he was heard to murmur: "Oh, God! In the next incarnation, let me come back to Fort Leavenworth as an Army wife."

An Army wife is just as much in the service of the government as her husband, because she plays an integral part in representing the Army for good or ill. A well-qualified wife is of immense value to her husband, and although there have been some disasters when wives were not up to what was expected of them, in many cases wives have greatly enhanced the value of their husbands to the government. The government really gets the full-time service of two people for the pay of one. The wife is definitely expected to pull her weight in the boat and in every way to uphold the fine traditions of the Army.

There is something about the Service, some indefinable thrill, that gets into the blood stream, and despite all the bad features and disadvantages, the average Army woman hankers for post life. She loves the glitter and the discomforts, the bugle call and the monotony, the excitement and tenseness that go to make Army life glamorous and thrilling.

I have greatly enjoyed writing and rewriting these pages about Army life—a subject very dear to my heart—and I offer this book to young Army wives of today and tomorrow in the hope that they may become better acquainted with the aims and ideals of the United States government in whose service their husbands have the honor of serving.

NANCY BRINTON SHEA

The
Army Wife

☆

Chapter I

THE CADET GIRL: AT WEST POINT—THE FLYING CADET GIRL

FROM time immemorial, brass buttons and a uniform have made a strong appeal to the feminine sex. "There's Something about a Soldier" sings in every girl's heart. It is no wonder, then, that Peggy's heart gets static in its beat when she looks at Ted's picture in his cadet uniform; because West Point cadets are outstandingly the best-looking, the most attractive and the handsomest embryo Army officers in the world. Why shouldn't they be? Isn't West Point conceded to draw the finest cross section of young American manhood? It is the cradle of the Eisenhowers and the MacArthurs.

Oh, the unforgettable thrill of being a "cadet girl"! The morning's mail brings that long-hoped-for invitation, a week end at West Point. Life is too wonderful! But in the next moment doubt and a million and one questions dart through Peggy's mind. Clothes, the paramount question in every woman's mind. What does one wear at West Point? Peggy's bank balance is devastatingly low at this point, and the trip will have to be carefully planned and managed on a shoestring. Her roommate, she remembers, spent a week end at West Point, but Sheila is such a vague sort of person. Her best story was the one about having to take a cadet, her host, to dinner and, what is more, pay for it herself. Just how much would this long-anticipated week end cost?

Upon a second perusal of Ted's letter, she notes that he has made a reservation for her at the United States Hotel Thayer. Thank heaven for that, but it sounds expensive. Also, he mentions that Mrs. Charles Barth is the official chaperon, and that she is charming to all the visiting "femmes." That is at least reassuring, but Peggy's difficulties have just begun.

(From now on, Peggy, I shall talk directly to you.)

To begin with, West Point is rather inaccessible, unless you plan to motor; and incidentally, a car will prove a great convenience during your visit, as the distances between focal points on the reservation are quite long. If you go by train from New York, take the West 42nd Street Ferry to Weehawken and board a West Shore Railroad train. One-way fare from New York is $1.10 plus 17 cents tax. Should you take the New York Central, you will have to detrain at Garrison and ferry across the Hudson River. The timetables of the railroads, motor busses and ferry service are subject to change without notice, so it is a wise precaution to check the schedule a day or so before your trip. The ferries are rather uncertain and, in inclement weather, extremely uncomfortable. They do not operate during the winter months. I ferried across from Garrison to West Point one cold, rainy Sunday in October and felt like Washington crossing the Delaware.

By all means, get off on the "right side of the tracks"! Whether your invitation says so or not, you are not expected to arrive before Saturday noon. There is usually a review at 1:10 P.M. on Saturday, except in bad weather, and the cadets are not free until after the inspection following it. This means that you will not meet your cadet until about two o'clock.

Many visitors prefer to use the modern streamlined busses

of the Mohawk Coach Lines, which operate between New York City and West Point via Haverstraw and Bear Mountain State Park. In addition to providing a comfortable, pleasant two-hour trip, they follow a scenic route of great beauty. The busses are filled with happy carefree girls anticipating a gay week end, and it is fun and rather puts one in the spirit of the occasion to travel with them. The New York terminals are conveniently located at Penn Terminal, 242 West 34th Street; Consolidated Bus Terminal, 203 West 41st Street; Capitol Greyhound Bus Terminal, 245 West 50th Street; and Washington Heights Bus Terminal, 181st Street and Amsterdam Avenue. On Saturday mornings the busses run every hour.

During the war, bus service became increasingly popular. In addition to passing through Highland Falls, with a stop at the gate directly in front of the Thayer Hotel, the busses also stop at Grant Hall.

Do not expect your host to meet you, because he will probably be in class or standing inspection. His week end does not start until after lunch in the cadet mess hall and the completion of his military duties mentioned above. The Saturday morning trains, busses and private cars are filled with week-end visitors: college girls, subdebs, probably a few young careerists. I assure you of this: the competition will be keen; so look your best. First impressions are important and lasting, even among women.

The United States Thayer Hotel is owned and operated by the government. Its purpose is to provide transient hotel accommodations at West Point for the public and more especially for the families and friends of the United States Corps of Cadets. It is important to make reservations, particularly for June Week, as the hotel is usually filled with visitors. The rates are slightly higher at graduation time.

Cadets have definite limits in the hotel. These usually include the lobby, reception rooms and the terrace. Cadets are not allowed to go upstairs or to use the elevators.

In the old days all cadet girls were accompanied by their mothers or a personal chaperon, but now it is accepted custom and perfectly proper for young ladies to go to the Military Academy alone. They could not be more thoroughly chaperoned if they were in charge of Mrs. Grundy herself. While at the hotel they are under the direct supervision of the hotel chaperon who lives there. The private homes, where paying guests are received, are conducted according to the highest moral standards. Otherwise the hostesses would lose their source of revenue. There is absolutely no impropriety in going alone or "solo," but naturally it is more pleasant to go with a friend or a group of girls.

Should you have no hotel reservation, go to Grant Hall and present yourself to Mrs. Barth. Don't try to walk from the railroad station; it is too long an uphill walk, and the taxi or bus fare is only twenty-five cents. If you have a hotel reservation, go to the Thayer and get settled. If your cadet has not mentioned a meeting place, he takes it for granted and expects you to meet him at Grant Hall.

Mrs. Barth, the official cadet hostess, will be awaiting you in her sitting room, which is located just off the main reception room at Grant Hall. Doris Barth is a charming Army widow who has spent much time at West Point. Her husband was Brigadier General Charles Henry Barth (class of 1925) who was killed when General Andrew's plane crashed in 1942. Mrs. Barth will understand any problem that you may have.

There will be a cadet officer of the guard on duty sitting behind a desk replete with phones and poop sheets. He will phone your request that Ted meet you in the visitors' room.

This communication is referred to as "calling him out." It facilitates matters if your cadet has been thoughtful enough to give you his company and telephone number.

If time hangs heavy, take a look at the Tudor Gothic interior of the building. The cadets are very proud of their reception room and they will be flattered at your interest. The room is paneled in oak throughout. The windows are Gothic with diamond-leaded panes, and the curtains which cover them are embroidered in handsome patterns of crewel-work. There is an air of elegance and charm in a beautiful setting at West Point, where romance still remains a gallant and chivalrous gesture.

If you crave a cigarette, smoke it in the adjoining Boodler's as smoking is not permitted in the reception room. Only ice cream and soft drinks are served in the Boodle Shop.

CLOTHES

Clothes, the all-important subject! Every woman knows that nothing can make or mar a week end for the feminine sex more completely than clothes—or should I say the lack of suitable clothes? Remember this: The Hudson Valley is very cold in winter and can be very, very hot in summer. Include a pair of comfortable walking shoes and, in winter, galoshes. High-heeled cut-out sandals may be the last word where town cars and taxis are available, but at West Point, where walking is the style, these will handicap you at the start as a hobbling nuisance with your cadet. Especially so, when he is anxious to see the kickoff and you are already late—when seconds count.

Try to limit your luggage to one piece, but if this impossible, at least reduce your clothes and your luggage to a minimum. Estimate your own strength, because you will

very likely have to carry your own bags. By careful planning
as you pack it is possible to eliminate many nonessentials.

Bear in mind that West Point is conservative; the Academy
is steeped in tradition and good taste. Bare midriffs and
strapless evening dresses are not considered good taste.

Either motoring or going by train, you will probably wear
a tailored suit, carrying a topcoat or a fur coat. Or perhaps
you own a three-piece suit with a change of sweaters. If
your wardrobe consists of sweaters and skirts, and a heavy
coat, then carry an extra spectator sports dress. Your prettiest
evening dress is for the hop on Saturday night, and with it
you can wear your fur coat or topcoat as an evening wrap.
The latter usually is too bulky to pack, and lacks warmth for
the cold nights. An evening dress is a necessity, as all the hops
are formal except tea hops. A guest arriving at Cullum Hall
in an inappropriate frock would cause her host embarrassment. In a very tactful and diplomatic manner, with the
true West Point touch, he would, no doubt, suggest that they
take seats in the balcony and observe the dancers from that
vantage point.

Summing up: One sports outfit, one daytime dress of
crepe, wool or velvet appropriate for dining at the hotel on
Sunday at noon and one evening dress should see you
through a week end. Should you be visiting an officer's
family, or be invited to tea or to a dinner party, this same
wardrobe will be adequate. A girl on her first week-end
visit is always tempted to take along every attractive item
she owns, but after the first visit the cadet girl reduces her
wardrobe to the essentials.

The Week End

The average week end will go something like this: Usually there is some athletic event on Saturday afternoon . . .

a football game, hockey, tennis matches or polo; or, upon your first visit, your host may want to show you West Point. In this case you will no doubt wind up on "Flirtation Walk," where, if you are the O.A.O. or "One and Only" girl, you will be escorted down the path leading to the river bank. Here is located the famous "Kissing Rock." It is a huge boulder that seems to be hanging by an eyelash, and the tradition is that, unless you confer upon your escort the kiss for which he has been longing, this great rock will come crashing down and send you both and the whole Military Academy to perdition. Needless to add, the story is a clever invention of cadets! To date, the time-worn Kissing Rock has never toppled, nor has the Military Academy felt the slightest tremor; but not so long ago a young lady toppled off it while surreptitiously watching her sister pledge her troth to a cadet.

When a cadet takes his sister, cousin or the One and Only of his "wife" or roommate to this romantic spot, he always escorts the fair maid along the upper path of Flirtation Walk, thereby omitting the Kissing Rock. Of course, it is to be assumed that no "drag" would be so bold as to suggest the lower path, no matter how badly she wished to visit the famous rock. In the evening, both upper and lower walks are off limits for cadets.

All the girls at West Point are known as "femmes." A particular date, or a girl who has been invited up especially, is called a "drag." You are a "drag"!

If you met Ted in the visitors' room, at the close of the afternoon he will return you there; then he will go back to barracks. If he called for you at the hotel, he will return you there, and you can dress for dinner. Remember this: The visitors' room is much closer to cadet barracks, and more convenient for the cadets as a meeting place. Also keep this in mind: A cadet spends much of his time walking and drilling, so don't make your visit seem like a postman's holiday to him.

Depending upon your personal preferences, you may dash into Highland Falls for dinner attired as you are in sports clothes, or you may don your evening dress and dine in state at the hotel. If you are particularly affluent, you may invite your cadet to dinner as your guest at the hotel; and you may feel well rewarded as he appears resplendent in his full-dress uniform and white gloves. You can tactfully arrange beforehand to have the dinner check put on your bill. A cadet is not permitted to sign chits, and all he has are his boodle checks, which are negotiable only at the Boodler's.

This dinner invitation is not expected or necessary; so do not feel obligated to extend it, especially on your first visit. The cadet mess is exceptionally good, and the boys enjoy the food there. Should you be invited by an officer's family for dinner on Saturday evening, then you could ask your cadet to have dinner with you at the hotel Sunday noon. You should ask him in advance, so that he can get a "D.P." (dinner privilege) or permit for dining out. If invited up more than once by the same cadet, it is desirable for the femme to show her appreciation by inviting her host to dinner—if she can afford it.

If your plan is to meet after dinner, take a taxi to Grant Hall, where Ted will be waiting for you in the visitors' room, to take you to the early movie. It is a short walk, and he will have tickets. After the movie, you will walk to the hop, which will be held either at Cullum Hall or in the old gymnasium. One of the "musts" here is that you go through the receiving line with your escort. In the receiving line there will be the cadet hop manager, one officer and his wife, perhaps more. Your escort gives your name to the cadet hop manager, who in turn introduces you to the officer's wife and to the officer. The hop manager presents you as Miss Carver. Shaking hands with each person in the receiving line, you say, "How do you do?" or "Good evening," and *smile*. It is just as necessary for a girl to give a firm handshake, with character in it, as for a man. Of course, no bone-crushing clasp is considered necessary, even if you are in the lady golf-pro class. An insincere smile is just as indicative of a person's character, however, as a clammy, cold-fish handshake. Courtesy to elders is a sound social investment. Don't greet your hosts as if they were inanimate objects; neither is it necessary to gush. Simply be natural, pleasant and sincere.

West Point belongs to the old school, and even at the dances there prevails a dignified, old-fashioned formality which is rather refreshing after the boisterous, rowdy balls given at some colleges today. And don't think that it doesn't set some of the femmes back on their heels! Those whom it sets too far back usually don't receive a second invitation. However, regardless of the strict rules and conventions, girls still love to go to West Point.

The drags themselves, whether they realize it or not, are very closely observed. The superintendent and the tactical officers at West Point regard it as important that cadets have the proper feminine associates. The fiancée of the yearling today will probably be the officer's wife of a few years hence. She has a definite responsibility, and she should be socially acceptable. This does not mean that she must be wealthy, a member of the Junior League or "in society"; but it does mean that she must fit in. She must be poised and well versed in the social amenities, able to adjust herself, to conform to conditions and to be at ease in any situation that may arise. She should know how to dress on any and all occasions and how to conduct herself at all times as a lady. Her future in Army circles may depend upon the impression she makes as a cadet girl.

West Point cadets are conspicuous for their gallantry, their good manners and the way they treat every visiting femme, regardless of her looks, her social antecedents and her deportment. However, the latter must be above reproach. Drinking is taboo, and there are special regulations in regard to smoking, which will appear later in this chapter.

The old system of program dances is still in vogue at West Point. Each hop consists of twelve dances, and when you arrive at the dance your program already will have been filled out for you by your cadet. Make a point of keeping your engagements and dances, regardless of your interest. Evening hops begin at nine o'clock and end at midnight. The receiving line is in formation one hour and a half after the hop begins, and cadets are expected to take their guests through it. In the Army, punctuality is of utmost importance. No one is fashionably late. Should you be invited to dinner at seven o'clock, your cadet will be on hand in plenty of time to escort you so that you may arrive on the stroke of seven. Not one minute before or one minute after. Don't bring discredit on your host by forcing him to be late. *Official Courtesy and Customs of the Service* specifically states that "a gentleman is always strictly punctual at all social engagements."

Don't let it go to your head if a cadet tells you that he wishes he could have all the dances on your program. Don't misinterpret the friendliness he shows you under these circumstances. Every cadet wants the girl he invites to be a big social success, and his brother cadets "stand by" and do their best to make you have a good time. Always say you enjoyed the dance, even if your feet feel as if they will never be the same again. This is a quite proper social untruth, and should not go against your conscientious scruples; but never thank a man for dancing with you. And don't do anything that may make you seem unappreciative of the efforts made by the cadet who is your host.

When the hop is over, busses and taxis will be waiting at Cullum Hall, the gym or wherever the dance is held, and the approved procedure is that guests take transportation at the hop building. Girls who live on the post or who are visiting an officer's family may walk home with their escorts, of course. Grant Hall is closed and deserted at this hour of night, so don't expect to pick up transportation there. You might as well pile in, and share a taxi with five or six other visiting girls back to the hotel. Regardless of how many ride, there is a straight rate of twenty-five cents per person. Don't expect your cadet to send you flowers; this is seldom done, the reason being that cadets cannot afford such luxuries.

On Sunday morning you may go to church or sleep late, but do not expect to see Ted until after church. The Catholic services are at 8:00, 9:15 and 10:30 A.M.; the Protestant services are at 8:50 and 10:55 A.M. Regardless of your religious tendencies, you should make a point of attending chapel once, at least. It is an inspiring service.

The stately chapel of gray granite hangs over the Hudson like a great gray eagle clinging to a cliff. Inside, stone arch after stone arch follows down the nave in stately procession. Old battle flags, torn by bullets, stained by rain and mud and blood, tarnished by time, form a tragic and glorious arch over the lads seated beneath. It is as if the ghosts of old warriors hovered above with hands outstretched in solemn benediction. The stained-glass windows, presented by each graduating class, pierce the gray monotone of the stone walls like so many rainbow jewels.

The organ peals, that most glorious of all organs, the clear, strong young voices of over a thousand young men sing, then follows the low rumble of subdued male voices repeating the Cadet Prayer:

O God, our Father, Thou Searcher of men's hearts, help us to draw near to Thee in sincerity and truth. May our religion be filled with gladness and may our worship of Thee be natural.

Strengthen and increase our admiration for honest dealing and clean thinking, and suffer not our hatred of hypocrisy and pretense ever to diminish. Encourage us in our endeavor to live above the common level of life. Make us to choose the harder right instead of the easier wrong, and never to be content with a half truth when the whole can be won. Endow us with courage that is born of loyalty to all that is noble and worthy, that scorns to compromise with vice and injustice and knows no fear when truth and right are in jeopardy. Guard us against flippancy and irreverence in the sacred things of life. Grant us new ties of friendship and new opportunities of service. Kindle our hearts in fellowship with those of a cheerful countenance, and soften our hearts with sympathy for those who sorrow and suffer. May we find genuine pleasure in clean and wholesome mirth and feel inherent disgust for all coarse-minded humour. Help us, in our work and in our play, to keep ourselves physically strong, mentally awake and morally straight, that we may the better maintain the honor of the Corps untarnished and unsullied, and acquit ourselves like men in our effort to realize the ideals of West Point in doing our duty to Thee and to our Country. All of which we ask in the name of the Great Friend and Master of men.—Amen.

It is an unforgettable service!

Before . . . and after . . . Sunday dinner at the hotel, the cadets and their drags usually gather in the ballroom, where they dance to victrola or radio music. Others go to the polo game, the cinema, band concert, organ recital, symphony concert, or swim or go for walks, depending on the season.

If you have been entertained by an officer's family, by all means be prompt in sending a note of thanks to your hostess. Training yourself to write these letters is very important. Don't be afraid that you cannot write a good letter. It can be very informal, but remember to send it. Even the most stilted letter is better than none.

Note writing is a little knack worth the trouble to learn. Once learned, it constantly surprises one at how easy it is. Courteous notes, particularly those of the thank-you type can be rose petals in one's path socially, making the way easier and more attractive.

Of course I don't need to tell you what to write to your cadet, but whether you enjoyed your visit or not the only courteous thing to do is to write him an enthusiastic letter of thanks, showing your appreciation.

The bread-and-butter letter to an officer's wife who has entertained you may be only a line or so:

Dear Mrs. Cane:

Thank you so much for including me with Cadet Worthing at your delightful dinner party last Saturday evening. The week end at West Point was wonderful, but I shall remember your party as being the high spot of my visit.

Thank you again, and please remember me to Colonel Cane.

Always sincerely,

Peggy Carver

Ten Don'ts for Drags

(From Kendall Banning's *West Point Today*)

1. Don't smoke cigarettes when in company of cadets except when and where your escorts are permitted to smoke with you.

2. Don't park your car if it contains a cadet. (Rules forbid cadets to sit in parked cars at any time, day or night.)
3. Don't urge a cadet to ride in a motor car after 10:30 at night. (He must be in barracks with lights out shortly after the hop is over anyway.)
4. Don't indulge in loud or daring clothing on the reservation. That goes double for behavior and conversation.
5. Don't ask to wear any part of a cadet uniform. In an emergency, a cadet may lend his raincoat to a femme, but visiting girls should provide their own rain gear and rain accessories.
6. Don't embarrass a cadet by expecting him to pay *any* of your expenses.
7. Don't ask a cadet to take you to Kissing Rock.
8. Don't demand all of the cadet's free time on Sunday. His free time is precious, and he may have other guests.
9. *Don't urge your cadet escort to do anything that is against regulations.* (Violations cost him too much in demerits.)
10. Don't bring or drink liquor on the reservation, much less offer it to a cadet. (The penalty to the cadet for drinking may be dismissal.)

A cadet is introduced as *"Mister Worthing,"* never introduced as "Cadet Worthing." It is unnecessary to introduce cadets to each other, but with the corps as large as it now is, it is a friendly gesture because they may not know each other.

The most popular girl at West Point today isn't necessarily the prettiest, the wealthiest or the glamour debutante; she is the girl who is natural, sincere and easy to look at. Cadets find the "glamour girl" exciting, but hard to live up to. She expects too much, and the social life at West Point is not fashioned along the lines of house parties and proms of the larger universities. Any young lady properly brought up, who knows how to observe the usual social amenities and who is reasonably attractive, has a sense of humor, enjoys sports and is an all-round natural femme, will have a good time at West Point.

JUNE WEEK AND GRADUATION

To the ladies who come up in June,
  We'll bid a fond adieu,
Here's hoping they'll be married soon,
  And join the army, too.
                    —"Army Blue"

June Week is filled with parades, sometimes as many as three in one day. At any hour of the day, in honor of visiting dignitaries, there will boom forth cannon salutes that almost make you jump out of your skin. The military bands work overtime, and in the evenings dance music issues from Cullum Hall, the gym, and the terrace at the hotel.

Thousands of visitors attend the graduation exercises. The address is always given by some public figure, such as the Secretary of War, the Chief of Staff, or even the President. As the diplomas, carrying with them the bachelor of science degree, are given out, each in order of rank or class standing, the graduates are cheered and applauded. The honor student, the athletic heroes and the lowest-ranking man in the class, known as the goat, receive the greatest applause.

If you are one of those who have come prepared with bridal attire for a wedding in the West Point chapel, June Week will take on an added importance and glamour for you. One could wish no more for you and your young lieutenant than that your whole lives should be one continuous June Week.

SUMMER TRAINING CAMP

Camp Buckner, named for the late Lieutenant General Simon Bolivar Buckner, Jr., and located six miles west of the Academy, is the summer training camp for the cadets. Here, among sylvan settings on the shores of beautiful Lake Popolopen, the yearling class spends a large part of the summer.

They work hard at military engineering, combat firing, amphibious maneuvers and tactical problems. On Wednesday afternoons, Saturday afternoons and evenings and Sunday they are permitted to have visitors.

Delightful week ends may be planned. Swimming, canoeing, fishing, boating, tennis and skeet facilities are available to the cadets and their guests. Usually on Sunday afternoons there is a water carnival. Parties of picnickers skirt the shore and swimmers dot the beach which follows the curve of a horseshoe inlet.

Having the correct sports clothes for a week end at Camp Buckner is very important! Shorts and slacks are *strictly nonregulation*. A spectator sports dress or skirt and sweater combination you will find appropriate. For the hops, which are informal, cotton or silk afternoon dresses are worn; the cadets themselves wear white uniforms. A bathing suit on the conservative side, comfortable sports shoes and your own bath towels plus the rest of your sports ensemble and equipment should see you through.

The camp hostess house is equipped with a powder room and large new dressing rooms for visitors desiring to change clothes. There is an attractive visitors' room, over which Mrs. Barth presides. There are no overnight accommodations at present. Guests commute to Highland Falls or stop at the

Thayer. Busses run on regular schedules between the hotel, Grant Hall and Camp Buckner. The bus fare is only twenty-five cents.

In every way Camp Buckner is a summer camp and life there is pretty rugged, so don't expect too much.

During the war air cadets were trained at Stewart Field, eighteen miles north of West Point.

THE AVIATION CADET GIRL . . . BOY MEETS GIRL!

San Antonio is affectionately called "the mother-in-law of the Army" because so many Texas girls marry Army officers. Fort Sam Houston, one of the largest medical installations in the country; Randolph Field, one of the nation's most important aviation centers; Kelly Field of legendary fame and the Indoctrination Division of the Air Training Command; Brooks Field; and the numerous nearby border posts and flying fields contribute their quota of eligible bachelor officers.

San Antonio is noted for its beautiful girls. Every year a new group of officers and officers-to-be reports to San Antonio and every autumn a fresh crop of debutantes makes its bow to society; so the most natural thing in the world happens. It's that trite old formula that seems to make the world go round—"Boy Meets Girl"—only, in this case, it is much more glamorous: "Handsome Army Officer or Dashing Flying Cadet Meets Southern Beauty." The society editors in San Antonio have a field day thinking up new ways to express it. In the famous San Jacinto Fiesta, held annually in April, there is always an Army duchess, and many escorts of the beautiful feminine members of the queen's court are eligible young Army bachelors. The Army always takes an active and important part in the social life of the city.

With the postwar transition of the Air Force in progress,

and with the future scope of the aviation cadet program to be decided by legislative action, I shall make my suggestions general enough to include all flying cadet girls, regardless of whether they are of a small group confined to only a few air installations or of one connected with several of the nation's training centers.

Rule number one for the sweetheart or close friend of a flying cadet is: *"Respect his flying training."* This is much more important than it may sound. In the first place, let's call your cadet "Bob," and assume that you, "Jane," are his One and Only girl.

Bob has been an airman of the Air Force for some time . . . and it may seem a long time to you that he has been away . . . but now he has successfully passed his entrance requirements for cadet training. This means a lot, for only airmen of the Air Force who merit advancement are accepted. Bob has successfully passed the rigid physical and mental examinations and his worth as an airman of the Air Force has been demonstrated by a fine record of past service. He has been accepted and is ready to take up his primary training. If he wants to tell you or write you of his worries and troubles, be considerate and lend an ear. He needs to tell someone how good he is, or how hard he is finding navigation and meteorology, and you are elected.

Or suppose you are the O.A.O. and "the girl back home." Before he left to enlist in the Air Force, you and Bob secretly became engaged and if all goes well you plan to be married when he completes his cadet training and receives his commission as an officer of the Army of the United States. The parting is very sad and tearful, and you promise to write every day. Also, you both may make a lot of silly promises about not dating anyone else. And Bob is off, to make a name for himself and to win those coveted wings. You promise to attend his graduation, if possible, and not so confidently Bob adds, "If I graduate."

Bob has been hoping for aviation cadet training ever since he saw his first Air Force bomber flying overhead, but this is the first qualm that he has experienced, the first time he has really considered the possibility of "being washed out." It is a serious realization. He has heard stories of how "tough" it is to get through Uncle Sam's flying school, but he doesn't know the half of it or what lies before him. I have no intention of trying to outline the course of discipline or instruction which our fair-haired boy will receive at Randolph Field, but I do plan to describe the flying cadet's program, so that you, Jane, may have a better and more sympathetic understanding and appreciation of his life as as a student.

BOB BECOMES A DODO!

A dodo, in the Air Corps vernacular, is defined as "a bird that can't fly, but runs at great speed!" All lower classmen when they enter Randolph Field or a similar basic flying school are known as "dodos."

The moment they set foot on the installation, their training begins, and I assure you each upper class goes out of its way to invent new "training methods" that are truly Spartan. The youth who considers flying training simply a breeze or who is inclined to be cocky will soon have his ego deflated, or if he is not able to adjust himself to the training, he will be "washed out." If the first week of discipline, which is said to be the hardest, proves too severe for the dodo and he can't take it, then he may be washed out without ever having set foot in an airplane. Flying airplanes in the Air Force demands a co-operative spirit!

The whole disciplinary system is related to that of the

United States Military Academy, and no beast detail of upper classmen ever worked harder than those at Randolph to harden up the recruits and whip them into shape. The training is arduous in every respect, with a lot of emphasis on physical conditioning, drilling and classroom work. Bob must assimilate a lot of knowledge before he flies and meteorology, navigation, maps and charts and aircraft engines are just a few of the subjects.

After you receive a few letters from Bob you will no doubt agree that he has a strenuous program. For any infraction of regulations he gets a demerit called a "gig." If he receives more than five gigs a week, he is required to walk the area or ramp. "Tour" is the name given this walkathon, and a tour consists of carefully pacing up and down the length of an asphalt surface at the rate of 120 steps per minute. Tours are walked off on afternoons which are ordinarily holidays for the cadets. "Hit the ramp, you dodos, is a familiar cry. Gigs are given for the most minor offenses or infractions, so the dodo thinks. At Saturday morning inspection, should the energetic upper classman find a bed not made correctly, shoes not shined properly, a spot on the window or mirror of the dodo's room, then gigs are handed out freely. Every Saturday morning there is a room inspection, followed by personal inspection, which includes rifle and uniform. Then there is a *review*. Reviews are also held whenever there are visiting dignitaries (generals from Washington or visiting foreign officers). They are impressive and very effective.

During this period of "processing," as it is called, Bob's emotions run the gamut. He asks himself, 'What is this place, anyway? Why did I ever come here? *When do I fly?* Why doesn't Jane write every day as she promised? Is she stepping out with my rival?" All in all, Cadet Bob is homesick, and desperately so. If he is worried about his O.A.O., he can't do his best and there will be a slump in his morale.

Now this is where the flying cadet girl can prove her worth. Write him cheery, newsy letters with all the home-town news. If you aren't much of a letter writer, then send him a subscription to the home-town newspaper. In return, he may send you the cadet newspaper, which will tell you in a general way what he is doing. Also, he will appreciate a little "boodle" now and then, in the way of a box of home-made candy or a cake.

The aviation cadet program is just getting started again after the postwar suspension of training, but the social life of the cadet will not be entirely neglected if the past record of these "fly boys" proves anything. In the past, it has been customary for the Flying Cadet Club of San Antonio to honor the new students with a tea dance at the end of the first two weeks of training. The dance is usually given at one of the larger hotels, and is called "the dodo tea dance." The upper classmen make up a guest list for this social function, and most of the dodos "drag blind"; that is, they are introduced to their dates at the dance. In this way the flying cadets make their social contacts.

Formerly there were four important dances during the year. These were reduced to the tea dance and the graduation dance during the war. Every four months a class graduates and a new class enters, so the dances come very often. The graduation dance is a traditional gala affair, usually a dinner dance.

Ten Don'ts for Flying Cadets Girls

1. Don't urge your cadet escort to do anything against regulations (such as taking you for an airplane ride).
2. Don't ask him to "buzz" or fly low over your home or school.

3. Don't encourage him to forget his troubles in alcohol (liquor and flying don't mix well).
4. Don't ask him to give you wings. These are supposed to be for his O.A.O. If he wants to give them to you he will, of his own volition.
5. Don't ask him to let you wear any part of the cadet uniform.
6. Don't expect corsages. Cadets have better use for their money.
7. Don't expect to enter barracks or his rooms. Post regulations are very strict on this point.
8. Don't telephone cadets. They have no time, and probably would not be called except in case of emergency.
9. Don't be selfish in regard to his time. His hours of liberty are few.
10. Don't fail to write cheery, encouraging letters often, if you live at a distance.

The flying cadet's liberty periods will be established as the cadet program gets under way. Remember that flying cadets are not officers. Their pay is meager, but enough to cover their normal expenses. A flying cadet receives from the United States government seventy-five dollars per month. His uniforms and flying equipment are issued, but he must pay for his own laundry and incidental expenses. After all deductions are made, $45 is about the maximum balance that he has for extras.

GRADUATION DAY

Graduation comes at last. Bob has completed his primary and basic flying training at Randolph and has been transferred either to Williams Field, Arizona, for advanced single-engine (pursuit) pilot training or to Barksdale Field, Louisiana, for advanced two-engine or advanced four-engine training. He has successfully mastered everything and is ready to receive his wings.

For weeks the word "graduation" has spelled the culmination of all that has occupied the thoughts and actions, night and day, of each flying cadet in the corps. During that time he has learned the mystery and the mastery of the airplane. From the shaking, bewidered dodo of the primary training school he has developed into a smooth, calm and accomplished pilot.

Bob's parents are going down for the graduation exercises and they have invited you to drive down with them. Or perhaps you and your mother decide to go. Unless you choose an aunt or some older person as a chaperon, this is about the only proper way that you can go to see Bob graduate. The flying school differs from West Point in that it has no official chaperon and no post accommodations; so you will have to stay in a hotel.

The cadets are occupied with their training until the day of graduation, sometimes making up flying hours or polishing their wing-overs or 360's, so they have very little free time for entertaining guests. No doubt, if you are the O.A.O., Bob will have saved his money, and after graduation he will be glad to entertain you. Should you accompany his family, don't forget that you owe them every consideration, and above all don't try to monopolize Bob. Remember that he is their son, and they are very proud of him, too!

The advanced flying schools are located in the South and West where it is hot from April to November; so wear a cool dress or lightweight suit if "your" graduation class is in the summer. A linen packable in some becoming color combination or a sheer is a good choice, plus a large hat for protection from the sun; and be sure to have sunglasses.

After the exercises, Bob will bring you his wings and ask

you to pin them on him. A nice gesture is to decline and give
his mother this honor and thrill. She will appreciate it, and
if Bob is your One and Only you will have this honor many
times in later years. If his mother pins his wings on, then
you may present him with his gold bars, the insignia he has
earned the right to wear; for now, at midnight, he will be a
second lieutenant of the United States Air Force.

Formerly, graduations and the aerial reviews held at flying
schools were something to be remembered, but the stream-
lining of the cadet program has forced a curtailment of this
activity. There will usually be a short program at the post
theater consisting of an address, one or two short speeches,
and then the awarding of diplomas and wings. The commissions are presented to the cadets in a large envelope,
which also contains orders placing them on flying status and
on active flying duty. Their commissions become effective at
midnight, the day of graduation. The next morning they
report for their flight as officers, in officers' uniform for the
first time, and *are they spoony!*

Chapter II

ARMY ENGAGEMENTS

For seven long years I've courted Nancy.
Hi! Hi! the Rolling River.

D URING wartime, service engagements are often of short duration, owing to the stress of the times. Certainly World War II produced a bumper crop of wartime weddings with the accompanying glamour and excitement of whirlwind honeymoons. The war wouldn't wait, and neither would young love! Many lovely wedding traditions had to be dispensed with because the youngsters were eagerly grabbing whatever happiness they could salvage.

In this postwar period, many young people are paying high today and will pay tomorrow and tomorrow for the wild wave of wartime marriages. Some of these marriages were entered into after an acquaintance of only a few weeks or in some instances a matter of days, and the ceremony was immediately followed by long war separations. In most cases there was no real engagement period at all and brief engagements became the fashion. Of course, we must be optimistic enough to believe that some of these engagements and marriages were "arranged in heaven" and that the bride and groom will live happily ever after. War or no war, long or short engagement, if it is true love and each understands the seriousness and sacredness of marriage, the marriage will be a happy one.

"Marry in Haste, Repent at Leisure"

Today, as far as military weddings are concerned, we are back on a peacetime basis. Long engagements are not unusual in the Service owing to regulations promulgated by the War Department.

A noted marriage counselor says, "In wiser and more ripened societies—societies not so close to the adventurer, explorer, pioneer stage—there is such a thing as being engaged. It is a recognized experience and a very pleasant one."

Waiting, with all the joyous anticipation of a wedding, is a time that *later* all married women look back upon as the most romantic and happiest days of their lives. Just as too early marriage robs the woman of a rightful time of fun, dancing, independence, youthful good times with other girls and boys, so this dash from an engagement into wedlock deprives her of one of the legitimate enjoyments of life.

Why be married at the immature age of eighteen? Why accept the first suitor who asks your hand? Why not complete your education and acquire training in some field so that if the need ever arises you can be self-supporting? Why not be engaged to each other for a while? It is a good testing time. Granted that HE is the ONE, why not have a year without rushing and planning and hurrying breathlessly to the altar? Why not enjoy friendship and companionship and happy times together, in the recognized and dignified status of being engaged?

It would be far better so! If young people would take time to learn what interests, hopes and amusements they share perhaps there would be fewer trips to Reno.

The War Department's nonmarriage regulations under

Statutory Provisions, Section 23 of the National Defense Act, September 18, 1946, reads as follows:

The Secretary of War, under such regulations as he may prescribe, may hereafter revoke the commission of any officer on the active list, initially commissioned after the date of this Act, who, at the date of said revocation, has had less than three years of continuous service as a commissioned officer of the Army, and each officer whose commission is so revoked shall be discharged from the Army; *Provided* That until July 1, 1942 the marriage of an officer shall not be a cause for revocation of commission but that after that date, under regulations issued pursuant to the authority contained in this Act, marriage may be a cause for revocation of commission only in the event that the officer marries within one year subsequent to the date of his original commission.

While these statutes may prove tiresome reading, it is well, my dear Peggy, to brush the stardust from your eyes long enough to realize the seriousness of the obligations confronting Ted if he is to make the Regular Army his career.

Upon first thought, this regulation seems unfair, but experience has proved that a junior officer of less than three years' service is not financially able to assume marital responsibilities and consequently his military career may suffer. After all, the government educated Ted first of all to be an officer; after that, when he has served his three years, he may consider matrimony.

In these days, young people seem to make up their own minds about marriage, though it is still customary in the best circles for an officer to call on the girl's father or mother, or whoever is head of the family, and ask for the girl's hand in marriage. Most parents, in these days, are "very well brought up" by their children; so it is unlikely that there will be disapproval voiced. Your father may wonder, "Is he good enough for our Peggy?" or "How can we bear to be separated from her?" but, like Elizabeth Custer's father, he may add, "Daughter, marrying into the Army, you will be poor always; but I count it infinitely preferable to riches with inferior society. It consoles me to think you will always be associated with people of refinement."

If you are definitely a home girl and have a family complex, then I should advise you not to marry into the Army, because you will probably be miserable, not to mention the unhappiness you will bring your husband. If your parents want you to make a wealthy marriage, don't marry an Army officer.

If the engagement is approved by the girl's parents, then the young officer should acquaint his parents with his intentions if he has not already done so. Letters will undoubtedly have been exchanged, and if he and his parents are close friends, they can usually read between the lines. However, he should write them specifically if it is impossible to have a personal visit. This letter may glow with happiness, and it is a thoughtful gesture to include or send a good picture of the girl of his choice.

Usually the boy's mother writes to the girl, or to her mother, his father to the girl's father, or, if possible, the young officer's parents should call at once on the parents of the bride-to-be. If the young man is an orphan, his nearest relative should take his parents' place and perform this act of courtesy for him. These social amenities should be carried out, and a definite understanding between the two families reached, before a formal engagement is announced.

The Engagement Ring

Annapolis has its traditional "Ring Hop" during June Week, at which the One and Only girl may receive a miniature engagement ring. West Point graduates also give a miniature of their class ring, often as an engagement ring. There are two reasons for this: first, sentimental, and second, because it is less costly than the customary solitaire. Some of these miniatures are very attractive. They usually carry the same stone as the officer's class ring. Some are of platinum, if the wedding band is to match. Set with a center diamond, and surrounded by sapphires, this is a pretty combination. Emeralds are expensive and break easily, though they are lovely. If the officer can afford it, he often gives a solitaire in addition to the miniature. In this case the miniature may be worn as a little-finger ring, but it has a very definite meaning. It is supposed to be worn only by an officer's fiancée, his sister or his mother. This custom is often grossly abused, however.

In days past, the engagement ring was not worn in public until the formal announcement of the engagement. Now it may be worn at any time, or some girls prefer to forgo an engagement ring and choose an elaborate wedding ring with the accompanying jeweled guard ring. Others of more simple taste like the traditional gold band of their mothers' day.

THE ANNOUNCEMENT

Several days before the announcement is to appear in the paper, the bride's mother either telephones the various daily papers or sends a written signed notice to the society editors. Most papers require a signed statement in order to avoid future trouble in the way of lawsuits. Depending upon the social prominence of the families, reporters and photographers will be sent out to get more information. At the same time, a signed copy of the engagement announcement should be sent to the Service periodicals—*The Army and Navy Journal*, 1701 Connecticut Avenue, N.W., Washington,

D.C., and *The Army Register,* 511 Eleventh Street, N.W., Washington, D.C.

Announcement of engagement for Service journals:

Mr. James Prentiss Carver and Mrs. Carver (or Mr. and Mrs. James Prentiss Carver) announce the engagement of their daughter, Margaret Jean, to James Theodore Worthing, Lieutenant, United States Army, son of Mr. and Mrs. Charles Louis Worthing of San Francisco, California.

Miss Carver attended Ward Belmont, Nashville, and was a member of the 1940 graduating class from Vassar. Lieutenant Worthing is a graduate of the U. S. Military Academy, 1936, and is stationed at Fort Sam Houston, San Antonio, Texas.

Local papers often carry a much more elaborate announcement, especially in the deep South where families are closely connected. Everyone is a cousin or related by marriage ties, so a complete family history is given by the papers of both the bride and the groom if they are of social prominence.

The officer may wish to have the announcement of the engagement in his home paper; so he should be consulted. Arrangements should be made for extra copies of the paper in which the announcement appears. Sometimes a dinner is given on the night the engagement is announced by the bride's parents, and some time between the salad and the dessert course her father may propose a toast to the health of his daughter and future son-in-law.

The engagement may be announced at a luncheon given by a friend of the bride or at an informal tea or cocktail party given by the bride's family, but it is never announced by the groom or any member of his family. At a tea or cocktail party the fiancé may stand with the family, and this is the form the announcement takes. Unless it is a surprise announcement at a party, either the bride or her mother announces the engagement.

There are many ways to make your party announcement, but guard against straining to be clever. Many girls and their mothers go to great lengths to dream up something original; however, I believe it is in better taste to stick to simplicity. Of course, it is your engagement and it is your party! One traditional manner is to have gay little boutonnieres (tagged with the two names) heaped artistically in a shallow basket, to be given to each guest as a surprise favor.

Don't announce your engagement farther ahead than a year; life is too uncertain! If it is an engagement of short duration, then allow the announcement to be made not less than six weeks before the wedding date.

Nine out of ten girls today skip the announcement party, but go ahead if this bit of fanfare will make you happy. Being a prospective bride puts you on a sort of pedestal, out of the realm of mundane things. Your family stands ready to give you the moon, and your relatives and friends are also standing by to help you make all your plans and dreams a success.

A formal white wedding is a once in a lifetime affair. Ever since you were a babe in arms your mother has been dreaming dreams of you on your wedding day. Don't let her down now. Be your gayest, happiest self; consult and make your plans with her. Listen to family ideas from your grandmother and aunts; you may think them old-fashioned, but then isn't marriage? Your mother will get a vicarious thrill in reliving her engagement days through your happiness. That is why it is so much easier on you and everyone concerned if you do not rush the wedding date. Reserve some time for yourself to relax and be wary, in the weeks before the big event, of letting your engagement pad take on the semblance of a railroad timetable. In all of this wedding welter don't treat the bridegroom as the forgotten man!

SHOWERS

Parties of this sort always seem to spring into popularity when there is a war in the offing. Why, no one seems to know, unless it is war hysteria.

At any rate, showering is not to be greatly encouraged. Brides should limit their shower parties to two and never accept a third. Usually the same friends are asked, as only one's intimate friends are supposed to be invited. It is never given by any member of the bride's immediate family, but may be given by a close friend of hers or of her mother's. More than two shower gifts, in addition to a wedding present, run into money, and there is usually criticism, whether voiced or not. Certainly it is inconsiderate and not in good taste for the bride to impose on her friends; so if someone insists upon giving a party for you, let it be a luncheon or tea, but by all means veto a shower.

Should your hostess consult you in regard to the type of shower and the guest list, choose a shower that will not burden your friends. A stocking shower, handkerchief shower or kitchen shower is much easier on the pocketbooks of your young friends than a lingerie or linen shower. The latter might be given by an older friend, which will include the older set and many of your mother's friends, whose budgets for this sort of thing are more expansive. But remember: Keep it down to two and no more.

As in the case of announcement parties, the hostess at a shower may let her ingenuity assert itself in any way she chooses. Sometimes the gifts are all heaped on a table or a teacart; she may have her attractive young daughter or son present the gifts; or if there are only a few guests and gifts, the presents might be hidden and a treasure hunt conducted. The leads should be very simple or the honoree will become confused and enjoy neither originality nor party.

When the bride opens her gifts, she must be very gracious and thank each person who has brought her a present. She must be careful not to give extravagant praise to one person's gift and be lukewarm over a lesser gift.

The shower is usually followed by an informal tea or buffet supper, at which time the fiancé, the escorts and husbands join the party. Bridal showers are seldom surprise parties, though they may be if the hostess so desires.

If you are marrying an Army officer and someone suggests a crystal shower, by all means change it if you can do so tactfully. Crystal is expensive and is very impractical when moving day arrives.

Personal Trousseau

Volumes could be written on this subject. Marrying an Army officer even complicates your choice of clothes. The first thing to do is to make an inventory of the clothes you have on hand, then another memo or shopping list to cover lingerie, hose, belts, scarves, purses, jewelry, gloves, shoes, blouses, coats, suits, dresses, rain gear and luggage. Of course, your wedding dress and your going-away outfit will be the highlights of your personal trousseau. The latter should be "a suit or costume that will proudly take you places for seasons to come." If you are fortunate enough to know for sure where your fiancé will be stationed the first year of your marriage, then consult a bridal counselor who can answer questions concerning the type of wardrobe you will need. If it is to be foreign service—Manila, Tokyo, Honolulu, Germany, Alaska, Italy—you will have some general idea, but don't overstock and here is why:

Orders are often changed overnight. An officer may be stationed in Georgia when the engagement is announced, and by the time the wedding trip is over he may have been ordered to Hawaii, Alaska or the Philippines.

The safest rule to follow is perhaps to have a nucleus of substantial clothes, using what you have on hand in the way of fur coats and the expensive items. Then save the money you might otherwise spend, and from the start establish a clothes fund or budget.

Fall weddings seem to lend themselves most advantageously to the choice of an all-around wardrobe. Of course, this is not always practicable or possible; but there are several economic reasons for my statement. Fall clothes, light woolens, etc., are usually heavy enough for most southern stations in winter. Heavy, fur-trimmed winter coats and suits are more costly and often of no use with a change of orders to the tropics. During the summer and at the end of summer, sales with wonderful values can be found that will give a complete spring and summer wardrobe to start on during the following seasons. You may have a trousseau that is suitable for Washington, but when you go to Puerto Rico or Honolulu, there will be many gaps in your wardrobe. Your evening dresses aren't quite right, somehow. You would like to buy the current style there. Very well, then, don't overstock your trousseau. Buy the essentials, and save your money for this future necessity.

On most Army posts the women wear exactly two types of clothes—sports clothes, either the spectator or active type, and evening clothes. In a city or on a post near a city, daytime dresses are needed for luncheons, cocktail parties and informal dinners, in addition to formal evening dress.

The following list will cover a minimum wardrobe for the Army bride on the average post; then she may add to or change the list to suit her personal preferences, her pocket-book, or climatic conditions.

1 evening wrap
3 evening dresses, formal (two of chiffon or lace, as they can be worn in any climate. If you are going to the tropics take at least four cotton evening dresses in addition to these formals. This is not extravagant!)
2 dinner dresses with either sleeves or jacket
3 pairs of evening slippers if they dovetail in with color scheme
1 or 2 short daytime or afternoon dresses for cocktail parties and teas. Matching accessories in purses, gloves and hats
1 tailored suit or three-piece suit, sweaters, blouses and accessories
1 topcoat or fur coat
3 or 4 summer day dresses for sports wear
2 winter dresses of wool or jersey
1 dressing gown (winter, warm tailored flannel), warm mules
1 dressing gown (summer)
1 negligee (the filmiest, loveliest one you can afford) or
1 hostess gown or hostess pajamas
2 bed jackets
6 nightgowns or pajamas
6 pants
6 brassières
3 girdles (if you wear them)
4 slips, 1 dark one
1 dozen pairs of stockings, various weights
2 pairs day shoes
1 pair walking shoes or golf shoes
1 raincoat and umbrellas
Beach clothes, shorts, slacks, sandals, 2 bathing suits, robe, beach bag
Riding clothes, if you intend to go in for riding or hunting: 1 riding habit, tailored by an expert tailor; extra coats and jodhpurs if you like them; custom-made boots and shoes

Plan your wardrobe with the help of the splendid suggestions in the fashion magazines and consult one of the experienced shoppers that all stores provide. Window-shop first; look about thoroughly, watch sales; then use common sense, make up your mind, know what you want, how much you can spend, and start out to shop. Everyone knows that the woman who must dress inexpensively must be far more exact than the shopper who has unlimited money to spend. Keeping the wardrobe sparse, and adding to it when a definite need comes along, is far more exciting than buying everything at once and growing tired of it, anyway. It is an odd fact, but a cheap dress with fairly good accessories will look fine while an expensive dress with cheap accessories will look cheap.

If the bride can sew, she may cut the cost of her trousseau considerably. It is foolish, however, to stock up with a large amount of clothes. Styles and stations change too rapidly, and it is far more comfortable to have the money in your bank balance for wardrobe emergencies that will surely arise. Be adamant in keeping a clothes budget, and under no consideration borrow from your clothes allowance to pay the butcher or to buy a new bed lamp for the guest room. If you do, you'll never catch up. Your personal appearance and wardrobe will suffer.

To this trousseau list, of course, you may add gorgeous undies by the dozens, or double the outlay of clothes if your circumstances and taste dictate. One warning: Although you are probably spending more money at one time on lingerie than you ever have before in your life—or probably ever will again—don't go on a lingerie-buying jag. Try to remember that these pre-wedding days, redolent of lily-of-the-valley, will be followed by bread-and-butter days when you may have to tub your lovelies in the community washroom of a crowded transport. Don't wake up with a laundry headache and yards of point d'esprit that will never be the same again unless your grandmother's charcoal fluting iron was among your wedding presents.

One important prop when you are shopping for quality lingerie is to buy by brand names. This means you can buy with confidence in whatever city you may be; though name-known lingerie doesn't mean the price is always the lowest, it does mean you can be sure the money you spend is getting the most, dollar for dollar. For instance, three good slips are better than six cheap ones and will outlast them.

The selection of your lingerie should not be totally emotional or helter-skelter. You are entitled to make it a little bit out of this world but also, remember, it must lead your day-by-day life with you. And life may be rugged at your first Army station! If you are slated to honeymoon in Alaska, include some warm flannel pajamas in your favorite pastel shades; also, long red flannels come in some very amusing styles of the gay nineties.

By now, you have some idea what type of clothes your fiancé admires, so you will be wise to plan your trousseau to please him. This is subtle flattery, my dear, and you will simply be completing his dream picture of you. There are certain things which Army men like in women's clothes; and one thing they don't like is anything that smacks of a uniform. Clothes regimentation was necessary during the war, but the war is over.

Here is a check list:

Army men like:
1. Sleek fit which shows off the figure. They are accustomed to well-tailored uniforms, and they are really quite observant as to the fit of clothes that are supposed to fit, such as suits.

riding clothes, boots. They know the cut, line and curves of bathing suits, too.

2. Gay, colorful hats . . . but not absurd, extreme creations.
3. Dainty, lacy, effeminate collars and immaculate cuffs. This is in direct contrast to the drabness of their O.D. uniforms.
4. Crisp house frocks at breakfast . . . rather than negligees with trains. The prettiest negligee in the world is under a dreadful handicap in the kitchen.
5. Dainty, attractive organdy aprons, crisp as lettuce in the kitchen, not the cellophane or Hoover variety!
6. Simple, smart, up-to-date costumes, but not extremes in fashion.
7. Feminine fripperies, such as froufrou lacy jabots, garden hats, full skirts, furs, snow-white gloves, sheer hose and high-heeled slippers. Southern men particularly like and often comment on these bits of feminine apparel.
8. Neatness: All the little points of good grooming are appreciated.
9. Good tweedy sports clothes; English oxfords and no fancy jewelry with tweeds.
10. Sensibly dressed women of whom they can be proud; over-dressed women embarrass their escorts as well as their hostesses . . . and themselves. The smart woman knows the occasion, and knows what is proper to be worn. If in doubt, it is always better to underdress, simply but effectively.
11. Smart, formal evening gowns. The Army likes to dress every night, and in a small command you see the same people over and over.

Men often have better taste than women. Instinctively they know what "does something" for us, perhaps without knowing why. Their opinion is entirely unbiased and usually constructive, so show attention and interest and be considerate of your fiancé's opinion and any compliments he may pay you concerning your clothes.

Should you be going to Alaska or to Fort Snelling, Minnesota, a fur coat or an extra-heavy coat would be your big expenditure. For Puerto Rico, Hawaii or the Philippines, you could eliminate tweeds, but it is always a great comfort to have at least one warm outfit for ocean trips even if you are en route to the tropics. The port of embarkation may be cold, and usually the first day or so at sea demands warm clothing, when you leave a cold climate for a warm one. If you sail from San Francisco during June, July or August you can always depend upon cold weather, and you will need a warm coat, at least.

If you can start off with a whole new trousseau, it is wise to divide your money like this: get a fur coat—and a good one since everyone will expect to see you in it for years. (Of course, you will probably be moving about.) Invest in one good town suit, a backlog tweed suit, extra sweaters and skirts. The shift from a cold climate to the tropics doesn't involve the sartorial headaches it used to.

Be sensible and check the place you are going before buying evening clothes: musts in many places, especially the tropics, are completely out of the picture in others. The cocktail dress is a good compromise, but play safe and include at least two long dresses for social affairs.

Regardless of where you go, you will need a good supply of sturdy, comfortable shoes. Beware of clothes which need the loving ministrations of an expert cleaner or a super-laundress. You'll be in luck if you find either. Take a gloomy view of the weather and go prepared with attractive rain gear.

If you can swing it, include one really super coat . . . the Stroock variety of peach-bloom camel's hair in palest peppermint pink, or tomato red, or café-au-lait beige. You can wear this over everything you own from sports right through the evening over your prettiest dance frock.

Planning your trousseau is a joyous event; every detail of the bridal outfit and the accompanying parts of the trousseau must be exactly right. So much will be shining, new and beautiful! Enjoy every moment of it, and plan to treat your wedding day as the beginning of your romance, not the end of it. The bride has illusions, visions, hopes . . . even as you and I.

LUGGAGE

One of the MUSTS in your trousseau is attractive, durable luggage, preferably of the airplane type. Airplane luggage is the lightest and most durable on the market today.

A good strong wardrobe trunk of a standard make is the first necessity. A combination hat and shoe trunk, the large size for large hats, will be worth its weight in rubies. These usually come with a tray to be used for lingerie and accessories.

A large wardrobe suitcase and an overnight bag or train box should complete the ensemble. If you have odd suitcases you will find they will prove useful in cross-country moves by car.

Your wedding luggage, however, should be matched and it is convenient when traveling to have a distinctive style or marking for easy finding, such as a black and white striped material. And if you tie a colored ribbon to the leather loop at the top of your wardrobe trunk, you can recognize it easily in a heap of trunks. This is a good tip on a transport, when you go below in a crowded, hot hold to find your trunk. Everyone else's will have a broad band on it! Your luggage, as much as your own appearance, represents you to your fellow travelers, so smartness is worth striving for.

<h2 style="text-align:center">LINENS</h2>

"Trousseau" is a French word, meaning the little *trousse* or bundle which it was customary for the bride to carry to the house of her husband. Today the word has come to mean the bride's personal wardrobe and her household linens. The things that make up a trousseau are usually bought or collected after the engagement is announced.

Young girls of the gay nineties spent their leisure time embroidering and making linens for a "hope chest" but the young women of today seem to have simpler and more practical tastes. However, some old-fashioned mothers and grandmothers start a young girl's trousseau and her silver collection when the babe is born, and on each birthday add to the hope chest.

It seldom pays to economize in buying linens. You'll be disillusioned with a bargain the first time it is laundered, because its beauty washes away with the sizing on its first trip to the laundry.

It seems safer to buy white linens in the Army because each set of quarters will have a different tiled-bath color scheme, and some of them are weird—brilliant blue tiles, or a sickly lavender, against which white is the only answer! With varicolored bath cloths and mats you will have a rainbow potpourri if you are not careful. Of course, the beautiful colored linens offered by the shops are most tempting, but the wise bride will fill her minimum requirements in standard white and trust that the colored towels and sheets may come in shower or wedding gifts. Also, after filling the "must have" list, save your extra money for linen closet accessories, shelf edging and the little niceties.

For the Bride with a Large Budget

1 dozen sheets . . . monogrammed linen or good percale, or
6 double sheets of a good grade of percale
6 single sheets
1 dozen pillowcases to match
4 blankets . . . lingerie blanket covers, trimmed in lace, if you like wool or down-filled quilts
1 dozen monogrammed linen face towels
2 dozen small linen face towels of good quality
1 dozen bath towels
1 dozen bath cloths
3 bath mats
1 three-yard damask cloth with 1 dozen napkins, best quality
1 silence cloth
1 two-and-a-half-yard banquet or buffet cloth . . . lace insets (or save wedding present check to buy this on foreign service, where linen is cheaper)
1 tea cloth, two yards square, the most elaborate you can afford
4 luncheon sets: 1 elaborate, 1 Italian linen, and 2 everyday
2 dozen lace-edged linen napkins for buffet suppers
2 dozen tea napkins
1 dozen inexpensive large-size hemstitched linen napkins for everyday use
1 dozen dish towels
1 dozen dishcloths
1 roll cheesecloth
Cellophane cases for best linen

Good linens last indefinitely and, while they may be as scarce and as hard to find as a *good* man, every bride knows the right thing when it comes along. Again, good brand names will be your best advisers.

The Smaller Budget

For the dining room:
1 linen damask dinner cloth, 8 or 12 matching napkins
1 supper cloth with 6 napkins, 8 preferred
1 luncheon or tea cloth, 8 napkins, 12 preferred
2 luncheon place-mat sets (17 pieces)
2 breakfast cloths, 4 napkins
2 bridge sets
For the bedroom:
6 sheets . . . 3 plain hem, 3 hemstitched
8 sheets, 72" x 108" if equipping twin beds
2 mattress pads
8 pillowcases, hemstitched
1 pair winter blankets
1 pair blanket covers
2 bedspreads
For the bathroom:
8 bath towels, 22" x 44"
6 small Turkish towels
6 washcloths
4 large linen towels
6 small linen towels
2 chenille bath mats
1 bathroom rug
For the kitchen:
6 glass towels
6 dishcloths
6 hand towels
12 dish towels

Rotate your linens. Linens will last longer, seem fresher, if you follow a regular rotation plan. It is so easy, too, merely a matter of stacking the freshly laundered sheets, towels, pillowcases at the bottom of each pile in your linen closet.

Here is something about sheets: Be sure to buy them long enough, so that there is plenty to tuck in, and to fold well over the blanket. If your better half has to yank the sheets to get them up around his neck, you can be sure they won't last very well. The more threads to the inch, the smoother, more fine textured the sheet. Look for this information on the label attached to the sheet. Also, look for the tab that states "torn" size dimensions. The word "torn" is advantageous in a sheet; "cut" sheets are apt to lose shape when laundered. "Torn" size is size before hemming. Percale sheets are finer textured and lighter in weight than muslin, but very durable. Pillowcases should fit easily, but not so snugly that they will soon be splitting at the seams. The most popular pillowcase sizes are 42" by 38½" and 45" by 38½".

You may as well start collecting housewifely tricks as soon as you have learned how to boil an egg. Brides of yesteryear thought it was clever to say they did not know how to boil water. Not so today! Anyone who can read a cookbook can cook. However, there is a knack to interpreting the cookbook and working with your mother and learning her cooking secrets will stand you in good stead. If your mother is not the housewifely type, then hie yourself to a good cooking school, or take a course in home economics. With your trousseau there should also be a fundamental knowledge of the cookery of simple foods and the rudiments of housekeeping. Whether or not you ever have to use this knowledge is beside the point; even on foreign service where you inherit a well-staffed household your home will function more efficiently if you know a thing or two about cookery and house management.

HAPPINESS HAS ITS PRICE

Love is something that comes to us without our working for it, but if we want it to stay alive and to be something beautiful, we must tend it with constant care. It would be wise if every young person might take a course in family relations before deciding on the wedding date. Another reason for an extended engagement!

During an engagement period, young people should become well acquainted with each other's ideals, tastes, faults. One should know exactly what kind of person he is choosing with whom to spend the rest of his life. We presume that you are contemplating marriage for keeps! No young couple should marry without having had several down-to-earth quarrels, when the true character usually asserts itself, and through the scratched veneer often shows the real disposition frightening. Far better to find this out before the wedding day than afterwards.

No young girl would think of applying for a secretarial position without training; no young man would attempt any profession without years of study and numerous degrees; yet some young people rush into marriage, which is one of the most important and most serious businesses in the world, with nothing more than a mere infatuation that they label "Love." Marriage is not a reform school, so remember this: The love of your life with bad habits is likely to retain them. A marriage ceremony is not going to perform miracles in either bride or groom as far as radical changes in character are concerned. Certainly nagging, laying down the law or ridiculing has never helped anyone to wish to be a better person. Real love, gentleness, understanding and loyal assistance are the only traits that can make a man or woman desire to change wrong attitudes and habits.

Peggy, I am presuming that you are a well-integrated young woman, and I am hoping that you not only have taken a full course in family relations but have consulted a counselor who is a gifted psychoanalyst. If he has pointed out your weaknesses of character and given you a good analysis, then you will be more understanding and better able to adjust to whatever kind of life lies before you.

There is an old saying that you never know anyone until you live with him, and this is true to a certain extent. However, there are some traits of character that cannot be masked. For instance, you will have to have a special kind and brand of love to make a success of your marriage if you choose a conceited man, with a Narcissus complex. He may love you dearly, but you will always take second place in his life. He may be generous provided he has an income large enough to take care of more than his own needs; otherwise, you may expect his golf, his polo, his club connections, his liquor cabinet and his friends to be taken care of before your requirements. More than likely, he will be a delightful host and a charming companion, but you can expect his vanity and conceit to demand that he come first in everything; you will be welcome to what is left. You may love him very much, my dear, but you will never change him. Of course, during a short courtship, he may be willing to make a great show of his generosity; but if you give him enough time, this selfish complex will betray itself to you. By the same token, search your own character for these traits.

The man who has a violent temper, which he was never taught to control in childhood, will continue to fly off the handle when provoked. Marriage will not make a saint of him! He may make promises, but it will take time, and an unusually even temper on his wife's part, to tone down his violence. His marks of cruelty, whether physical or mental, will leave scars that are hard to forget. This goes for the fault-finding type of man, too. Should you be the same immature, spoiled type, you won't have much chance of a happy marriage . . . unless, when one becomes angry, the other makes it a rule to remain calm, regardless of what happens.

The man who drinks too much before marriage seldom reforms afterwards unless he honestly desires to help himself. Alcoholism has a tendency to advance, and when it becomes a psychological problem then it is a disease—just as fatal and serious as cancer or tuberculosis. The man or woman who drinks to excess does so to forget unhappiness, a sense of frustration, financial troubles, or as an escape from work or responsibility that is resented. Of course, a drunkard must not be confused with the man who takes a highball for conviviality, or even occasionally gets "high."

If you like to drink, too . . . then watch out! A man who drinks will usually drink less if the woman he is with drinks nothing. There is a happy medium, of course, but women seem more allergic to liquor than men, so let your conscience be your guide on this score. Social drinking is one of the dangers of the age. If you take your stand early in your marriage, you will have a better and a happier home.

Another source of unhappiness in marriage is the lack of freedom of religious belief. Certainly everyone has a right to worship as he pleases, and your views should be compatible on this subject. A decision should be made before marriage about the religious training of any children you may have. Whatever you arrange should be honestly adhered to, and don't plan secretly to change the arrangements later or to try to convert your husband to your belief against his wishes. Roman Catholics feel very strongly on this subject, and that is why a union with a non-Catholic is not encouraged by the church. Arrive at a definite understanding, then live up to it.

The man who is a gambler at heart will never be changed by a marriage ceremony; he will never give up the idea that the very next time he might hit the jackpot! Again, don't

confuse a gambler with a man who enjoys a weekly evening
of poker with his brother officers, or who likes to bet on the
ponies occasionally. You will understand what I mean if
your young lieutenant tells you on the first day of the month
that he owes his salary for last month's repeated losses at
gambling. You will never know where you stand financially
with this sort of uncontrolled spending. No Army officer
can afford to gamble, unless he has an outside income, and
it is definitely frowned upon by senior officers. Even senior
officers have been dismissed from the Service as a penalty
for gambling.

The engagement period is one of the happiest, yet one of
the most serious and important, phases in your life. Your
whole future depends upon your selection of the right man!
Don't be afraid to pray for guidance, and take time to listen
for the answer to your prayers. The Bible says, "Ask and ye
shall receive." That in itself is a prayer, and God will help
you if you sincerely try to help yourself. Prayer and love
are the greatest forces in the world.

I do not suppose there ever was a thinking bride who at
the last moment, or certainly at some time during the engagement, did not have a few qualms about marriage and her
choice of a mate. This is only natural, but after you have
checked over the afore-mentioned habits, weighed his weaknesses against your own and made a sincere effort through
prayer, then relax, and God will give you your answer.

Should it be a negative answer, then break the engagement
by all means. Don't be a coward and let anyone persuade
you to undertake a lifetime job that you can see is marked
ahead with milestones of unhappiness. It takes strength of
character to do this, but it is the only sane thing to do. You
can find that strength in prayer.

By this time I hope you are sure in your heart that Ted is

the One and Only man in the world for you. If you are proud of his good looks and military appearance, don't be afraid to tell him so. He may laugh at the idea, but underneath he will be enormously pleased that you think so. One last thing: Never criticize your fiancé or later your husband in public if he should make an error. Also, don't hoard the mistake all evening, then pop up like toast in a Toastmaster the moment you are alone to remind him of his error. This is not the way to start off in step with each other.

Make your prenuptial dates treasures of memory that you both will always cherish. It is a woman's world again, your fiancé fell in love with you because you are *you*. He is the center of your world, just as you are the center of his. And no person or outside influence should be allowed to mar or interfere with the beautiful design for living that you two have planned for the rest of your lives. Earn the right to your happiness and let nothing take it away from you!

Chapter III

THE MILITARY WEDDING

HERE COMES THE BRIDE!

ILITARY weddings differ slightly from the usual formal
weddings. There is nothing more glamorous, however, than a full military wedding, with the handsome groom, his best man and his brother officers as groomsmen all in full dress or evening dress, wearing the traditional
Army blues. Gold braid, gold belts, dazzling epaulets, bril-
liantly lined evening capes, and flashing sabers make a wonderful background for beautiful bridesmaids in gowns of
delicate shades and the exquisite bride in her white wedding
gown. The whole scene resembles a court of yesteryear and
takes on a note of brilliance.

During war periods military weddings are most popular.
But because of sudden orders and the difficulty of officers'
getting leave, it is not always possible to have an elaborate
wedding. Sometimes plans have to be altered completely,
owing to the movement of troops or an unannounced flight
or mission.

Decide first of all with your family what type of wedding
you will have, whether it will be formal, military, semiformal
or informal. Try to plan it without spending your father's
next year's income or leaving your mother with a nervous
breakdown. Next, your fiancé included, decide on the date

and time. June is the traditional bride's month, though April and May are popular and the autumn season is increasingly fashionable. It is not appropriate or in good taste to plan a large church wedding to take place during Lent, Holy Week or Advent (the three weeks preceding Christmas). Marriage license bureaus carry on a thriving business every day of the year, however, so the month and date is up to your personal taste and convenience.

An invitation is always a nicer compliment than an announcement. The words are self-explanatory and the only thing that an announcement explains is, as Emily Post says, that "you were not invited to the wedding"; however, there are circumstances in which the latter is preferred. For example, when a wedding is limited to the family and close friends, or when a date has to be set at the last minute, announcements should be sent to the friends both near and far who will be interested in the happy news. The bride and her mother should consult a good stationer and decide upon the style and type of engraving, paper, etc. Be open to suggestions, but avoid fads in engraving styles, and, even if you have to forgo some necessity in your trousseau, insist upon engraved invitations or announcements.

It is a good idea to request that the envelopes be sent to you ahead of the invitations or announcements so that you can have them addressed and ready.

This is also a good time to order your calling cards. You will need them in returning calls at your first post. In the rush of the wedding plans you may forget to order them; so take this opportunity and you will be glad to have them on hand. Officers always have their own personal cards for calling purposes; so yours should read, simply: "Mrs. James Theodore Worthing." Avoid using initials or abbreviations; for instance, neither "Mrs. James T. Worthing," nor "Mrs. J.

Theodore Worthing," is in good taste. The entire name should appear on a visiting card.

If you want to have joint cards made, remember this: Socially, a lieutenant is still called "Mister." He is called "Lieutenant" officially, but the calling cards should read "Lieutenant and Mrs. James Theodore Worthing." This appears to be a contradiction, and it really is. The old Army still calls a lieutenant "Mister" on social occasions, but during World War I it became the vogue to address him by his official title at all times. Either form is correct, though the old Army usage is preferred by everyone except the lieutenants. Individual calling cards are still proper, though joint cards are being used more and more, for calling. They were formerly used when sending flowers to funerals, as enclosures with gifts, etc.

Some stationers suggest to the bride the use of engraved thank-you cards; but of course you know that every gift you receive should be answered by a personal note in your own handwriting.

The proper form for an invitation to the church ceremony is:

Mr. and Mrs. James Prentiss Carver
request the honor of your presence
at the marriage of their daughter
Margaret Jean
to
James Theodore Worthing
Lieutenant, United States Army
Wednesday, the eighth of October
at five o'clock
St. Paul's Episcopal Church
San Antonio, Texas

"Request the *honor* of your presence" is the form used for church wedding invitations. If the wedding is to be in the home or at a club with a reception following the ceremony, the form "Request the pleasure of your company" is used.

Different localities seem to favor various hours for weddings. In the East, high noon is the fashionable hour for a formal wedding, and the wedding is usually followed by a breakfast, a reception, or a luncheon. In the South, late afternoon or evening weddings are popular on account of the climate, and are usually followed by a reception with dancing, or a buffet supper.

If the reception is to be at the bride's home, probably many who are invited to the church will not receive an enclosed invitation to the reception. Unless it is a garden party or one has an enormous house it would be impossible to invite all the church guests. Most people understand this, but great tact and care must be exercised lest an old friend of either family feel slighted. The invitation to the breakfast or reception is enclosed in the wedding invitation and reads like this:

Reception
Immediately following Ceremony
29 Arlington Drive

R.S.V.P.

The Full Military Church Wedding

I shall now describe an elaborate church wedding, as a standard, in the hope that it will cover any situation that may arise. It is given in detail only as a guide, so that a smaller wedding may be fashioned after it.

We shall assume that the bride-elect is from a very wealthy, socially prominent family. The setting is an historic old cathedral at which the bride's family has always worshiped. Perhaps a bishop will officiate, or some other high prelate assisted by several clergymen. A vested choir with a renowned soloist will furnish the music, and the entire church will be elaborately decorated by a florist. The chancel will be a bower of flowers, and the pews for the families and distinguished guests will be designated by ribbons or sprays of flowers tied to the pew ends. Should the groom be an Army boy and, say, serving in his father's regiment at the time of the wedding, then the colors, that is, the American flag and the regimental flag, might be so placed that the couple stand under them during the ceremony. There will be a colorful canopy or awning leading from street to church, and the florist will provide white canvas for the aisle inside.

This seems a good place to stress the vital importance of a wedding rehearsal. The bride always directs her rehearsal but never takes part in it, as it is considered bad luck. Someone else is her proxy. By all means have the organist present.

One thing about a military wedding is that the head groomsman is the one to set the organist straight about the marching tempo and to see that the whole ceremony moves smoothly with military precision—if there are no young children in the party to complicate matters.

The wedding day dawns! After collecting their bouquets at the bride's home, the bridesmaids proceed to the church. There they await their entrance cue in a room off the vestibule.

The groomsmen arrive at the church half an hour before the ceremony begins. The officers, having deposited their caps and military capes in a room off the vestibule, don gloves and assume their posts at the different aisles. Offering an arm to every lady, whether they know her or not, the groomsmen escort the bride's family and friends to the left-hand pews, and the groom's family and friends to the right-hand pews. High-ranking Army officers and their families attending the wedding should always be seated as befits their rank.

It is a nice gesture to send cards denoting seating—the day before the wedding—to closest friends or most distinguished guests ("Second Pew, left," etc.) These are presented to groomsmen.

After the groomsmen have seated all of the guests, the bride's mother enters and is escorted to her seat by the head groomsman. The doors are closed and no one is seated during the ceremony. The groomsmen march in in pairs and station themselves beside the first few pews in the nave of the church.

Next come the bridesmaids in pairs, and at the chancel they also divide and stand on the steps or go up into the chancel.

The maid or matron of honor is next in the bridal procession, and she stands on the left at the foot of the steps opposite the best man. If there are flower girls, they precede the ring bearer and separate at the chancel steps, standing in front of the groomsmen and bridesmaids.

The bride and her father drive to the church together. They wait with the bridesmaids until it is time for them to join the procession.

The bride enters on her father's *left* arm—then poor Dad doesn't have to stumble over a mess of veil and train to get to his seat. Authorities disagree on this point, and for the bride to enter on her father's right arm is equally correct, but at the rehearsal try out both entrances. Father will agree with the first plan, whether you do or not; but after all, it is up to you! It is your wedding.

The proper wedding marches are: processional, Wedding March from *Lohengrin* by Wagner; recessional, Mendelssohn's Wedding March.

Musical selections should always be of the classical type. Selections from any of the old masters, such as Wagner,

Brahms and Schubert, are always appropriate to be played by the organist during the half-hour preliminary period while the guests assemble.

Leave all popular favorites to be played or sung later at the reception where sentimental tunes can be as light and gay as the dancers desire. Should the bride or groom have a special anthem or hymn which he or she desires to have sung, it is a welcome innovation.

Wagner's "Evening Star" from *Tannhäuser*, Mendelssohn's "Spring Song" or Friml's "Toujours l'Amour" are favorites while "At Dawning," "I Love You Truly" and "Oh, Promise Me" still seem to thrill the most sophisticated of guests. If there is any doubt as to selection, consult your organist.

On the first note of the Wedding March the clergyman, followed by the groom and best man, step from the vestry into the chancel. The groom removes his right glove, holds it in his left hand, and stands at the head of the steps to await the bride. If there are several steps to the chancel, the groom goes down the steps to meet her, which seems more gallant. The guests like to see him smile as he watches his bride come up the aisle. Some bridegrooms look glum and scared!

When the bride and her father reach the steps of the chancel, the bride is met by the groom. She changes her bouquet to the other hand and puts her right arm through the groom's left arm. Her father moves back, then steps forward again when the clergyman asks, "Who giveth this woman . . . ?" The father then joins his wife in the first pew.

At this point the bride and groom, maid of honor and best man move forward to the altar. The bride hands her bouquet to the maid of honor, and the best man passes the wedding ring to the groom, who in turn hands it to the clergyman.

During the ceremony the clergyman returns the ring to the groom, who places it on the bride's finger at the words "With this ring." In a double ring ceremony, the maid of honor hands the groom's ring to the bride, who places it on his finger as soon as she has received her ring.

The final words of the ceremony having been pronounced, the handsome groom kisses his lovely bride, the clergyman says a few congratulatory words in which he wishes them happiness, and the recessional music begins. The maid of honor hands the bride her bouquet, and straightens her train. The bride and groom leave the chancel, and at the head of the steps they pause for a moment. Then the best man escorts the maid of honor, each groomsman escorts a bridesmaid, and it is a nice custom to have two of the groomsmen return to escort the two mothers from their pews to the door of the church before the ribbons are released. Even if there are not ribbons, the guests wait for the parents to leave, as there is ample time for this courtesy. The ushers form in two lines facing each other at the entrance of the church, and stand at attention as the guests file out.

Of course, the mothers may prefer to walk out with their husbands, but it gives a more military touch and it is a nice courtesy to have them escorted by one of the officers in the wedding party.

The ancient and traditional ceremony of the bride and groom walking under the arched swords of the officer ushers is always expected. At some weddings you will see this ceremony performed in the church, but never in a Roman Catholic Church. Would you like to know the reason for this? The practice of drawing swords at the altar or in the chancel of the church is entirely wrong. Because of the old law of right of sanctuary and refuge, as well as the very nature of a church, it is considered a flagrant breach of military etiquette to draw a sword in church.

The "arch" should be made outside the church if possible, but if inclement weather or street traffic should prevent this, then the crossing of swords may take place in the vestibule near the door. Civilian ushers line up with military ushers. The senior usher should give the order, "Draw sabers."—*Naval Customs, Traditions and Usage,* by Admiral Leland P. Lovette

In a military wedding, the groomsmen break ranks in the vestibule of the church; the bride and groom wait at the entrance of the church until the ushers are in formation. At a given command from the head groomsman an arch of swords is made, and the bride and groom walk beneath. This is very impressive and a beautiful introduction for the bride into the Army. Only the bride and groom pass under the arch of sabers; it is not proper for any other members of the wedding party to take part in this traditional ceremony. The flower girls, maid of honor and bridesmaids wait until the head groomsman orders:

1. Return
2. SABERS

I have seen the arch of sabers at many weddings in Protestant churches, and it is really up to the clergyman to make a decision on this. It is a little easier for the bridal party if it is held in the church, but it is equally effective if the arch is made outside on the steps of the church. Everyone loves to see the bride enter her new life under an arch of swords; there is something romantic and beautiful about the ceremony.

The bride's father, if he is not in the Service, wears a morning coat or cutaway and dark gray striped trousers. Very light gray buckskin gloves are usually worn.

The bride's mother, although she has all the responsibility of the wedding, does not seem to take an active part. She is the hostess at one of the most important events over which she will ever preside. "She is the official hub of the wedding and the stage manager; the diplomat without portfolio." A bride's mother should have great dignity; she is the lovely mature forecast of her daughter in the years to come and a symbol of her family's tradition. She is the last person to enter before the procession, and she should be becomingly and beautifully gowned. The groom usually send the bride's mother, also his own mother, a corsage. Perhaps a pale gray-blue or lavender chiffon, lace or velvet dress with a small matching hat might be worn. Upon rare occasions, the mother has been known to take the father's place in giving the bride away—when the father was deceased. This would be in very bad taste if the father were living and divorced.

The parents of the bride always sit in the first pew on the left, facing the chancel. The parents of the groom always sit in the first pew on the right. The immediate families occupy the pews behind these; then the honor guests and specially invited friends, who should have pew numbers, sit within the ribbons of the first twenty pews designated. If the groom's commanding officer and his wife are present—also any officers from his regiment—they should be seated as honor guests immediately behind the groom's relatives.

Invitation to a Post Chapel Wedding

Every bride naturally wants and should have her wedding at her own home church or in her own home; but the War Department doesn't always take the bride's wishes into consideration. Many Service brides get a thrill out of being married in a military chapel. The wholesale weddings at West Point on Graduation Day attest this fact, but unless you are an Army child or have some close family connection living on the post, it seems more proper to have the groom and groomsmen come to the bride, if possible. No matter how simple your home or how small the home church, unless circumstances over which you have no control direct otherwise it is in better taste for the bride and her family to stage the complete wedding.

This particular situation might arise: Your engagement has been announced to a flying cadet at Randolph Field, and the wedding is to take place the day of his graduation, the day he gets his wings and comes into the Army as an officer. He has received orders to proceed on foreign service immediately after graduation, and there is not time for him to fly east to your home even for his own wedding! Believe it or not, the War Department is just that hardhearted. You might as well learn it right now. The government regards women only as camp followers.

I like Elizabeth Custer's fine description of camp followers. In *Boots and Saddles* she says that whenever in the old days an officer's wife put down an emphatic foot or a group of pioneer women declared that they were going to take some decisive step to which the officers were opposed—something perhaps involving their safety—the officers would sportively look up the rules in *Army Regulations* for camp followers and read them to the offenders as they would the Riot Act. "The 'regs' still hold, I believe, and provide that the Commanding Officer has complete control over all camp followers . . . with power to put them off the reservation or detain them as he chooses." She also adds, "Though army women have no visible thrones or scepters, nor any rights according to Military Law, I never knew such queens as they, or saw more willing subjects than they govern." Understand, this was the "old Army of frontier days" when the C.O.'s wife was treated as a queen; however, even in these days, I must say Army women fare rather well whether or not the War Department is conscious of their existence or their wishes!

Getting back to the post chapel wedding—if you are to be married at your fiancé's station, you should be accompanied by your parents and as many of your immediate family or close relatives as is practicable. If you are an orphan, then your guardian or your closest relative should accompany you.

Facilities are available on a post, and it is possible to have a very lovely wedding. However, decorating the church, and all the expenses incident thereto should be borne by the bride's family. Your fiancé may, in your absence, have to make all the plans and arrangements with the Army chaplain, the organist, soloist, or choir; but remember, these expenses are taken care of by the bride's family.

It is a great help and a pleasing gesture if the groom will detail one of his groomsmen to assist the visiting parents in these cases. They come from afar and do not know about florists in the vicinity, how to find the chaplain, or how to go about the hundred and one wedding details that will necessarily come up. There are many things in which they will need help, and sometimes they need transportation.

Some young couples dispense with music and decorations, and have only their families and the officer's brother officers present. He always invites his commanding officer and his wife any any other ranking officers under whose direct command he serves. If he belongs to a regiment, it is customary to send invitations to each officer of the battalion in which he serves, or to each officer of the group of which he is a member.

The post chapel wedding might be followed by a small wedding dinner or reception at the Officers' Club; or this may be omitted.

The Home Wedding

For sentimental reasons, the bride may choose to be married at home or in the home of a relative or close friend. The military theme may be carried out, as in a formal church wedding. Home weddings at dusk, the house lighted by pale candlelight, can be particularly lovely. Spring flowers used in profusion or autumn leaves artistically arranged as a background may take the place of an expensive florist's services. An old-fashioned garden makes a perfect setting for a beautiful wedding.

In these trying times most men, particularly fathers who have the bills to pay, throw up their hands and balk at the mention of a big wedding. No wonder the poor dears are frightened if your plans are to compete with the wealthiest girl in your set; but you can still have a lovely wedding, making it as simple or as elaborate as you choose.

Dress

Here again the bride decides on the theme of her wedding. A note of informality, or the size of the house or garden, will determine the number of attendants, the number of guests, etc. There is a tendency in modern fashion for brides to choose delicate shades, such as ice blue and shell pink, and this is quite a personal matter; yet tradition decrees that white is really the color of the wedding gown. For the home wedding, white satin, bengaline, taffeta, velvet, crepe or any of the summer materials such as organza, *mousseline de soie* or chiffon are appropriate. The conservative bride marrying an Army officer should, with an eye to the future, choose a material and style of dress that with slight alteration can be converted into an evening dress. Sometimes the gown is made so that the long train is detachable. If the bride wishes, for sentimental reasons, to keep her wedding dress, then she may make it as elaborate as she wishes. Often she chooses to be married in her mother's wedding gown, and if there is not too great a difference in style and length, this is a perfect solution. The veil may be of rare lace, an heirloom in the family, or it may be of layers and layers of tulle arranged with orange blossoms or plain shirring.

For a home wedding in the evening (provided the groom, best man and groomsmen own Army blues) nothing can be more regal than to have them in full dress or special evening dress with gold belts, and capes. At the present time, however, most junior officers, unless they have served in Washington or have been White House aides, do not own complete blues, so you can compromise and the men will wear either the white dress uniform in summer or white mess jackets and black trousers . . . or the field service uniforms of O.D. The O.D. (olive drab), also called the field service uniform, is quite proper for weddings, even in the evening. At any rate you will want a military wedding. The officers who act as groomsmen or ushers will wear the same uniform as the groom.

THE EARLY MORNING WEDDING

Among Catholics, early morning weddings are quite usual and, regardless of the hour, may be as elaborate as the bride wishes. Sometimes in view of boat or train schedules an early hour is chosen and the ceremony is usually followed by a breakfast, either formal or informal. (A simpler wedding seems in better taste at such an hour, but that is also a decision for the bride to make.) In summer, the bride might wear organza or *mousseline de soie* rather than heavy satin; her veil could be of tulle instead of lace, and if she carried a bouquet or a sheaf of flowers gloves would be omitted. If she decides on a corsage bouquet, then gloves are proper. Her attendants might appear in the simplest sort of organdy dresses, the groom, his best man and the groomsmen in white uniforms. An all-white wedding in the early morning is a pretty sight, and the white uniform with its gold insignia is very effective.

If a white wedding is in the cards for you, of course satin is still the classic material for the wedding gown, but lace in its sheerest qualities is also highly favored. Frosted white organdy and marquisette are two leading fabrics for spring wedding gowns. A veil of illusion or heirloom lace intertwined with flowers such as lilies of the valley, orange blossoms and white violets may be arranged in a becoming coronet.

The bride decides on the number of bridesmaids, their costumes and flowers. Everything should blend with the general theme of the wedding. In the customs of yesterday affluent brides often gave the bridesmaids their dresses and all the accessories, but it is seldom done today. Sometimes she pays for all the garden hats or, if she is wealthy, has all of their slippers made to order along with her own. In any case, she should take into consideration the financial status of her attendants and make their necessary expenditures as small as possible.

One bride, several days after her engagement party, gave a small luncheon at her home and invited the girls she wanted to be in her wedding. Of course, by tactful planning and a knowledge of their desires, she knew that they could and would be glad to serve. Then they discussed plans and color schemes, exchanged ideas and had a glorious time! For what girl doesn't thrill at the mention of a wedding? It would be a serious mistake to ask a limited number and then have someone decline for financial or other reasons. The bride would be embarrassed about asking a substitute. No one is flattered at being a second choice. It might be better to ask them before the luncheon.

It is customary for the bride, if she has a sister, to choose her as either matron or maid of honor. If there are several sisters, all of them may be included, even as junior bridesmaids.

If the bride has no sisters, she chooses her most intimate friend. It is a nice gesture to invite the groom's favorite sister to be a bridesmaid. A bride, if she wants the whole stage to herself, may have no attendants; she may have only a maid of honor; or she may have a maid of honor, a matron of honor, four bridesmaids, or six bridesmaids. At one very elaborate Army wedding there were twelve bridesmaids. A dozen bridesmaids seems somewhat theatrical. The usual number is four or six.

No attempt will be made to suggest bridesmaids' costumes with the changing trend of fashions. Several years ago, rainbow weddings were the vogue. The bridesmaids dressed in the various hues of the rainbow; later came the fashionable all-white wedding, but this tends to take away a little from the bride's glamour. Tomorrow, the vogue will be something else; so the bride is free to set her own style. The only suggestion is: The bridesmaids' dresses and accessories should be alike as to materials, gloves, slippers, hats, flowers, and should complement or be of the same or similar material as the bride's dress. They may vary in shade to carry out a particular color motif. The dress of the maid or matron of honor is just a bit different, perhaps a trifle more elaborate. But remember, the bride's dress is the *pièce de résistance*—she is the central figure, and it is the big moment of her life! No one can or should try to eclipse her! Tactfully

suggest to your bridesmaids to go light on the make-up, to
strive for that natural debutante complexion.

Your bridesmaids will bless you if you select a style and
type of dress that they can do this and that to, and appear
in a second time without being marked as a member of so-
and-so's sextet.

Junior bridesmaids' dresses are usually of some simple
material and made in such a way that the little girls may
use them afterwards as party dresses. Ring bearers are seldom included in modern military weddings, but if you have
a little nephew whom you want to have in your wedding,
a simple white linen suit would be appropriate for him.
Train bearers also are seldom seen at a military wedding,
because they usually get excited and complicate matters—
for instance, by playing with the groomsmen's sabers or
doing something equally amusing but distracting.

The term "groomsmen" is still used in Army circles. The
bride and groom talk over the wedding plans together, and
the groom selects his best friend from among his brother
officers as "best man." In civilian circles it is customary
for the groom to ask the bride's brother to be his best man,
but this is seldom done in a military wedding—unless the
brother is in the Service. The number of ushers or groomsmen coincides exactly with the number of bridesmaids, and
they act as escorts for the bridesmaids at the reception.

You need have no worry about the dress of your fiancé
or his brother officers, once you have both decided on the
type of wedding it is to be—formal, informal; home, chapel
or church—and whether traditional blues, O.D. or white
uniforms will be worn. Army officers know exactly what
to wear on every occasion and are meticulously neat and
well groomed, especially when on parade!

Marriage at Parsonage or Magistrate's Office

This ceremony is not a wedding but merely a marriage. Street clothes are usually worn. The groom may wear uniform, though civilian clothes might be less conspicuous and preferable. An elaborate wedding dress does not seem appropriate, though a small breakfast, luncheon or dinner is in keeping.

The Second Marriage

Young war widows, and there are literally thousands of them, often ask about a white wedding. They still cherish the idea of a real wedding with all the formality which they probably had to forgo owing to the exigencies of war. Everything is against it, my dear!

Since the days of the ancient Romans white has symbolized virginity and purity, and it should be a custom preserved for a first-time bride alone. Weddings are formed upon just such charming traditions.

If you desire a festive wedding, then compromise by choosing a delicately tinted pastel gown of floor length with a short floating veil-like headdress. Ice blue is a popular color for a wedding of this type.

An older widow who prefers a small church wedding to whom only the close friends of the bride and groom are invited often chooses gray, a soft shade of blue or violet or perhaps a tailored suit. If a white dress is worn, it should have a touch of color in trim or flowers to get away from the traditional white which custom has reserved for the first-time bride.

Of course, by the same token this tradition applies also to divorcees who marry for the second time even though their maiden names were restored by the court. In other words, no woman rates two white weddings!

FLOWERS

Although the bride may select the flowers and make arrangements with the florist, the groom pays for:

Flowers sent to the bride
Corsage sent to the bride's mother
Corsage sent to his mother
Boutonnieres if civilian clothes are worn by groomsmen

The bride's family pays for:

All flower decorations for church and home
Flowers for bridesmaids
Flowers for flower girls
Flowers for maid of honor or matron of honor
The organist
The soloist

Now for the bride's flowers! Remember, Army men do not earn very much, and you won't want him to spend his all on flowers. Fifteen dollars is the average for the wedding bouquet, and if you go into a huddle with your florist, he will wax enthusiastic and patriotic and, with a few suggestions from you, will arrange something lovely. As a suggestion, how about white gladioli treated like orchids; or tulips with their petals turned back, their leaves forming a fan as a background; or fragrant freesias on top of a prayer book with a shower of satin ribbons, freesias knotted into them; or Easter lilies or calla lilies. Or, for five dollars you should get something heavenly in white sweet peas, camellias, gardenias or a spray of white lilacs.

A recent bride requested the florist to make her bouquet

into sixteen small bouquets, with a beautiful orchid in the center. When she threw her separated bouquet to the waiting bridesmaids, each of them received "a bouquet that is supposed to bring them an early bethrothal" and the bride kept the orchid to wear on her going-away suit.

FEES

The groom pays the clergyman. The lowest fee is usually ten dollars, and, depending upon the groom's rank and circumstances, varies from ten to a hundred dollars. The amount is enclosed in an envelope, and the best man gives it to the clergyman in the vestry immediately after the service. An Army chaplain will not accept a fee; so it is not offered, which leaves ten dollars more for the honeymoon. Naturally the wedding trip and ring are the responsibility of the groom.

GROOM'S GIFT TO BRIDE

This is purely optional and depends upon the groom's financial circumstances. Most second lieutenants in the Army have all they can swing to finance their small part in a wedding. However, if the groom can possibly afford it, a *small* personal gift of jewelry, something she can wear, will have a certain sentimental value. West Pointers often give their brides a pearl-studded "A" pin. If there is an heirloom in the family in the way of a string of pearls, a ring or an old-fashioned pin, or some piece of jewelry which a doting grandmother passes on to her favorite grandson, he may give this to his bride.

THE HOME RECEPTION

Properly speaking, the only persons in the receiving line are the bride, the groom, and the wedding attendants. The

mother—also the groom's mother—usually greets guests at
the door, while the bride's father and groom's father mingle
among the guests. However, there are many solutions to
this problem. At a recent military wedding reception at the
Officers' Club, both the mothers and the fathers of the bride
and groom received with the newly married couple. The
bride and groom stood between the two families, and the
attendants followed the groom's parents.

The party may be as simple or as elaborate as one wishes,
but at a military wedding party it is customary to have a
bridal cake, the first slice of which the bride cuts with her
husband's saber, his hand over hers. It is also customary
to drink a toast to the bride. This toast is usually proposed
by the best man. Again the groomsmen draw their sabers
together—1. Draw; 2. Sabers—and cross them over the bride's
head, while the toast is drunk by all the guests. These parties
are usually very gay with music, and if space permits, dancing follows. The groom always dances first with his bride,
then with the attendants in the wedding. When the crowd
thins, the bride whispers to her maid of honor to assemble
the bridesmaids in the hall. They all gather at the foot of the
stairs, and about halfway up the bride tosses her bouquet.
They all try to catch it, but the lucky one is supposed to be
the next one to go to the altar. The bride, accompanied by
her mother and bridesmaids, goes up to her room, where she
changes into her traveling ensemble. The groom goes to a
room that has been reserved for him in the bride's home,
changes his clothes and waits until he is summoned and
told that the bride is ready. Then they come downstairs
together, say good-by to all of the relatives and the remaining guests and leave. Many young couples wish to keep
their wedding trip plans secret; so they skip the leave-taking
except of their parents and slip out without the knowledge

of the guests. They miss a lot of fun, such as the rice shower or having their car placarded with newlywed signs and old shoes, but perhaps if they are shy they prefer to avoid this fun at their expense.

For the reception at home it is always easier to have a caterer handle the dinner, supper or refreshments if you can possibly afford it. A reputable caterer brings his own serving men or maids, the food will be good and perfectly served and if necessary he can furnish dishes and extra silver. There is enough excitement in the house, what with extra house guests and the wedding and all. The catering task is too much to expect of the bride's mother or any hostess unless it is a great house with trained servants in abundance.

If you cannot afford to have a caterer, then by all means keep the refreshments as simple as possible. The wedding cake could be baked beforehand or ordered, and punch can be made a few hours ahead. Champagne punch is not necessary at all, but it somehow seems to go with weddings. If you prefer a simple fruit punch with iced tea as a base, then stick by your principles and serve it.

Wedding Reception at Club

When the guest list is very large, and the bride wishes to include more friends at the reception than can be accommodated at her home, the wedding party is often given at a club or hotel. All the details, such as decorations, menu, music, can be taken care of expertly by the club, and the bride and her mother are relieved of this responsibility.

The receiving line, formed near the entrance of the ballroom or lounge, includes the parents of the bride, the parents of the groom, the bride and groom, then the bridesmaids. The groomsmen are not in the receiving line, and sometimes the fathers of the bride and groom prefer to mingle with the guests. In this case, the mothers receive with the bridal party.

If there is to be a dinner, there is a center table—the bride's table—at one end of which she and the groom are seated. At the opposite end sit the bride's father and the groom's mother, next to him the bride's mother, and, on her right, the groom's father. At the left of the bride's father is seated the clergyman's wife if he has one; if not, then the grandmother of the bride or some close relative. The best man sits on the bride's right, and on the groom's left is the maid of honor; then the ushers and bridesmaids and relatives make up the rest of the table. The wedding cake is the centerpiece, and when it is to be cut, a waiter places it before the bride, or if it is a narrow table she may go to the center and cut the cake. At a large dinner of this sort the bride usually cuts only one slice with her husband's saber. Individual boxes of wedding cake are at each place and are to be taken home by the guests; the bridesmaids are supposed to put them under their pillows and dream on them for good luck.

The other wedding guests are seated at small tables either in the dining room or on the terrace.

As to menus, the club will be glad to suggest a suitable one. Few people can afford to entertain on a very large scale, so buffet suppers are increasingly popular. Young people like the informality and would much rather have a good orchestra for dancing than a fine dinner. At these parties, the simplest of refreshments are served. All the young ask is that there be plenty of it. Chicken salad in piping-hot rolls, and champagne punch were served at one reception, augmented, of course, by coffee, tea and other beverages. Small cakes, an ice, and mints could be added.

GIFTS TO THE BRIDESMAIDS

This custom is gaining in popularity, it seems, but it is by no means obligatory. Depending upon the bride's circumstances, she may give some little trinket, but it is nice to give something lasting, no matter how small. One recent Army bride gave each of her attendants a miniature silver pin in the shape of a spoon that was a replica of her pattern of silver. Evening accessories aften are given, or something that is to be worn in the wedding by the bridesmaids. Evening bags are popular, as are fans, charm bracelets, compacts, or some similar trifle. The groom usually gives to his groomsmen some small gift—studs, links, cigarette cases or leather traveling accessories.

WEDDING PRESENTS

Wedding invitations are usually mailed three weeks before the wedding date. Very soon, gifts will begin to arrive at the bride's home. She would have on hand a gift book—it can be bought at any good stationer's—and as each gift arrives, she or her mother should fill in the date the present is received, the article, the name and address of the donor, where bought, and the date the gift was acknowledged.

This is a systematic and methodical way to keep a record, and will be a wonderful help when everything seems to arrive at once and you feel overwhelmed. Too, it is much nicer, and you can write a more enthusiastic note of thanks if you write immediately to the person who was kind enough to remember you. If the presents start coming in too fast, put them in a special room and do not open them until you are free to record them.

A bride must write a note of thanks to every person who was generous enough to remember her. The omission of this is the one thing that the sender may forgive but will never forget, and your youth will not excuse you. Telephoning is out; in your enthusiasm you may express your first thanks in this manner, but the written note must follow, no matter how simple it is. It may be only one line, such as: "Thank you for the beautiful present you and Major Singleton sent me." But send it, even if only a line. You must.

Of course, a typewritten letter or note should never be sent, and worst of all is the engraved card of thanks. Do not let any silver-tongued engraver entice you into buying these cards, which would be an engraved admission on your part of not knowing the social amenities.

Some people frown upon displaying the presents as a vulgar exhibition intended to show one's popularity; others think it is quite the thing; so you can let your conscience be your guide. If the presents are displayed at a wedding reception, they are usually shown in the library or in an upstairs bedroom from which the furniture has been removed. White-covered tables are arranged, and special tact should be used in grouping the presents. Cards are usually left on, though that is also a matter of taste. Checks are never displayed but one clever bride whose uncle had sent her a generous check decided to spend the money for a love seat. She bought a miniature, attached his card and placed it among the gifts. It attracted considerable attention. Usually silver is arranged on one table, glass (heaven forbid that an Army bride receive much of this lovely commodity) and china on another table.

Suppose the bride received a dozen or so pairs of candlesticks or salts and peppers. There is nothing wrong with exchanging these gifts for something else but the exchange should not be made until after the wedding. Stores cooperate and are usually glad to make the exchanges if too long a time is not allowed to elapse between the purchase and the exchange.

After a bride decides upon her pattern in silver, the leading jewelry store usually makes note of it. In small towns it is customary for the store to keep a list of the silver purchased, and, should a customer ask for advice, the salesman is able to make suggestions. In this way duplicates are avoided. For the same reason it seems best not to have silver engraved. All wedding presents are sent to the bride's home, and by law they belong to her.

In some Army towns, where a Service engagement is announced the leading stores invite the bride to come in and select her pattern of silver, china or crystal. The stores keep a gift book for "Mary Jones," and when hurried friends telephone in for a gift, the obliging saleswoman can tell them the pattern, what she needs most, what she has already been given, and the purchasers may consult their own desires and purses in the matter. Much time and effort can be saved and, above all, Mary will be pleased. Instead of a houseful of two-, three- and five-dollar gimcracks Mary will have lovely sets of matched silver, plates and glassware that will be a godsend when she gives her first Army party.

This method may seem very mercenary, and by some will be definitely frowned upon; but it is practical. The trained salespeople handle the situation most tactfully, the friend who has only three dollars to spend can send Mary one oyster fork and she will love it if it matches her pattern. When she opens the package, instead of frowning and thinking (if she does not actually say it), "Oh, my!" she will beam and say, "Oh, how lovely! Now I have eight of my set."

When eager-to-please relatives and friends beg you to tell them what you want for a wedding present, don't just be namby-pamby and evade the issue by saying, "I'd love anything!" How stupid. . . . Always consider the person's financial status and never suggest anything beyond his means, but don't hesitate to give out ideas. You will receive enough white elephants that won't fit in with your Army future anyway, so be specific when you are asked.

Checks are by far the best presents because you can convert them into exactly what you want and need for your new home. Here are some practical ideas for gifts: electric percolator, electric grill, iron, hot pad, electric blanket, electric clock, pair of boudoir lamps, table radio, luggage rack, blanket covers, silver picture frame, large ash trays, cigarette box. If I were you, I should prefer to buy all of this type of bric-brac in either silver or Steuben glass or a good matching crystal . . . with someone's fat check. Sterling silver is the most lasting of wedding gifts; discourage anyone's giving you a set of china, no matter how fine, unless it is an heirloom or something in open stock. It is better, in the Army, to buy china as you need it, and you will have opportunities to buy imported china from time to time at various stations.

Some really lovely dessert plates or a salad set might be a welcome addition. But the heirloom china will prove more than a white elephant, until the quartermaster has broken the last piece! That may occur on your first Army move or the last one you have in some thirty years of nomadic life, depending mostly on whether or not Buddha smiles on you.

Avoid fads, such as chromium gadgets, pewter or all-wooden table service. A piece or so is fine, but a set will date you. I was married in the "polychrome age," which was long before your time. Fortunately my set was all destroyed in an Army fire, and I replaced some of the gifts in silver as time went on. Good silver is lasting and a good investment. Formerly only the bride's monogram or initials were used, but today it is deemed proper to use the bride's future initials. Simple block letters are considered smart, or a single Old English initial. Again, don't go in for fads if you expect to enjoy your silver in the days to come. Choose a conservative pattern with simple marking. Very plain silver was quite the vogue a few years ago, but it scratches easily; so choose something that you really like and that won't be too expensive when you are ready to add to it. If you can possibly afford it, buy sterling flat silver. Even if you have to start with only two knives and forks, better to have four of the essential pieces in sterling than round dozens of everything in plated ware. You can continue adding to them until you have a dozen of everything. If it isn't "looking the gift horse . . ." you might also ask for a non-tarnish silver chest in which to keep your silver; however, the usual flannel bags are easier to pack.

Here is a list of what you should get with the checks you receive, or if relatives ask you frankly what you need in silver:

Flat silver in sterling:
4 luncheon-size knives and forks
4 bouillon spoons
4 butter spreaders
4 salad forks
12 teaspoons
3 large table or serving spoons
1 steak or carving set

Later, you can build your service up to twelve or eighteen, with additional dinner-size knives and forks, cream soup spoons, iced tea spoons, ice-cream forks, after-dinner coffee spoons, and a large-size carving set.

In a good heavily plated silver you can use:

1 silver meat platter
1 silver vegetable dish with two or three compartments

1 silver bread tray
1 or more silver sandwich trays, nut and bonbon dishes

Of course, if some fairy godmother presents you with a silver tea service, and you receive in addition a beautiful tray to go with it, be grateful . . . but the first thing to do is *insure* it.

If china is in order as a gift, then the dinner setting should include: dinner, salad and butter plates, cream soups and saucers, teacups and saucers.

A FEW WEDDING TRADITIONS

An old tradition newly important to modern young brides and grooms is the custom of double wedding rings, a slim band for her and a wider band for him . . . tangible tokens of their troth.

The diamond solitaire is the visual symbol of an engagement, a symbol that all brides have dreamed of from little girlhood, a symbol of happiness shared by two people. Army men often have a diamond set in a miniature of their class rings.

The bride's cake—that towering, gleaming, iced confection—is one of the long-cherished legends of every wedding and is an established wedding tradition.

The groom's cake is traditionally dark with rich fruits. Small pieces are individually packed in white boxes tied with white ribbon, and often the bride's and groom's initials or monogram are embossed on the box in silver. Each guest is given a little cake to take home and dream on . . . another touch of wedding magic! If boxes are not available, squares of waxed paper and paper napkins embossed with the given names of the bride and groom are provided.

The bride wears formal white kid gloves, slit for the third finger, left hand.

The lace-edged bit of linen may be a dainty wedding handkerchief, sometimes new, sometimes old, but generally fitting part of the jingle . . . "something old, something new, something borrowed, something blue."

A superstition is that the groom should never see the bride's wedding dress until the ceremony. Happy the bride the sun shines on! But all brides are happy, even if it pours rain, for it is *their* day!

The Wedding Trip

This is the event of your life. There will never be another trip to compare with it; so forget everything, and be happy. Army officers can seldom offer their brides a very expensive, luxurious trip; but that doesn't matter so long as you are young, in love and congenial. Sometimes orders for foreign service makes it possible to have a glorious honeymoon to Hawaii or the Orient. More often a few days' leave between stations is all that can be taken. Whatever fate has in store for you, be a good sport and adjust yourself to any circumstances that arise. Above all, don't forget . . .

"You're in the Army now."

Wedding Anniversaries

First year...Paper
Second year..................................Calico, cotton
Third year..Leather
Fourth year...Silk
Fifth year...Wood
Sixth year..Iron
Seventh year.......................................Copper
Eighth year..............Electric appliances (very practical)
Ninth year..Pottery
Tenth year..Tin
Eleventh year.......................................Steel

Twelfth year...Linen
Thirteenth year.......................................Lace
Fourteenth year......................................Ivory
Fifteenth year.......................................Crystal
Twentieth year.......................................China
Twenty-fifth year....................................Silver
Thirtieth year.......................................Pearls
Thirty-fifth year.............................Jade and coral
Fortieth year..Rubies
Forty-fifth year...................................Sapphires
Fiftieth year..Gold
Fifty-fifth year...................................Emeralds
Sixtieth year......................................Diamonds
Seventy-fifth year.................................Diamonds

Chapter IV

CUSTOMS OF THE SERVICE FOR THE BRIDE

Over hill, over dale,
As we hit the dusty trail,
And those caissons go rolling along!
—Artillery song

WHEN the wedding trip is over and the bride realizes that she and her husband are nearing an Army post or Air Force installation, the place that is to be their first home, she gets a distinct thrill. At last they arrive and are stopped at the gate by a sentry! If the officer is reporting for duty at a new station, he will direct the taxi to take him to post headquarters or he will drive his own car there.

First, he registers and reports in for duty. You will remain in the car, Peggy, until Ted returns with the keys to the quarters you will occupy. Ten to one, the quarters will not be ready and you will have to stay at the hostess house or a hotel in the near-by town until the quarters are vacated. None of this procedure is very romantic or what you had pictured.

Again, if Ted is an officer returning to his station with his bride and has made friends on the post, your reception may be entirely different. In lieu of the rolling caisson mentioned in the song above, a group of Ted's friends may have decorated a jeep for your inaugural ride around the post. The jeep will be equipped with a loud horn which will be blown

81

constantly as you make your first tour of the post; the drivers of the cars following in the procession will also blow their horns so as to acquaint everyone with the fact that this is a bridal procession. Soldiers will stop their work to wave a greeting, Army wives will dash to the windows to get a glimpse because everyone loves a bride! The procession will probably draw up at the Officers' Club where a little informal welcoming party will have been arranged by some of Ted's friends for you to meet dozens of officers and their wives, some of whom will be your lifelong friends. There is something fine and lasting about the first friends and contacts a bride and groom make in the Army. Once you are within your own particular social ivory tower, you will find the Army a true democracy. It's a very special kind of democracy, as you will find.

Time marches on, but not too many years have elapsed between this day of mechanized cavalry and artillery and the time of mounted regiments. Let us look back twenty or thirty years to the colorful reception given an Army bride. As the proud young officer with his pretty bride approached the post, nervously she asked her husband why there were so many people at the gate. He smiled, but by this time the colonel of the regiment, his wife and many of the officers and their ladies had surrounded the horse-drawn Dorehty wagon or conveyance to extend a greeting and welcome to the bride. The regimental band immediately struck up "Here Comes the Bride." In the old days, in the mounted branches, the officers greeted the bride and groom by riding out on horseback beyond the post to meet them. Then the officers and ladies of the groom's regiment gathered at the quarters of the commanding officer where a reception was held and an "Army toast to the bride" was drunk.

Until the next bride arrived, this one was considered the

bride of the regiment. She was given the seat of honor at the commanding officer's right at the first large dinner party; often she was in the receiving line, and she invariably got a big rush at the first hop and was the belle of the ball. If the groom had been with the regiment even only for a few weeks, they were given a regimental wedding present, usually a silver platter, a coffee service or some piece of silver on which was engraved the crest of the regiment. This was always a treasured gift because of the sentiment attached to it.

A few regiments today hold an annual reception to honor brides who have come to the station within the past year.

The 9th Infantry, formerly stationed at Fort Sam Houston, is a very colorful regiment, and the old traditions are still carried out. The Infantry Punch Recipe has been handed down for many years, and on special social regimental occasions the famous punch bowl is used. It is a huge silver bowl, large enough for an average man to sit in with his legs folded beneath him, and it is of solid silver! This gorgeous treasure belongs to the 9th Infantry and was acquired during the Boxer Rebellion in Peking.

After the reception, during which the bewildered bride met so many people she was in a complete daze, a few of the groom's closest friends and their wives accompanied the young couple to their new home or quarters. The groom carried his bride over the doorstep, kissing her as he crossed the threshold. The guests, equipped with all the makings for another welcoming toast, stayed for one round of drinks and then departed. Alone at last!

This description of the bride's reception to an Army post is, of course, confined to peacetime! With the great wartime influx of young officers and their brides, regiments and commands could not possibly carry out these old social customs without permitting their work to suffer. In wartime many of the customs of the Service are necessarily curtailed, and to the bride a great part of the sociability, the tradition, and the glamour is lost.

The postwar bride will come back into her own, no doubt, with all the traditions of the Service and others added. According to *The Officers' Guide*, "The newly married couple is conducted around the post over a suitable route terminating at their quarters, the band playing appropriate airs. On arrival at the destination the bride and groom dismount and all officers PRESENT SABERS TO THE BRIDE. When possible the new home should be made ready for occupancy prior to their arrival by friends or members of the garrison."

Often, several wives go in together and stock the frigidaire with the essentials, such as butter, milk, eggs, bacon, and the kitchen shelves with coffee, sugar, salt, pepper, bread and other necessities. Another method used on foreign duty is for a member of a committee to supply the above foods and charge to the officer's commissary account.

QUARTERS

"Quarters" is the Army term used for residence, apartment or dwelling which an officer and his dependents occupy. It may mean anything from a shelter—and I mean literally a shelter, such as a Quonset hut—to a comfortable, palatial home.

If you are not stationed on an Army post, you will probably live in town. This may mean an apartment or a house, a motor court or a trailer! A second lieutenant with less than five years' service with dependents is allowed $60 rental allowance; over five years' service, $75. A first lieutenant with less than ten years' service gets $75; over ten years' service, $90. A captain with less than seventeen years' service is allowed $90; over seventeen years' service, $105. A major with less than twenty-three years' service receives $105; over twenty-three years' service, $120. The rental allowance remains $120 on up through the grade of general of the armies!

It is unnecessary to go into the pay scale and variations here, but if you live off the reservation, the term used is "being on commutation." It means the officer must commute from the post to his quarters and receives a rental allowance (which is seldom adequate even if he can find suitable quarters). An officer in the Army is expected to live in a good residential part of a town or city. Generally speaking, it is more desirable to live on a post and forfeit the commutation. Sometimes an officer has a choice; but if there are quarters available, the rule is, they must be occupied.

The average set of quarters on an average post of today for a junior officer or company officer consists of a living room, dining room, kitchen, two bedrooms and a bath, and sometimes a maid's room and bath. If the furniture is available, the following pieces are issued: living room—a desk and chair, also a folding table; dining room—dining table, eight chairs (two arm and six side chairs) and a buffet; kitchen—a stove, refrigerator and kitchen table; bedroom— G.I. cots or beds, mattresses, two dressers, one chiffonier, one dressing table and bench. At least you can get along with this, and you should have to buy very little to be comfortable. A comfortable divan, the new sectional type, would be practical, and with several substantial chairs and the addition of lamps, curtains, pictures and rugs, will make a very livable set of quarters.

To a bride of my day this would have sounded palatial. My first post was Fort Sill, Oklahoma, and we arrived one cold day in January in a typical Oklahoma dust storm. After the customary festivities of arriving were over, and the guests had gone, I looked around at our quarters with a sinking heart. It was a small four-room box with beaver board walls and the woodwork painted a deep Java coffee brown, of which my gallant young lieutenant seemed very proud. The eight-by-ten living room contained a fat little heating stove, two barracks chairs and a rough pine kitchen table. In the bedroom, my husband's faithful striker, Valinchus, had placed two G.I. (government issue) cots or bunks neatly made up with issue sheets and O. D. (olive drab, also issue) blankets. In the one tiny closet he had hung all of the lieutenant's uniforms, and around the room he had made a little fence of his boots. (Vaguely I wondered where my trousseau was to be stored!) The dining room contained a similar pine kitchen table and four barracks chairs, and the six-by-nine kitchen had room only for its one imposing item, an Army coal range.

My husband seemed happy, and proud of our home. He pointed out with pride how much Valinchus had done in his absence. The floors had all been scrubbed and painted, the stoves polished, the windows cleaned; there was a neat woodpile at the back door, and had I noticed the "new window shades"? That was a special favor from the Q.M. (quartermaster) although they were also G.I. I went to sleep that night praying that it would look better in the daylight. It didn't—it was shabbier than ever!

My experiences would make a pioneer woman of the frontier days smile. If you are interested in stories concerning the lives of pioneer women in the old days, I recommend to you *Boots and Saddles*, by Elizabeth Custer, and *Tenting on the Plains*, by the same author. When your lot seems drear, go to the post librarian and ask for some of the books written by officers' wives of frontier days. These brave women fought prairie fires, experienced pestilence, earthquakes and Indian raids, lived through floods, stagecoach holdups, grasshopper scourges and mutinies.

A very short bibliography of books written by Army women includes:

Reminiscences of a Soldier's Wife, by Ellen McGown Biddle, gives a graphic description of the hardships and terrors to which Army women were subjected during the early days of the settling of the West.

Vanished Arizona, by Martha Summerhayes, wife of General Summerhayes (retired), tells a very amusing and entertaining story of her experiences with Indians, rattlesnakes and buffalo herds in the wilds of Arizona.

With Custer's Cavalry, by Katherine Gibson Fougera, is dedicated to the memory of Elizabeth Custer, and is a fascinating book of memoirs of the late Katherine Gibson, widow of Captain Francis M. Gibson of the famous 7th Cavalry, U.S.A.

Army Letters from an Officer's Wife, by Francis M. Roe, is a humorous and spicy account of the old days.

These books and others that are listed in the Bibliography will furnish entertaining reading for a rainy afternoon, and in addition will give you an insight into the customs of the "old Army."

Another must on your reading list about the old Army days is *The Immortal Wife* by Irving Stone. It is the inspiring story of Jessie Benton Frémont, her ambition for General Frémont, her courage in following him to California and to the ends of the earth. It is a beautiful love story with an Army background.

Furnishing Army Quarters on a Limited Budget

The Army bride whose husband has acquired or collected nothing in the way of house furnishings is well off, whether

she realizes it or not. Of course, it is even more desirable
if he has a nice bank account and gives her carte blanche
for the furnishing of their first quarters, but only if she has
had some training in interior decorating and knows how to
budget the dollar. (Many shops nowadays will help make
a furnishing budget.) Otherwise she will make some ghastly
mistakes and poor buys, which will rise to haunt her at every
move. So perhaps it is just as well that the second lieutenant's wife does not have carte blanche at first. Let her use
her resourcefulness.

Be it ever so humble, there'll never be another place like
that G.I. furnished Quonset, or the unfurnished garage apartment in some small town where you first set up housekeeping. Nor will there ever be another dinner like the first one
served on a G.I. table or a rough packing box, but in fine
style . . . with your best silver and china and a bottle of
champagne maybe, by way of being festive!

Right off, learn to use your best possessions together every
day; don't hold back for company. Remember, you'll want
to keep your husband as long as you do your silver! It was
remarkable the way Army brides converted dreary furnished
rooms into attractive, livable places during the war. One
young bride let me in on a secret which I shall pass on to
you: really lovely accessories.

You won't be able to do much about the outside of the
quarters, and if you live on a post where there are rows and
rows of duplexes you dare not distinguish your domicile by
painting your front door a Chinese red or a turquoise blue.
The quartermaster even frowns upon a distinguishing brass
door knocker, unless one agrees to leave it as government
property. (You see, the door knocker's nails might leave
holes in the door which even putty would not cover!) You
might as well learn early in the game that any improvement

you make on government property is not supposed to be removed. And I might as well admit that I have a penchant for color, and I like a lipstick-red door with white trim and a huge brass knocker and pots of English ivy on either side.

The welcome to your home is right at the front door. An unswept front porch, strewn with old newspapers, leaves, toys is not a very inviting approach. Make your windows interesting; they are the eyes of your house. Curtains of the cheapest sort of material can look effective if enough material is used. The effect of amplitude even with cheesecloth lends a more luxurious air than even very expensive fabrics stingily used.

There is nothing lovelier than crisp white muslin or organdy curtains, crossed over the upper sash and looped back to show a pot of blossoming perky cyclamen or pink azaleas. This is one way to make your quarters different from the other sixty-three sets in a row! Keep your window treatments simple.

Your home, no matter if it is a one-room efficiency apartment or a bare set of Army quarters, is a distinct revelation of your personality. Your living room paints your portrait as a homemaker, and is more of an index to character than any palm reading would ever reveal. It is much more than a collection of furniture and fabrics; it is your background. There is no doubt that a home has an individual atmosphere just as a person has an individual personality. The moment one steps inside the door of a house one senses something of that atmosphere.

You don't need "Welcome" on the front-door mat if you can achieve hospitality, eagerness and delight when you respond to a guest's knock or ring. If you have a maid to answer the door, does she smile when she admits a guest? If you have a dog, teach him to wag his tail in welcome, rather than tear to the front door and frighten the visitor by his ferocious manner or barking.

Have your front hall brightly lighted; it gives a cheery air to the house. Place a big bowl or a battery jar of greens such as laurel or ivy on a table in the hall if you can't afford fresh flowers. If this isn't convenient, you can always have a bowl of bulbs or some flowering plant. One of the first things I always do in settling a new home is to invest in five or six potted plants. They work wonders, besides giving me a lift. If you have only one mirror, hang it in the hall over a console or table. Both you and your guests will enjoy a last-minute look to give you and them the assurance and poise needed!

A Few Army Trade Secrets

Your furniture arrangement can make or break a room. Don't place anything cater-cornered. This means a sofa, radio, piano, desks, tables and chests. Select your end tables the same height as your sofa and chairs. Buy end tables and straight chairs in pairs.

Use only one bold pattern in any room. With gay flowered chintz for draperies and slip covers, use a plain rug and keep walls plain.

Hang your pictures with thought and care in groups; otherwise they will look like postage stamps. Always hang a large picture or a group of smaller ones over something.

Lamps should be tall enough to give a good shaft of light for reading, sewing or writing. Lamps are tremendously important, and so are lamp shades. They date a room as nothing else can.

Hangings should reach the floor, and glass curtains may reach the window sill or drop below it to the floor.

Beware of dinky gadgets that are ineffectual. For instance,

choose sturdy book ends that will really hold books, large ash trays, and vases and bowls that are practical.

Men like feminine women but they like functional houses. A happy household is a synthesis of both; and the wise homemaker early learns to make her house work for her rather than vice versa.

The Living Room.

Your living room can be completely charming without being expensive if you will use your wits and a sewing machine. Of course, not every bride is skilled in using a sewing machine, but this is a good time to begin. Plan your living room to be really lived in. If your husband is six feet three and you are five feet two, select furniture that will fit each of you. Low chairs in which a tiny person can lean back blissfully may be more than a headache to an ex-football player.

Provided the quarters have the usual G.I. furniture, a desk, table and chairs, you will want at least two comfortable chairs as soon as you can afford them.

A good divan is always expensive, but don't buy a cheap new one. One old Army trick is to use a G.I. cot, upholster the ends with G.I. pillows and make a well-fitting slip cover for it. If you aren't expert enough as a seamstress yourself, then hire someone to do it. It pays. Don't omit the pillows and plenty of them! One clever bride, with her husband's help, made good modernistic bookcases and end tables out of packing boxes. Often Army women use "target cloth" for curtains. This is usually obtainable through the Ordnance Department, is very cheap and dies beautifully. Until you can afford good rugs such as Oriental or Broadloom, don't buy any. Make string rugs, dying them to match your color scheme, or use hooked rugs. Grass rugs or the invaluable *lauhala* mats are in order in the tropics.

When your budget will stand it, invest in a comfortable divan or two love seats for your living room. A good plan is to watch the used furniture ads in the papers, haunt the secondhand stores, or the antique shops if you are collecting. Or go to the express company and the storage company sales that are usually held twice a year. There you can often pick up really good, well-made, expensive pieces of furniture at your own price. Get a good decorator to come and help you plan your living room. Pocket your pride, tell him what you have to spend and be honest; then you can take his suggestions and do the best possible.

By all means, consider the new sectional furniture . . . the kind that can be separated and used as individual pieces, or in twosomes form a love-seat, or with three or four units make an extra-long sofa on which Ted can stretch full length. The only difficulty is that it appears bulky; however, soon it may be made of light plastic material.

Never buy faddish furniture or something for the particular house you are occupying. Remember, you may move tomorrow! Avoid massive or very heavy pieces. You will pay excess on every move, and that runs into money. By the same standard, avoid very light, frail furniture, or brittle antiques that won't stand packing and hard moves. The old saying, "Three moves are equivalent to a fire," is very true in the Army.

If you buy really good chintz, have it lined as a protective measure. It is wise to consult a good decorator before investing. Even with short windows, make your hangings three yards long so that they will fit any window, any place you may move. When buying material for three windows, it is wise to buy enough for a fourth. Three sets of curtains often prove awkward.

Recently I saw a large picture window framed in a drapery of philodendron ivy plants. Place one on either side of the window, letting the leafy tendrils climb up the casing. Philodendron will grow and thrive in spite of you, and soon you will have a complete frame and cornice of shining green leaves. It really is a novel way to grow your own draperies.

The Dining Room

On almost every post, furniture for the dining room is issued. Should you be compelled to buy it, then a drop-leaf table or a gate-leg table that can later be used in a living room or hall is preferable to a dining set. Odd chairs work out to better advantage later. If there is any possibility of your going to Panama, China or the Philippines, spend very little on china. An inexpensive set of dishes that can be used in the kitchen later is desirable. Assuming that you received your flat silver as a wedding present, and that some fairy godmother gave you a silver tea service, start to fill in your silver slowly, buying one good piece at a time. Cheap hollow ware bends badly in moving. We are also assuming that you have a good supply of linen in your trousseau.

Card tables are all right for card playing, but even the strongest and most sturdy are wobbly and rickety for dining. Don't join the card-table-using fraternity except for parties.

Begin using your sterling silver and your wedding presents from the start so that you and your husband can set a standard of living graciously. To live with your own beautiful possessions in close daily contact makes life richer and fuller. It is the little routine things like eating breakfast together and using your spode breakfast service that you will treasure the longest.

Colorful place mats can make an attractive table. Personally, I loathe paper napkins, and it isn't too much trouble to rinse out small napkins, but that is a matter of personal choice.

Country drug and grocery stores still keep candy in big, square unembellished glass jars. Try buying a pair or two of them. Minus the covers, they are stunning for holding flowers on dining table or sideboard. Artificial flowers, no matter how beautiful, cannot take the place of fresh ones and are never in good taste as a home decorative note.

Kitchen Utensils

There are two schools of thought in regard to equipping the kitchen. If you plan to do without a servant, then buy good utensils and all the labor-saving devices that you need, as you need them. For example, an electric mixmaster is an expensive piece of equipment but worth the price if you go in for cooking in a big way. Insist upon the best in cutlery, as cheap knives cost more in bad tempers than the monetary difference warrants, Don't count on being able to find even a paring knife in some of the small-town stores.

If the Q.M. issues cooking utensils, your husband may insist upon drawing them for you to use. Submit if you must, but I warn you, the meat forks are a yard long, the china plates, cups and saucers will wear you out lifting them and the two-gallon teakettles and huge skillets will make you old before your time! If this setup is for you, then by all means hie yourself to the dime store and outfit your kitchen for a couple of dollars.

The Bedrooms

If G.I. cots are all that you can draw for the bedrooms, cover the bed ends with attractive cretonne or quilted chintz, make a pretty bedspread, and you have a grand decorative disguise. A folding Q.M. table with a skirt of the same chintz will suffice for a dressing table. One very clever bride thumbtacked a foundation of peach sateen to the table, then used a pair of inexpensive dotted net curtains as the overskirt. The ruffled sides formed the valance, and the ruffled ends formed a pretty finish for the front of the table. Padding was used for the top, over which she became "quite extravagant" and put quilted peach satin, and over the whole placed a slab of inexpensive glass; thus she had a beautiful dressing table for a few dollars and a little ingenuity. Wardrobe trunks, slip-covered, often have to serve as wardrobes and chests of drawers.

For the bride who has received a goodly supply of wedding presents, the furnishing and decorating problem is much simpler. Especially if she has been thrifty and saved her wedding checks. However, never buy right off! Study your quarters and their possibilities, and remember a good decorator is a wonderful help, but never give him carte blanche unless you can afford it. If you are stationed in or near a large city like New York or Washington, some large reputable firm may supply your furnishings on a budget plan. However, this is sometimes dangerous for young people. They get into debt. But that is a vital point that requires special emphasis, and will be taken up later.

Here is a scoop! When you run up against the impossible in a set of Army quarters, or you have to make a garage over into a livable home, or when you can't make up your mind, or if shortages and lack of money flout your best-laid decorating schemes, there is a new service sponsored by *House Beautiful* with Elaine Neal as its consultant. You send her your floor plan, placement of windows, doors, fireplace, if any, and present arrangement of furniture. Include floor dimensions and ceiling height. A snapshot helps if you can send one, and she likes you to tell her something about yourself, your color preferences and taste, and how your family lives. The fee is two dollars per room, and this service is limited exclusively to mail. Address your letter to Elaine Neal, *House Beautiful*, 572 Madison Avenue, New York City, 22, and allow at least three weeks for a reply.

Early in your Army housekeeping you will need to develop a philosophy for living, all your very own. It will pay dividends if you learn early to enjoy and to be grateful for what you have each day, because that elusive tomorrow never comes. Try to see the best in your home each day; it may be a Quonset hut but there are bound to be compensations. There will probably be a view which some millionaire would envy, but no amount of money could buy it because the land belongs to Uncle Sam, and you are his ward for the present. It is your view. Be glad if your quarters are small; your household duties will be less and you can spend more time on other activities you enjoy. Again, should you draw a field officers' set, enjoy that for the time it will be yours. Perhaps you can now have Great-Aunt Susie come for a visit since you have an extra bedroom and bath on the first floor. It may lend itself to a house party, and all of your civilian friends will be impressed and envy you. Just take whatever comes in your stride and you will enjoy the Army!

It is said, and it is practically a scientific fact that to be loved makes women beautiful, and houses blossom in exactly the same way. If you love your home, whether it is a penthouse or a prefabricated shelter, it will have charm.

Consult your husband and get him interested in the arranging of each set of quarters as you move about from place to place. Encourage his interest and make him feel that he has a part in planning the appearance of your home. Men have

good taste and they are practical. At first he may say he does
not know about such things, but that is because he is diffident.
While most Army men dislike department store shopping,
perhaps you can persuade him to go along if you make him
feel you really need his help in going to a furniture store or
decorator's shop to buy a rug or a certain piece of furniture.

Men like big comfortable chairs by the right kind of light,
table tops and chair arms that glasses won't stain and that
are kept free of gimcracks. Put your ivory elephant bridge,
if you must have one, somewhere else. Have large, easily
cleaned crystal ash trays, a crystal cigarette box large enough
for at least one pack of cigarettes and a lighter kept filled
with fuel on a near-by table. If your husband enjoys working
at a desk so disordered it looks as if a cyclone had hit it, then
try to find a niche for the desk where it is not in public view.
It's easier than finding a new husband, and anyone with
literary inclinations dislikes heartily having his papers rear-
ranged into orderly stacks.

Everyone appreciates some degree of privacy and a modi-
cum of personal independence. Try to arrange for both your
husband and yourself to have one inviolate corner. It may
be possible to set aside a corner of a seldom used guest room
for your desk or sewing. Should your husband's hobby be
woodwork, maybe he would like a portion of the garage for
his workbench and tools. These are the little things that
sometimes make or break a marriage.

If it is at all possible, have separate dressing rooms and
separate closets. You may have your dressing table and
clothes closet as fussy with froufrou as you like; but remember that your husband, sharing the bedroom, may enjoy a
more conservative room. His dressing room and clothes
closet, the latter equipped with detachable slanting shoe
racks, large wooden hangers that will keep his uniforms in

shape, tie racks and separate boxes for military headgear, should be done in a monotone accented by a masculine color. Nothing la-di-da here. He will enjoy a special light to shave by in the bathroom, too.

If you are in crowded quarters with only one closet to be shared, then at least partition it off. If there is an extra closet in another room, by all means separate your clothes. Nothing is worse than to have to hang your favorite evening dress in the same closet with your husband's riding or field boots! For the man in your life, be as efficient as his secretary in keeping his wardrobe closet as compact as his office files. If he has long been a bachelor, the orderliness may be a shock to him at first, but he will grow to love it and to depend upon you.

A smooth-running household always has a well-arranged linen closet. Sheets are stacked in neat piles and confined with attractive ribbons or decorative bands to match the color scheme of the closet. If there is a guest closet, it can support a daring scheme of decoration such as rows of garment bags in transparent plastics piped with brilliant lemon yellow and gray stripes to match hatboxes and garment boxes. All of these you can learn to make yourself, and they can be carried from place to place.

Learn to do your housekeeping when your husband is at work, your homemaking, the task of being relaxed, devoted, attractive and an interested wife when he arrives at the door.

RANKING OUT AND BEING RANKED OUT

This is an old Army custom that, I am glad to say, on many posts is obsolete today. I shall quote a little incident from Martha Summerhayes' book, *Vanished Arizona*, that will illustrate it:

Arriving at Fort Russell, Cheyenne, Wyoming Territory, in April, 1874, to join my husband's regiment, we were met by two gallant officers in the uniform of the U. S. Infantry, who gave us welcome, and to me, a bride, a special welcome to the Regiment.

One of the officers, Major Wilhelm, who was to be Jack's Company Commander, said that Mrs. Wilhelm expected us to lunch and we were to be their house guests until we were settled. Soon after luncheon, Jack said to Major Wilhelm.

"Well, now I must go and look for quarters; what is the prospect?"

"You will have to turn someone out," said the Major.

About an hour afterwards they returned, and Jack said,

"Well, I have turned out Lynch; but as his wife and child are away, I do not believe he will care much."

"Oh," said I, "I'm sorry we have to turn anybody out!"

The Major and his wife exchanged smiles, and the former remarked,

"You must not have too much sympathy; it's the custom of the Service. It's always done, by virtue of rank. They'll hate you for doing it, but if you don't do it, they'll not respect you. After you've been ranked out once, you will not mind turning others out. Army women are accustomed to it."

The commanding officer of each post is free to have his own policy in regard to quarters, but few today believe in "ranking out" an officer, once he is settled, unless it is absolutely necessary. At some posts, like West Point, quarters are reassigned once a year, and there is a general moving day. Should you be ranked out, don't be hurt or insulted; "it's only the System." Remember that quarters are part of your husband's pay, and it is only fair that longevity should count in this regard. When your husband is a field officer, you can expect better quarters. The old saying R.H.I.P. ("Rank hath its privileges") is applicable here, but it should be followed by "Rank also hath its obligations"!

There's an old Army superstition, "Plant parsley and you'll move." Well, I committed the unpardonable sin of planting parsley, and I moved regularly. Then, on one very undesirable station, I had parsley growing everywhere—in window boxes in the kitchen, in small pots for decoration, and in the flower garden. But the god of superstition turned a deaf ear, and even the W.D. left us unmolested. It may work for you, however!

CALLING

During the war years both official and social calling was curtailed to a great extent, and large receptions took the place of individual social calls. It is interesting to note that in the postwar Army many feel that a combination of a general reception, where a newcomer might meet the personnel of the garrison, and a selective system of personal calling should be worked out. Another school of thought has it that the commanding officer of each post should dictate the policy of social calling. Others dislike calling altogether and would like to see the custom abolished.

"A period of adjustment and readjustment must be survived." Solutions for many present-day problems occasioned by great increases in personnel will be found. When reporting at a new station, an officer should consult the adjutant to find out the policy of calling and returning calls.

At smaller Army installations perhaps the officers and their wives of the group or branch to which your husband is assigned may call.

Receiving Callers

Shortly after your arrival on a post, and as soon as people feel that you are settled, you may expect callers. However, should they call before you are completely settled don't feel uncomfortable or apologize. Everyone realizes what settling means, and if you have sufficient G.I. chairs in which to seat your guests, that is all that is necessary. In days of not so long ago it was customary for an officer, captain or above, to post a card on the bulletin board at post headquarters announcing that he was settled and ready to receive callers.

Today calling on large posts is almost impossible, and is often confined within a regiment or to one's intimate friends. So if no one calls on you at first, don't feel neglected. A large reception at the Officers' Club, nowadays, serves as a general introduction and replaces the excessive number of calls.

The customary hours for calling are in the evening between eight and nine o'clock every weekday except Friday and Saturday, and on Sunday afternoons from four to seven o'clock. For receiving callers in the evening an officer should be dressed in dinner clothes, either a tuxedo, mess jacket or uniform; his wife need not necessarily wear a dinner dress, but she should change to something other than the dress she has worn all day.

If there is a servant on duty, she may answer the door; otherwise it is proper for the officer to go to the door, and his wife rises to greet the guests. The visiting officer will introduce himself and his wife to your husband, who in turn will present them to you. Of course, the correct formal greeting, as you know, is "How do you do?" but when meeting callers in your own house, it is gracious to be a little more effusive by adding, "It is so nice of you; do come in."

Don't worry about what to use for conversation. The callers, being old-timers on the post, will usually start the ball rolling. They will probably ask you how you like your new station. If you like it, be sincere and say so; if you don't like it, be very noncommittal, yet tactful, because you may change your mind later. Try to keep the conversation general, and suggest to your husband beforehand that he avoid getting off in a huddle with the visiting officer to talk shop. Army men are prone to do this; then we find the women talking servants and children. A very dull evening was had by all!

The proper length of a call is about twenty minutes, never longer than thirty minutes, unless you are intimate friends. Cards will be left, two of the visiting officer's one for you and one for your husband, and his wife will leave one card for you. This is the easy way to remember about cards: A lady *never* calls socially on a man; so she leaves a card for each adult woman only. An officer leaves a card for each person called on.*

Returning Calls

Either save calling cards or keep a list of all callers. The latter is a safer method, because sometimes people fail to leave cards, or the cards are lost. Formal calls should be returned within a week or within two weeks. In the case of someone you particularly want to find at home, you may leave cards or not and return a second or a third time. You must be careful about returning calls; many older officers attach great importance to this.

How very important first impressions are in the Army! A young officer is the cynosure of all eyes in his regiment, and his bride is equally so in the social circles of the Army. Colonel Moss, in his *Officer's Manual*, says, "You cannot observe with too much care the social customs of the Service, the customs that are so essential to the good fellowship, contentment, harmony, and happiness of the garrison."

Having made your call, leave the required number of cards on a card-tray table in the hall. Once you have risen

* It is customary to leave one joint card, and the officer leaves one of his visiting cards for each person called on.

to leave, do so by all means. Say good-by or good night, but don't linger. In the Army, that is called "doing a rug dance."

The Important First Calls

Upon reporting to a station, it is customary to find out from the adjutant the commanding officer's policy in regard to calling. Unless the commanding officer has indicated that he does not wish to be called upon, the new officer and his wife pay a social call upon him and his wife, and also upon the new officer's immediate superior officers. In a regiment, this would include the commanding officer and also the executive officer.

If the post C.O. is a general officer, he may or may not return this call personally. Often he has his aide return calls on the junior officers. Some C.O.'s prefer to set aside one afternoon or evening during which they are "at home" to callers. Others obviate all calling by giving a reception. The latter method is in force today at all large posts.

POST ACTIVITIES

Even the smallest of garrisons has its Woman's Club, of which the commanding officer's wife is usually the honorary president. All the activities of the post are concentrated in this organization. It is very important for every officer's wife to take an interest in it. You don't need to be a joiner, but if you have any special gift or talent, don't hide it under a bushel! Of course, it is not very good taste to advertise one's accomplishments; if you are an asset, others will soon realize it. It is well to avoid cliques, and to go slowly in picking one's intimate friends, but by signing up for the various activities in which you are interested you will probably find congenial companions, some of whom may grow into lifelong friends.

The Red Cross ranks number one, these days, on the list

of club activities. Even if you can't sew a straight seam, you can wrap bandages or learn to knit. Do your bit willingly when you are called.

Bridge we always have with us in the Army; if you enjoy playing, join the club. If you have never played, you should take lessons and gain a little experience before joining. To play a good game is a social asset.

Golf is a very popular sport, increasingly so among women. If you play, you will naturally join the Golf Club group. If you desire to play, again as in bridge, take lessons before joining in competition.

Dramatics—If you have histrionic ability or are interested in the theater, by all means sign up. The dramatic group always has lots of fun, and it needs prompters, make-up artists, and decorators for sets. When a post is too small to support a dramatic club, but a little theater is functioning in the near-by town, join it. You will be very welcome.

Tennis and swimming—These sports appeal to the junior matrons, and with a sufficient number of groups, tournaments, meets and various good times are planned.

Reading Club—A circulating library in which the newest books, both fiction and nonfiction, are available, is a great convenience, as Army posts are often far from the lending libraries in town.

There are many other activities, such as collectors' groups, art groups, music appreciation, and many more too numerous to mention here. If you are especially trained and good in something, find a few congenial souls and start a group yourself. Foreign-language classes often study French or Spanish, and at Fort Leavenworth there is one ambitious group studying Russian!

In the Women's Activities Group at Fort Leavenworth the Red Cross, P.T.A., Girl Scouts, Brownies, Teen-Agers, Teen-

Towners and Junior D.U.S.A. (Army Daughters) are all represented by wives of military personnel on the Women's Activities Board.

While making a survey of the major Army installations in the United States, I learned some very amazing and interesting facts. The general answer to my question, "What do you enjoy most about Army life?" was the following: going to and living in new places, meeting new people and different peoples and renewing friendships with former Army friends.

When I asked, "What disadvantages do you find?" one spirited young woman rose and in a belligerent tone snapped, "The inability to reply to newspaper columnists' anti-Army campaigns."

Things You May or May Not Know

1. It is considered unmilitary for an officer to carry an umbrella.
2. In the Army it is not customary for officers in uniform to be the motive power for baby carriages.
3. Most officers when in uniform avoid carrying bundles unless absolutely necessary. (Come, come, Colonel, the war is still on as far as extra delivery boys are concerned and it won't hurt your prestige to carry home the groceries for the little woman.)
4. While there is no rank among women in the Army, a junior officer's wife should always show courteous deference to older women and especially to the commanding officer's wife, though in no way that smacks of "boot-licking" or currying favor.
5. Special courtesy should be shown to older women, especially to wives of retired officers. A younger woman should rise when introduced to an older woman. As you

were taught in childhood, offer your chair or perform any little courtesy that the occasion warrants, but avoid any affectation or show of manners for which you may be criticized.

6. Always wait for the guest of honor to leave, before saying good-by to your hostess.

7. Avoid gossiping, promoting rumors or listening to gossip. No good ever comes from malicious gossip, and often reputations are torn to shreds. In this regard "Silence is golden." Colonel Moss explains gossip in this manner: "The germ of gossip may be likened unto the germ of cancer . . . As the latter contaminates and rots healthy flesh, so the former contaminates and rots the social fabric, harmony and happiness of post life." There have been cases where commanding officers have taken extreme measures in regard to women gossips. Some have been barred from posts and forced to live apart from their Army friends.

8. A lady's name is never mentioned in an officers' mess, and this rule is "as good as it is old." There is a certain chivalry among Army officers, and the rule is so strictly observed that young officers, upon occasion, have been silenced by their brother officers for speaking ill of a lady's reputation in public.

9. Should your husband confide in you or tell you details of official business, use tact and common sense in keeping it to yourself.

10. Don't be a busybody, a meddler, carry tales or scout for trouble. Such behavior will act only as a boomerang, and Army wives have definitely hurt their husbands' official prospects by such conduct.

11. Pay attention to small details. Write letters of condolence,

congratulation, notes of thanks for gifts and courtesies *promptly.*

12. Don't criticize your new station, your commanding officer, his wife, or any member of the command in the presence of outsiders.

A Summing Up

Many of the "young" commanding officers' wives on foreign service—and they are young by Army command standards—are finding it hard to play teacher, so several have appealed to me for help. Here are some of the questions young officers and their wives ask:

1. When and upon whom should they make social calls? The commanding general or commandant of a post or field dictates this policy in regard to calling protocol through official channels, usually through his adjutant. It is customary for him either to meet the officers of the command and their wives at a reception, or to designate certain nights for calling and the hour at which he and his wife wish to receive. As explained earlier, an officer upon reporting to a new station should inquire and receive information from the adjutant as to the commandant's wishes in this matter.

In the case of your group commander or some officer with whom you are closely associated, it is expected that you will call the first or second week that he and his family are in residence. An officer should feel free to ask the adjutant any question of a semiofficial nature; that is part of his job—to see that the command runs smoothly.

2. Do cards take the place of a call if the person called upon is not at home? Yes, but it is a nice gesture to make a second attempt at finding the person at home.

3. How long should a call of an official and social nature last? The proper length of time for this type of call is twenty

minutes or not more than thirty minutes, unless you are an old friend and the hosts insist upon your staying. To keep consulting your watch or to watch your host's clock is not very flattering.

4. How soon should formal calls be returned? Formal calls should be returned within a week or ten days; not more than two weeks should elapse.

5. Why does the Army insist upon calling? The Army doesn't. It is left up to the wishes of the commanding officer. Usually, it makes for friendliness and most people enjoy it unless they are antisocial.

6. Who entertains first? Don't let this one worry you! If you are a new arrival, wait until you are entertained. Certainly, you are not expected to entertain "the rank" until you know the score, and they have entertained you. By entertaining first, you place others in the position of having to return the obligation. It is customary for the person residing longer on the post to entertain you first; however, this is not too rigidly followed, so just use tact and common sense.

7. In what manner should you entertain? This question is covered in full in Chapter VI; however, remember to keep your parties appropriate to your husband's rank. Remember that all generals were once second lieutenants and they know just how far Army pay can be stretched. In addition, generals have their financial problems, too! A simple breakfast, an informal dinner or a buffet supper may repay the most formal of dinners. No longer does the Army believe in "an eye for an eye; a tooth for a tooth in lieu of a lunch for a lunch and a banquet for a banquet"! Keep your entertaining on a simple but attractive scale.

8. How soon should obligations be returned? Formal dinners should be returned in some way within a month. If you know your prospective guests well, you need not stand on ceremony.

Social Customs for Army Bachelors

I am including this item in the hope that some generous young Army wife may lend you her book! Perhaps you are one of the thousands of young college men who came into the Army before or during the war; you like the Service and have decided to make the Army your career. Not through any fault of your own, but owing to the irresponsible age in which you were brought up, you have taken all social courtesies more or less as your due, or certainly for granted without any sense of obligation. Well, the Army is shaking down to a peacetime status, and whether you know it or not, Lieutenant Brown, you have certain very definite obligations as a bachelor, and Army hostesses expect certain things of you. Your manners and the way you handle the social amenities have a distinct bearing on your official record as "an officer and gentleman."

1. You are expected to make social calls, the same as a married officer. It is a nice gesture to pay a social call if one of your married friends or the commandant has a young lady guest. If she is an L.P. (an unattractive lady) you need not do more. If you like her, then you might invite her to a movie at least, or to the officers' mess for dinner.

2. If you are invited to a dinner party, your social duty is to dance with your hostess, the lady you escorted and all of the ladies at your dinner table. (Now this is not just being Mid-Victorian, because Army wives have memories like elephants where courteous bachelors are concerned.)

3. Army bachelors sometimes take the attitude that they are doing their hostess a favor by attending the party. Have a care on this score, young man. You may bring a bride to this or some post and be faced with a similar situation. It is a boorish attitude.

4. Army bachelors have social obligations just as married

officers and their wives have. Sometimes two or three bachelors go in together and give a cocktail party or dinner at the club to repay their obligations. Keep a check on your obligations.

5. Dinner calls are also a gracious gesture, and should be made within a week after you have attended the party.

6. Should a bachelor officer ask permission of the hostess to bring his girl to her party, then in some way he should show his appreciation of this hospitality. A nice thing to do is to send cut flowers the morning of the party, or to send his hostess a corsage. The bachelor should be thoughtful enough not to make his request at the last minute, because it may change the entire seating arrangement, in which case the hostess is well within her rights if she courteously explains the situation and asks him to bring her some other time. Having accepted, the bachelor is expected to attend, alone.

7. If the party is being given on the post, and the invited bachelor wishes, it is a courteous thing to ask the hostess if there is any young lady visiting on the post that she would like him to escort to the party.

Bachelors of the old Army built up quite a reputation for their gallantry; they were greatly in demand and there was a certain chivalry and glamor that matched their good manners and gentlemanly courtesy. The above suggestions may seem like trivial points to a man, but somehow these little acts of courtesy oil the wheels of the social organization in maintaining a congenial Army post. Army wives do resent rude, thoughtless and careless bachelors; on the other hand, a courteous, well-groomed and considerate Army bachelor is welcomed everywhere and his presence gives a certain fillip to any social gathering.

Chapter V

THE BUSINESS OF OPERATING
AN ARMY HOUSEHOLD

Soup-y, soup-y soup-y
Without a single bean,
Pork-y, pork-y, pork-y
Without a streak of lean,
Coffee, coffee, coffee
The weakest ever seen!
—"Mess Call"

Basic Principles of Household Management

SUCCESSFUL Service women are perhaps among the most resourceful, the most versatile and the most efficient of managers in the field of homemakers. An army officer's wife *must* be successful if she is ambitious and wants her husband to wear stars some day—on his shoulders, of course!

But to be successful combines all the qualities of being a financier, a culinary artist, an interior decorator, an expert in marketing and buying, the perfect hostess, a devoted wife and mother, a social success and a woman who can make a second lieutenant's pay stretch to the nth degree without ever breaking. A pretty big order, isn't it?

But Army women have a knack of being able to do these things and also to make a home out of a tepee, a nipa shack or whatever Uncle Sam assigns their husbands as quarters.

Another thing that would play havoc with the average civilian household is the frequent moving or change of station, sometimes upon a few hours' notice.

An Army wife never complains when she has to leave the spring garden she has so painstakingly planted. She smiles and hopes that the family who inherits it will enjoy her pansies, tulips and hyacinths, and that she may find something growing in her yard at her next station. That is the Service! The only tragedy that upsets the seasoned Army woman is to be separated from her husband.

Most Army homes have an indefinable charm—a charm that reflects the personality of their present owners, regardless of shabby furnishings, bare walls or lack of servants. There is an inviting atmosphere, a total lack of pretense and a sincere hospitality that makes the guest want to linger.

The old adage, "A rolling stone gathers no moss," is disproved by Army people long in the Service; they are inclined to collect too much in material goods. With the opportunity to collect treasures on foreign service, many of the senior officers make their homes most fascinating and interesting. Some of these houses contain museum pieces and priceless treasures in the form of Oriental rugs, exquisite Chinese handmade linens and embroideries, wonderful collections of silver and china, bronzes, Japanese lacquer, Chinese ancestral scrolls, teakwood chests and cabinets, and inlaid mother-of-pearl screens that would cost a fortune at home.

The young second lieutenant and his bride, upon their first call at the commanding officer's quarters, are simply overcome by all this grandeur that spells vast wealth to them. Peggy and Ted should cheer up, though, because in their later service all of these lovely furnishings may be theirs too, if they know how to spend and save wisely. The success of their household organization depends upon one little word, *system.*

SYSTEM IN THE ARMY HOUSEHOLD

Every successful business in the world is built upon system, and without system a business does not continue to thrive. The Army household is a business, and the Army wife is the business manager. The keynote of her housekeeping should be "efficiency."

Now, since you are installed as the manager of the Worthing Firm, Peggy, provide yourself with the proper business equipment. I mean take over the Army desk that is usually issued, or find a substitute as your business desk. Equip it with pens, pencils, scratch pads, a calendar, paste, a foot ruler, yardstick, tape measure, scissors, stamps, post cards, stationery, a checkbook, account books, cookbooks, card catalogue, and a typewriter if possible. If you are naturally of a methodical turn, half of your battle is won. Have special drawers in the desk for files, document boxes, and household inventories. In conclusion, a place for everything, and everything in its place.

Fortunate indeed is the Army wife who has specialized in home economics because homemaking in this day is a highly specialized art, a definite business and a profession. To the Army woman, however, no set of rules, budgets or standards will apply. Living conditions at every station are different, and to succeed she must be highly intelligent and have a generous amount of good common sense.

Hard and fast rules cannot be given, but doing her housework on schedule will be a big help to the bride. To have her household machinery well oiled and running smoothly requires systematic planning. A convenient time once a week should be set aside in which to make schedules for the coming week.

Suggestions

1. Ask your husband to bring home to you a copy of *Post Regulations*. Read it carefully and acquaint yourself with the orders. Each post has a different set of regulations concerning life on the post, and you will save yourself a lot of grief and perhaps embarrassment by complying with these orders, for instance: parking regulations, speed laws on the reservation; garbage disposal; the regulations in regard to pets; quarters maintenance—and the officer's responsibility in regard to upkeep. You can get into serious difficulty by hanging pictures except from the molding (if that is mentioned in *Post Regulations*). The rules regarding servants, peddlers, magazine agents will be set forth, specifically. Regulations regarding deliveries of commissary, laundry, post exchange purchases, and much valuable information will be given in this pamphlet.

2. Make a tour of the post, and acquaint yourself with the P.X., the commissary, the bakery, the laundry, the garden, the chapel, the stables (if you ride) and the various offices.

When You Are Your Own Maid

1. After removing breakfast dishes, clean living room and dining room (be prepared for morning callers).

2. Make beds and clean bedrooms.

3. Kitchen: Prepare vegetables for luncheon or dinner, and let them cook for a while as you wash the breakfast and dinner dishes of the night before. (Of course, some housekeepers will be horrified at this, but twice a day is enough for any bride to wash dishes.) Depending upon your hour of rising and the time of breakfast, two hours should give you time to do this work thoroughly, leaving time for a couple of sets of tennis and a swim. (If you stop to finish

a detective story, remember to deduct it from your leisure instead of skipping your household duties.)

4. Prepare lunch; eat; wash or stack dishes.

5. Leisure: Learn to budget your time so that you can include rest, recreation, personal beautifying and mental improvement in your "Design for Living."

6. Prepare dinner; dine, clear table and stack dishes in covered container. (Don't ask or expect Ted to help you with the dishes. He is working for the government.)

This last suggestion was the only thing in the first edition of this book on which I received an *adverse* criticism! The young bridesgroom officers offered congratulations, but somehow the brides did not agree. I still believe that just as a man keeps his job separate from his home life, so should an Army wife keep her housekeeping job separate from that of homemaking.

Of course, the war brought many changes. For the first time in their lives many men found a sense of achievement in work which before they had considered "women's work." If your husband likes to cook, then surrender the kitchen whenever he offers to take over. There is nothing "sissy" about a man helping about the house. If he enjoys drying the dishes and offers to help, again be agreeable and don't forget to be appreciative. But don't *expect* him to do your work, in addition to his own military duties.

You will find that a thorough cleaning of one or two rooms each day is better than letting your cleaning accumulate for the week end or "blue Monday." Go through the entire house daily, but learn to finish one room before going on to another. Try to keep your living room in order at all times, so that if a caller should drop in unexpectedly, you will not be thrown into a rush of explanations. This is easily done if, before going to bed, newspapers, ash trays, card table, cards, sewing or whatever may have been used is put away and chairs are straightened. Then at least the living room will not overwhelm you the next morning.

Of course, there will be particular days that you may set aside for special cleaning, baking or mending, just as your mother and your grandmother did before you; but it will help greatly if you will be methodical and use a little will power about complying with the routine schedule you make for yourself.

Home management is no hit-and-miss proposition! It is an important business and requires just as capable handling as any career.

Learn in the beginning to organize your work. Find the short cuts and be anxious to try out timesavers. At least give new ideas a trial, and don't feel obliged to manage your home just the way your mother did. Times are changing and if she is progressive she has probably changed some of the tried and tested methods with them. Subscribe to several of the leading women's magazines; they are to the housewife what a service or trade journal is to your husband. This is a means of learning what is new in the homemaker's field.

An Army wife soon learns that the small decisions are hers; don't worry your husband about the commissary order being late or the dairyman's passing you by. Substitute something from your emergency shelf, and learn to keep these petty annoyances to yourself. No man likes to clutter his mind with such details, and little irritations like these all come in the realm of housekeeping and are the gremlins that beset every housewife.

Servants

This is a chapter in itself, but a bit of advice that has been passed on by an experienced, older Army matron is this: "If servants are plentiful, and you can afford them—take advantage of your good fortune and 'live the life of Riley,' because there will be many times in your Army career when you will have to do the cooking, washing, raise a family, perhaps, without any help at all. The Army is like a 'grab bag.' You never know what you will draw next; so take advantage, my dear, of any ease that comes your way."

A servants' file, in which is kept a record of servants' qualifications, comments of former Army employers and a wage scale, is a wonderful help. Would that more posts maintained an employment agency! In *Post Regulations* there will be special mention of rules for servants.

If you can afford a servant, then, before you employ her, have a definite understanding with her as to her duties. Be fair and honest in regard to her duties, what you expect of her, her salary and her free time. With conditions as they are now, one can not be too demanding, but your household will be judged, at least in part, by the appearance and manners of your maid. If you do not know what to expect of a maid, there is a very entertaining and helpful little book called *Maidcraft*, by Lita Price and Harriet Bonnet, which will help both you and the maid. It is a splendid guide for the one-maid household.

It is a great help to a servant and to the housekeeper to post a work schedule in the kitchen as it saves time in giving daily specific orders. If you have no servant, then the system may help you in budgeting your time for leisure.

PLANNING MEALS

Menu planning in advance is almost a necessity if your household includes a maid; if not, it is equally important. It saves time, money and the need of thinking each day what to have for the next meal. Planning ahead makes more economical purchasing possible. Try making out practical menus for a week and you will be convinced of the value of the system.

Always plan your meals when you are hungry, and not just after having eaten a large dinner! Army housewives should consult their social calendars and their plans for the coming week before making menus.

Most of the buying will be done at the commissary or at the post exchange; however, on Fridays and Saturdays there may be advantageous sales of foodstuffs in town. Watch for sales in the daily papers. It is a good idea to make a personal visit to market once a week. If you market at the same town grocery regularly enough, the grocer and butcher will learn your needs and value your patronage.

This is not true of commissary buying, however! You take government issue and like it. It is also a good plan to visit the commissary at least once or twice a month; but beware of the first few days of the month. The government stores are overcrowded at this time with enlisted personnel who are stocking up for a month, and the waiting lines of customers appear endless. Thoughtful housewives also delay their larger orders of staples until after the fifth day of the month. The deliveries are overcrowded, and the sales forces at the commissary will appreciate this consideration.

Post exchange markets are usually run on a concession basis, and often the produce is a fraction higher than at the markets in town. You are paying for the convenience of post service, if this is the case. Many housewives market personally at the P.X. grocery every day, then join a group of their friends for the famous "Coca-Cola hour" in the restaurant, where the news of the day is discussed. Have a grocery pad and pencil conveniently placed in the kitchen, and insist upon the maid's keeping a close check on supplies, especially when they are getting low. You may choose to double-check this yourself on the weekly inspection. If you did not receive a good cookbook at one of the showers, then invest in one immediately. There are hundreds on the market, but one of the most reliable is *The Boston Cooking School Cook Book*, by Fannie Merritt Farmer. Another good one is *The Joy of Cooking*, by Irma Rombauer. The latter is particulary helpful on meal planning.

Weekly Menu

These meals are planned with three ideas in mind: foods and staples that can be bought at commissaries; simple dishes that any bride can cook with the aid of a cookbook; and the use of leftovers. The women's magazines of today are filled with delicious tempting-looking foods that are pretty to look at, and no doubt delectable to the palate; but few of these recipes are for the Army bride! Why, you ask? Well, there are several reasons. First, the household budget won't stand for fresh mushrooms at eighty cents a pound, squab cooked in sherry, stuffed lobster à la Béchamel or Knickerbocker suprême of chicken; second, even if the bride has an unlimited bank account of her own, often she is stationed at some outpost or on foreign service where it is impossible to procure fresh watercress or celery, and sometimes even lettuce is a decided luxury. Fresh States produce comes high in Manila, Guam and Hawaii. Lettuce costs from forty to fifty cents a head in the Philippines, while States beef in Honolulu is almost prohibitive in price.

What do Army people do? Well, they still eat, and eat well; because Army wives soon learn to plan their menus around native products. In Hawaii, with luscious avocados selling at two for five cents during the season, delicious sun-drenched pineapples for the small sum of ten cents,

native breadfruit (marvelous when baked), papayas growing on the reservation and to be had for the picking, the
Army family menus are built around these low-cost native
foods.

In the Philippines, fish and chicken are normally inexpensive; so the meat problem is simple. On the Mexican border,
Army wives learn Mexican cookery. Each station has its
own regional food problems with the attendant attractive
advantages in offering something new that is edible and delicious. So that is why the seasoned Army housewife only
looks at the pretty pictures of food displayed in the magazines, and glances over the recipes. Few of these are practical
for her unless she is stationed in a large metropolis with
wonderful market facilities.

Sample of Weekly Menu

Breakfast	Luncheon	Dinner
Sunday:		
Fruit or melon	Roast chicken (or)	Sandwiches
Ham	Chicken and dumplings	Tea
Waffles, syrup	Wild rice	Cake
Coffee	String beans	
	Salad (or) dessert	
Monday:		
Orange juice	Creamed chicken on	Lamb chops
Broiled bacon	toast	Baked potatoes
Toast, coffee	Fresh vegetable salad	Green peas
	Tea	Salad (or) dessert
Tuesday:		
Tomato juice	Bouillon	Baked beans
French toast	Eggs à la Benedict	Brown bread
Syrup	Head-lettuce salad	Frozen fruit salad
Coffee	Dressing	Coffee
Wednesday:		
Grapefruit	Homemade veg. soup	Meat loaf (or) pot roast
Sausage	Toast	Creamed onions

Eggs	Hot gingerbread	Carrot, apple, raisin
Toasted rolls	Whipped cream	salad
Coffee		Coffee, mints

Thursday:

Orange juice	Cup of soup	Cold roast (or) loaf
Ham omelet	Baked beans	Potato salad, celery
Toast	Green salad	Sliced tomatoes
Coffee		Cake, tea

Friday:

Fruit juice	Bouillon	Fruit cup
Soft-boiled eggs	Tuna salad, sandwiches	Broiled fish
Toast	Tea	Scalloped potatoes (or)
Coffee	Cake	Macaroni—cheese
		Beets (or) cauliflower
		Dessert

Saturday:

Grapefruit	Hamburgers on toasted	"Out" or company
Cinnamon toast	buns	Clear soup (or) salad
Coffee	Baked beans	Tomato stuffed with
	Salad	cheese (or)
		Tomato stuffed with
		shrimp
		Fried (or) baked
		chicken
		Mashed potatoes (or)
		wild rice
		String beans
		Dessert, coffee

After making up the menu, it is wise to go over it with the maid in this fashion: Explain to her that the creamed chicken which appears so extravagant on Monday's luncheon menu will be made from the chicken left over from the Sunday dinner. The vegetables for the salad and the peas for Monday dinner will be bought on Saturday. Assuming that you have a daily order for milk and bread, your order on Monday will include lamb chops and a complete list of staples for the week. The latter may be ordered on Satur-

day, but Monday or Tuesday seems a better day for ordering
staples, as the deliveries are not so crowded. Glancing over
the list, you will see that your staple order must include:

1 lb. bacon	1 can of fruit salad
1 syrup	1 box of gingerbread mixture
1 salad oil	cinnamon
2 cans tomato juice	1 lb. coffee
bouillon cubes	tea
2 cans of baked beans	macaroni
brown sugar	cheese
1 can tuna	rice

Check lard, sugar and condiments. Your marketing list
of fresh vegetables and staples for the week will read:

	Emergency Shelf:
1 dozen oranges	Canned soups
2 grapefruit	Canned meats (whole chicken
1 lettuce*	or chicken à la king)
1 lb. fresh tomatoes*	Canned fish
1 lb. green peas (for 2)	Canned vegetables
1 celery*	Canned fruits
Potatoes	Canned juices
Eggs	Canned specialties — ancho-
1 lb. bacon	vies, caviar, cocktail sau-
Sausage	sages, brown bread, plum
Onions	pudding, sandwich spreads,
String beans*	preserves, jellies
Beets*	

During the days of meat rationing and the shortage of
canned goods these menus were of little use; however, the
meats, canned goods and "fancy groceries" are rapidly re-
appearing on commissary shelves and are back in circula-
tion. Any Army woman who was a good Victory cook, who

learned the vitamins necessary for a well-rounded diet, will have no difficulty in following the suggestions.

It is far easier to market on an Army post than in a crowded city. Many Army wives found this to be true during the war; an Army line seems nothing in comparison to the long queues at food stores in a crowded capital like Washington.

The items marked with a star (*) will be on the daily order, as it is necessary that they be fresh and bought the day they are to be used. Menus should be planned so that they are elastic enough to include a guest (this can be managed with the help of an emergency shelf). Also they should be elastic in case you are invited out for meals or your household plans are changed. If you can stick to this method of planning, you will find it a great saver of time, energy and money.

In the Army, especially in the Air Force, there is no such thing as an unexpected guest. Once he arrives and accepts your invitation to share potluck with you, it is up to the housewife to use her ingenuity in preparing a good lunch or dinner. The emergency shelf is a lifesaver, and should be well stocked with standard canned goods and a few delicacies that will turn a plain dinner into a company dinner, and make your husband marvel at your cleverness.

A Few Suggestions on Marketing

1. Special sales can save you money, but be sure the quality is high, even though the price is low.
2. Don't forget on your market list any staples you may need, and with which your kitchen shelves, pantry and emergency shelf should always be stocked.
3. If you shop in person you'll always know what you are

getting; and don't fail to ask the price of things before
you order.
4. Learn the different cuts and grades of meat. Cheap cuts
are delicious if properly cooked.
5. Give yourself a good course in marketing from books.
There's no use learning the hard way when experts have
tested and worked out an easy way that is yours for the
asking at any good library.

There are scores of books on the subject of marketing
that the librarian will suggest to you. In stressing the advantages of system, I am not urging you to make a fetish of
it, but it does deserve your consideration if you desire to be
a successful Army housewife.

THE FAMILY INCOME

In the Army, where there are so many demands on an
officer's pay, careful planning and co-operation in handling
the family income are absolutely necessary for families, especially in the junior grades.

Debt is something that is feared by all officers of the Army.
The government orders an officer to pay his official bills in
full by the tenth day of the month, and all other bills should
be paid not later than the fifteenth of the month.

An extravagant wife, or one who has no sense of the value
of money, can cause her husband to be court-martialed and
dismissed from the Service. Many otherwise happy families
have been wrecked on this rock of debt in the matrimonial
sea.

Any method of handling the family income has its obvious advantages and disadvantages. Since the Army housewife does most of the family buying, she is really the purchasing agent and a business partner. The only fair and

businesslike method is to have a joint bank account opened in the name of both husband and wife. The joint account is preferable as the wife's signature would then be legal in case of the death of her husband. Find out the state banking laws wherever you are stationed.

Plan your budget so that there will be no necessity to ask your husband for money, either for household or personal needs. Some Army families follow the "allowance" plan—a household allowance and a personal allowance for the wife and each of the children. The word allowance in this case smacks of condescension, which may be proper toward children but is not applicable to the wife or partner. However, this is a mere technicality, and if the housewife approves, this method may be as good as any.

Charge Accounts

The "chit" or charge system is often referred to as "the curse of the Army," and it is literally true on foreign service, particularly in Manila. There, one seldom carries money; signing a chit is so much easier, whether it be for a Scotch and soda at the club, a *calesa* ride or an Oriental rug at one of the East Indian stores. The Hindus are only too eager to charge any merchandise to Missy, and "she can pay any time she chooses, three months, six months, or even a year from now." They know your husband must, as an Army officer, pay his just debts and, as becomes the tropics, there is no hurry. Eventually, the first of the month comes, and the bills start rolling in.

The bride is in tears! She had no idea she had spent so much, and her husband is bewildered at first, then angry, and finally frantic when he realizes that he will have to borrow money to meet these bills. Quick, angry words probably follow—all because these young people had no definite financial plans. Perhaps the bride has come from a family where she had carte blanche at the leading stores; then it is going to be for her a real test of character to pass up the tempting buys. The only safe way to meet this situation that I know of is to save toward the purchase of, say, the Oriental rug, then pay cash and it is yours; or to work out a budget which includes installment buying of large items such as an automobile, an Oriental rug, or house furnishings. In a good partnership between husband and wife neither would be so dishonest as to take advantage of the other. For instance, the wife would not charge articles that she would like to have when she knows she has not the money to pay for them. It is obvious that the credit system is not at fault, but there is something morally weak in the people who abuse it.

Charge accounts have several advantages: To have a charge account means that your credit standing is good. As I have explained, an Army officer or his family, upon presenting the proper credential, finds no difficulty in opening accounts anywhere. Charge customers receive special service and courtesy, for example, advance notice of sales. Goods may be bought on approval and returned to the store if not satisfactory, and the customer has added prestige when she says to the saleswoman, "Please charge it to my account."

Cash System

One objection to the cash system is that money must always be carried and small change kept on hand. Often necessary purchases are neglected because of the difficulty of getting change for a bill. Accounts of each penny or dollar spent must be painstakingly kept; otherwise, losses and mistakes occur. With large amounts there are the added dangers of pickpockets, burglars, carelessness and fire. Even with large stores it is sometimes hard to get cash returned. They prefer that you make another selection of goods and sometimes refuse to return the money. However, a cash basis may be a fine system for individual families, and it is highly recommended for persons who are inclined to be extravagant.

Household Bills

All household bills should be paid once a month, and by bank check. Your canceled checks will be your receipts, and these may be kept in an inexpensive filing case or pasted in the checkbook opposite the corresponding bank stub.

In signing personal checks, Peggy, you should use the same formal signature you gave the bank in opening your account. If it is "Margaret Carver Worthing" or "Margaret Worthing" then use this form, never "Mrs. James Theodore Worthing."

Installment Buying

Installment buying should not be considered until the Army family has a small savings account. Since you have an assured income, and are not in debt, there are times when it seems wise to buy an expensive item, such as a piano, a set of books or an automobile, on the monthly payment plan. Be sure to find out how much interest you will pay, and the monthly carrying charges. At all times, in your savings account there should be enough money to take care of two future monthly installments. Emergencies and unexpected expenses have an unhappy way of popping up the second month the installment is due. To agree to installments that make too large a dent in the pay check is obviously foolish.

Borrowing

Never borrow money from friends or relatives. The proper place to borrow money is from a bank. Another form of borrowing is to ask tradesmen or stores to carry your account longer than the customary time. However, it is advisable for young officers, if they are in debt, to send each firm a small amount each month, if only five dollars, toward payment of the account. If you are honest, you will write and explain your difficulty and make an effort to pay something each month. Your credit rating will remain unhurt.

Beware of "loan sharks," and *make it a rule never to endorse* or sign a note for anyone, or ask anyone to endorse a note for you. Endorsing is a vicious custom in the Service. An officer hates to turn down a brother officer who is in financial difficulty, but too much cannot be said about the undesirability of such a legal obligation. If you can afford to lend the actual cash, and care to, it is better than to guarantee to pay a note, no matter how good the "risk" may be.

Budgets

Until you have had at least five or six months' experience in running a household, it is rather futile to make out a budget. Before a workable budget can be made, it is necessary to have some kind of record of expenditures on which to base it. This shows the value of the proper kind of household accounts. The past month's accounts may be made the basis for the following month's budget, until a fairly definite standard of expenditures has been determined. Perhaps too much is being spent upon food, and not enough for clothing!

Moving around from place to place as Army people do, it is difficult to make a general budget that will meet all conditions. Standards of living vary with different individuals and in different localities; so, for the Army couple, their best plan seems to be the trial-and-error method. Try out various suggestions as to budgets and settle upon the one that fits your needs whether in Alaska, Hawaii or the Middle West.

Savings and Investments

Every family should have a savings bank account. Many Army officers try to keep the equivalent sum of a month's pay in their savings account for emergencies such as an unexpected change of station. There are all sorts of attractive savings plans, which your banker will be glad to recommend.

Investments should not be made without consulting your banker. His advice may save you many dollars. However, if you have extra money with which to speculate on the stock exchange or "play the market," that is your own affair.

Insurance

Army officers usually carry government life insurance, in which rates are lower than the corresponding forms in civilian companies. In addition, they may carry as much as they feel they can afford. The monthly premiums are deducted from the government pay check. Investigate the Army Mutual Aid Association, War Department, Washington, D.C. Life insurance is safe; it cannot be swept away by a crash.

Fire insurance is most necessary. If your husband does not already have the maximum amount to cover your possessions, don't delay getting it. Write at once to the Army Co-operative Fire Insurance Association, Fort Leavenworth, Kansas, for necessary blanks and information. The yearly premiums are most reasonable, and it is splendid protection.

Automobile insurance, at least against public liability and property damage, is imperative. Almost all post commanders demand that an insurance certificate be presented before a pass is given to operate a car on the reservation. Many states also demand that owners of automobiles carry automobile insurance. The United Services Automobile Association of Fort Sam Houston, Texas, is a mutual company of long standing, organized and managed by Army officer personnel. Its premiums to Army personnel are lower than those of most automobile insurance companies and its service is of the highest.

Marine insurance is expensive, but a fine thing to have when traveling to and from foreign service. It is wise to read very carefully the regulations and restrictions governing it.

For educational insurance, see Chapter VII.

Safe-Deposit Boxes

Every family should maintain a safe-deposit box in some bank or trust company vault and should keep in it all legal papers, such as birth and marriage certificates, wills, insurance policies, and other valuable property. A yearly household inventory should be filed with the fire insurance policy.

There are three ways in which a title may be taken to a safe-deposit box. Each has its merits, and each its disadvantages. The first is individual ownership, in which case the box is absolutely private to the owner but, in case of his death, it can be entered only in the presence of a representative of the probate court.

The second method is joint tenancy for a husband and wife, in which case each may enter the box independently of the other. However, if either party dies, the box is sealed and may be opened only in the presence of a representative of the state tax commission, the purpose being to discover any assets which may be held subject to inheritance tax.

The third method and probably the best for Service personnel who are married is "individual ownership with appointed deputy." This is nothing more than the first method except that the box owner appoints a deputy who may enter the box. Actually, the owner gives a power of attorney to the deputy, but it is limited in scope to entry and use of the box.

The third method is advantageous to officers and families leaving for occupation duty. A relative or attorney may be appointed as deputy and may open the box in case necessary papers should need to be forwarded.

Power of Attorney

During the war many Army wives were given the power of attorney. Legal blanks for this purpose are available at Army posts and at banks. It permits the wife to obtain automobile licenses, and enables her to dispose of joint property in an emergency.

Income Tax

It is a common and erroneous belief in civilian circles that Army and Navy personnel are exempt from taxes. Under the present federal personal income tax law a husband and wife may file a joint income tax return. If the wife has an income from any outside source, she must keep an accurate record of sums received, with the date of receipt and source of such income.

The Value of System

The Army family which earnestly tries to run its establishment on a business basis will find that system and efficiency bring proportionate returns, as they do in a thriving business. It takes will power to save, but the pleasant satisfaction a bank account gives you in case of emergency, and Army life is filled with emergencies, more than makes up for the minor self-denials to which you condition your character.

Try saving where it hurts least! For instance, if you want to have "orchids on your budget" learn to walk, instead of taking a bus. The walk will help your figure, and when you get home, drop the dime in your piggy bank. When buying a dress, shorten it yourself instead of paying several dollars for minor alterations; set the money aside, however, and save it for something special. Take advantage of movie matinees as the prices are lower than in the evenings. This applies to the theater in town, not on a post. Avoid white elephants; they are always expensive, whether in dress, novelties or gimcracks. It is the little extravagances that make the dents in your budget.

Has Anyone Told You?

That dresser drawers of your handsome mahogany G.I. furniture sometimes get stubborn. It helps to rub a candle stub or soap along the sliding edges. They will move in and out much more easily, even when heavily packed.

That camphor placed in chests, trunks or drawers will keep mice away. Placed in a silver chest, it will keep silver from tarnishing.

That heavy linoleum makes an ideal covering for kitchen tables, and ledges in butler's pantry. If waxed, it can be cleaned easily.

That brooms and brushes, to keep straw or bristles from bending, should always be suspended from a nail, by placing hook in top of handle.

That before driving a nail into plaster, if you place it in hot water for a few minutes, it will not crumble the plaster of the government quarters. (Of course, you aren't supposed to drive nails!)

That discarded washed powder puffs are splendid for cleaning silverware.

That piano keys may be whitened by rubbing them with a cloth moistened with milk.

That if your nonexistent maid should set a hot dish or a glass on your fine mahogany G.I. dining table which leaves a ring, it may be removed by applying the following solution: Spread a thin paste made from salad oil and salt over the marred spot, leave for an hour or two and then rub off gently with a soft, clean cloth.

That a set of cleaning essentials, including broom and dustpan, kept upstairs as well as downstairs, saves many extra steps.

That rubbing your hands thoroughly with vinegar removes the unpleasant odor after peeling onions. I learned this much too late in life! One Sunday afternoon at Kelly Field I was busily engaged in making potato salad when a pair of foreign envoys came to make a social call. Hastily I discarded my apron and answered the door. The polite Spanish colonel kissed my hand, much to my chagrin!

That to rid the house of cooking odors from cabbage, cauliflower, Brussels sprouts, onions, place a teaspoonful of ground cinnamon on a hot iron skillet and let it stand over low heat for a few minutes.

That whenever you have a number of letters to seal, ice cubes help.

That if you want dripproof candles, freeze them before using. They will never drip and will last twice as long.

Chapter VI

ENTERTAINING IN THE ARMY

Then drink, puppy, drink, and let every puppy drink
That's old enough to lap and to swallow;
For he'll grow into a hound and we'll pass the bottle round
And merrily we'll whoop and we'll holloa.

Army Hunt Song

I N THE Army there is an informality in extending invitations that is not found in the fashionable circles of civil life. The social life on a small post resembles that of a large family, and one of its chief charms is the free manner in which an Army community, say an entire division or Air Force group, submits to transfer from a city to foreign service without breaking up any of its social activities. In fact, it seems to knit the families closer together, and develops a camaraderie the like of which is found in no other organization.

The telephone is the means of conveying many invitations; for a large party, however, the hostess finds telephoning her invitations quite a chore. Allowing for busy signals, leaving messages for those not at home and conversing with those at home takes more time than writing notes, she finds. If the hostess has plenty of time, she may call and deliver the invitation in person, but it is not good form to issue invitations to a party at another party which you are attending. The persons invited may forget your asking them and not show up at your party.

134

Few army people are so formal, except on legation duty or in Washington, that they send out engraved invitations for dinner. Blank forms may be filled in, as:

Colonel and Mrs. William Adams Blaine
request the pleasure of
Captain and Mrs. James Theodore Worthing's
company at dinner
on Friday, January the eighth
at eight o'clock
308 Sumner Place

The acceptance or refusal should be written within twenty-four hours and should follow the same form as the above, which wording, you will note, is always in the third person.

A formal invitation is never written entirely across the page, in longhand running style, as an informal invitation is.

Your acceptance or refusal on a good grade of plain white notepaper should read:

Captain and Mrs. James Theodore Worthing
accept with pleasure
Colonel and Mrs. William Adams Blaine's
kind invitation to dinner
on Friday the eighth of January
at eight o'clock

If it is impossible for you to accept, the form for regret used is:

Captain and Mrs. James Theodore Worthing
regret that they are unable to accept
Colonel and Mrs. William Adams Blaine's
kind invitation to dinner
on Friday the eighth of January

Remember, in the Army a formal dinner invitation must be answered within twenty-four hours. Delays are very annoying to a hostess, and she might like to ask someone else in your stead who has better manners.

The Informal Written Dinner Invitation

Dear Mrs. Worthing:

Will you and Captain Worthing dine (or have dinner) with us on Friday, the eighth of January, at seven o'clock?

Looking forward to the pleasure of having you with us,

Very sincerely,

Helen Adams Blaine

The Informal Note of Acceptance or Regret

Dear Mrs. Blaine:

Captain Worthing and I accept with greatest pleasure your kind invitation to dinner on Friday, the eighth of January, at seven o'clock.

Thanking you for your kindness in thinking of us,

Sincerely yours,

Margaret Carver Worthing

Calling-Card Invitations and "Informals"

For luncheons, brunches, teas, cocktail parties, buffet suppers, informal dances and picnics, notes are seldom written. Calling cards or "formals" are used:

Wednesday, Jan. 15

at one o'clock

Mrs. William Adams Blaine

Lunch   Bright Shawl Tea Room

or:

Mrs. William Adams Blaine

Lunch   The Bright Shawl
R.S.V.P.   One o'clock
                                                         Wednesday, Jan. 15

This invitation requires a written answer at once, the same as a dinner invitation.

R.S.V.P. (*"Répondez, s'il vous plaît"* . . . reply, if you please) on an invitation commands a reply. The hostess does this in order to be sure of the number for whom to make reservations.

or:

Colonel and Mrs. William Adams Blaine

Cocktails   Officers' Club
5 to 7   Wed. Nov. 15

This invitation requires an answer, though people are very lax about answering written invitations to cocktail parties.

A tea:

To meet
Mrs. Horace Manners
Mrs. William Adams Blaine

Tea   Thursday, May 5

This is the informal invitation that does not require a written answer unless you cannot attend. Then a written note of regret should be sent.

THE TELEPHONE INVITATION

Invitations should not be left with servants or children. However, you may leave your number and ask to be called. It is not necessary to indulge in long conversations, if you have any choice in the matter. Formality should be ob-

served with older people or those with whom you are not
on intimate terms. For instance, no junior officer's wife
should call an older Army woman or a senior officer's wife
by her first name unless she has been invited to do so. Note
that the colonel's wife will usually address you formally,
until she knows you quite well. The conversation will go
something like this: "Mrs. Worthing, this is Helen Blaine
speaking. Will you and your husband have dinner with us
(or with Colonel Blaine and me) on Saturday evening, at
eight o'clock, at the Officers' Club?"

You might say: "Yes, we'd love to," or "I'm sorry, but we
are going to the Blakes'." It isn't very polite to say, "We have
another engagement," but you may say the same thing in
another way, as: "We have just accepted the Blakes' invitation." It isn't necessary to tell where you are going, and in
some cases it may be better not to mention names.

TELEPHONE ETIQUETTE

In a social telephone conversation, never say, "This is
Mrs. Worthing calling"; say, "This is Helen Worthing calling." However, when you answer the telephone, before you
know who is calling, it is quite correct to say, "Mrs. Worthing
speaking."

Should you be calling a business firm, of course, you would
say, "This is Mrs. Worthing." In telephone conversation
where you are giving an order to the commissary or P.X.,
the accepted form is, "This is Captain J. T. Worthing's order,
Mrs. Worthing speaking." Then give your address, quarters
number, etc., before you give your order.

If you have a servant, teach her the correct form for answering the telephone: "Captain Worthing's quarters, the
maid speaking." Have a telephone pad near by and instruct
your maid to ask courteously if there is any message, or the

caller's number, in case you are away from home. If you are at home, the maid may politely inquire, "Who is calling, please?" so that she may relay the information to you, and save you from going to the phone if you are very busy at the time. Long conversations over busy Army trunk lines are not to be encouraged.

THE BRIDE GOES TO HER FIRST ARMY LUNCHEON

If it is a small home luncheon, often your hostess greets you at the door, and if there is a guest of honor, she introduces you to her and to any other guest you may not know. You speak graciously to everyone present, but to those seated in an adjoining room a nod will suffice. If the luncheon is given at a tearoom, a club or a hotel, you look about for your party, then go first and greet your hostess. Sometimes cocktails or a glass of dry sherry is served before luncheon is announced. At a formal luncheon there will be place cards showing you where to sit.

If it is informal, such as a bridge luncheon, the guests may be seated at bridge tables and served a plate lunch. Or, in buffet style, the guests may serve themselves, then find places at tables or sit about the living room informally with their plates in their laps. (Most unsatisfactory unless there is a goodly supply of small tables about.)

After luncheon, if there is no special entertainment provided, guests usually sit and converse from twenty to thirty minutes, then bid their hostess and the guest of honor good-by and leave. When one guest says good-by the others invariably follow; but at Army gatherings the younger women always wait for their elders or the ranking officer's wife to make her departure.

What to wear! A bride wears one of the prettiest day-time dresses in her trousseau, with her most becoming hat and accessories. If the luncheon is given at a hotel in a city, street clothes or a suit will be appropriate.

BREAKFASTS AND BRUNCHES

With the servant problem what it is, many Army people find a solution in easy informal entertaining by giving a hunt breakfast or brunch. These are very popular because they are inexpensive and the service can be kept simple. Sunday is a popular day. The party can be very festive on a cold day with a great open fire, after a brisk ride on horseback or a strenuous round of golf.

The guests arrive in sports clothes and bring along with them good hearty appetites. They are ready for plenty of sausages and eggs, waffles, or whatever tempting menu the hosts may offer. Hot Tom and Jerrys in winter before a blazing log fire put everyone in a jolly mood, and in summer iced drinks may be served before brunch or breakfast is announced. The food should be served before twelve-thirty; otherwise the party, not of its own accord but in conformity to social custom, becomes luncheon and a more elaborate menu should be offered.

If you ride, go in your riding clothes, or any becoming sports clothes you may own. Officers usually add a sports coat to their golfing togs.

TEAS AND TEA DANCES

The invitation to tea always suggests a small cozy party, yet there is nothing very cozy about a gay tea dance for several hundred people, or a formal tea served by a caterer. Most small teas given by Army women are informal, however, and are enjoyable affairs. On this occasion the hostess uses her loveliest tea cloth and tea service, and the quarters are shining and at their very best. In other words, everything is "on inspection"; it is a party for the feminine world. Wear your dressiest afternoon dress, a gay large or small hat, white gloves (if they are fashionable) and carry a card case or small purse. If you are returning from town, and must wear a suit or tailored outfit, be sure that you are perfectly groomed, that your blouse and gloves are fresh, and, if you can, add a gardenia; it will improve your morale immensely.

The tea table, with a coffee service at one end and a tea service at the other, will be presided over by an intimate friend of the hostess, or the ranking officer's wife present. This is a courtesy usually extended to the C.O.'s wife and executive's wife, if they care to serve or pour.

After greeting your hostess and the guest of honor, go into the dining room, and from the buffet or serving table select a plate, cup and tea napkin—or perhaps the cups and saucers are in front of the deputy hostess who is pouring. The older woman will probably greet you with some pleasantry if she knows you, otherwise she may simply ask, "How will you have your tea?" The guests help themselves to sandwiches, cakes and confections, which are arranged on the tea table.

Try to have a short visit with you hostess and a few words with the guest of honor, but under no circumstances monopolize their time. All guests converse with each other, whether or not they have been introduced.

A half-hour or, at the most, forty-five minutes is long enough to stay at a tea of this sort. Thank your hostess, say good-by to the guest of honor and, if you can gracefully do so, to the deputy hostess who served you.

One calling card should be left for your hostess and one for the guest of honor on a tray that will be conveniently placed in the hallway.

The Intimate Tea

This is the type that might be described as cozy. Your commanding officer's wife may ask you in for tea alone, or she may invite from one to a dozen guests. The hostess usually presides at a small tea table that a servant places before her. If there is no servant, then one of the younger guests passes the cups of steaming tea, while another may volunteer to pass the sandwiches and cakes.

You may be asked to bring your knitting or sewing, and many choose this delightful, informal way of entertaining. The refreshments can be very simple—bread-and-butter sandwiches, tea and cookies.

The Formal Dinner

With conditions as they are, it isn't likely that you will be the recipient of many formal dinner invitations. Little dinners of eight, informal home dinners of six and buffet suppers have taken their place. However, general officers and ranking officers who maintain well-staffed households entertain formally as in days gone by, and you may consider yourself honored if you are invited to one of these "at home" dinners. Formal dinners are now usually given at clubs and in private dining rooms of hotels.

The seating at a formal dinner in Army circles is always according to rank, with the exception of the guest of honor. The experienced hostess—and no one except an experienced social leader should attempt to entertain at a formal dinner —will draw up a seating chart. Undoubtedly she will have to consult the *Army Blue Book* so that Captain Brown of the Engineers will not be disgruntled because Mr. Jones of the Infantry occupies his rightful place at table. If the seating is according to rank, then the hostess must be consistent and follow the book.

Wear your best dinner dress or formal evening dress. A dinner dress with a suggestion of sleeves or a long dress with a jacket seems to be more apropos; however, some women feel that a formal dinner calls for bare backs and bare shoulders. Long white or colored kid gloves may be worn but, of course, are removed in the powder room. Your husband wears formal evening dress (blues) or civilian evening dress (tails) if he owns them; or, if he possesses neither, then a dinner coat, though the latter is not correct, strictly speaking, except in tropical climates.

Your hostess will be standing near the door and will greet you upon your arrival with some gracious remark and a smile of welcome. Remember this: The perfect guest owes his hostess the courtesy of entering into the spirit of the party and should strive to be entertaining and at his best. It does not mean that one should attempt to "take over" or to be the center of attraction. What most social gatherings need is a few trained listeners, and your popularity will depend upon your poise, your graciousness and your charm. No man, young or old, is impervious to a beautiful woman who is a good listener. People love to talk about themselves, if you can get them to open up. A grim-visaged, crusty old colonel may prove a delightful dinner partner if you are a mind reader and can direct the conversation to his pet hobby. All he needs to have is a pretty and intelligent listener and he "will become lost in the impenetrable forest of his own verbosity." The bride or young woman in the Service who is a good listener and a close observer can learn more at her first formal dinner party than can be included in this entire book.

Never be late to dinner. If you are invited at eight o'clock, be there at eight, not five minutes before or two minutes after. In military circles, being "fashionably late" is taboo. If you arrive early, your hostess may not be ready to receive you, and you will interfere with her last-minute duties and plans. Arriving earlier than you were asked is really worse than arriving a few minutes late. If an unavoidable accident delayed you, your hostess will not wait more than twenty minutes before dinner is announced, and then you are expected to take your place and start your dinner at whatever course is in progress.

During dinner be careful to divide your conversation equally between the men on either side of you. In the good old days, the hostess used to accomplish this by a social trick called "turning at table." For instance, during the soup and fish courses she talked with the gentleman on her left. All of the guests watched the hostess, and the signal for everyone to change conversation partners came when the hostess turned and began to talk to the gentleman on her right. This seems a bit farfetched today, but it is a point that should be watched by the younger generation. There is nothing more awkward than to feel like a fifth wheel, and to be neglected by an inconsiderate dinner partner. Of course, if you draw a Sphinx for a dinner partner, who prefers to be left alone with his food, that is something else. However, you should make several attempts to engage him in conversation. Your dinner partner is the gentleman on your left.

After dinner, the ladies and gentlemen return to the living room or drawing room for coffee and liquers. The art of conversation is indulged in, if there is such a thing today. One clever Washington Army hostess is proud of the fact that at her parties "the Army and Navy planes are left in the hangars, all Cavalry horses remain in their stables, good servants exist only in heaven, and the dear little children at

home are in their beds, where all good children should be."
This Army wife directs the conversation without appearing
to do so—one of the fine arts of the perfect hostess.

After an hour the guests take their departure. The ranking
guest leaves first, and immediately following, the others say
good night. It is enough to say, "Good night, and thank you
so much!"

At the dinner for eight, these same suggestions would be
applicable.

The Buffet or Cocktail Supper

The buffet supper is, perhaps, the most popular form of
entertainment in Army circles today. Its informality appeals,
many more guests can be entertained and the service is
simpler for the hostess.

At any social function of this sort it is proper to wear
evening dress after six o'clock. Of course, if there is an
especially informal entertainment afterwards, such as a skating party, you dress accordingly.

Cocktails, if any, are served, and then supper will be announced. Everyone proceeds to the dining room, where the
table is set as for a tea table. Plates, silver and napkins will
be near by on a serving table. The platters of meat and the
hot dishes and salad will be on the table, but the hot rolls,
relishes and coffee may be passed. If the hostess does not
ask deputy hostesses to serve the salad or vegetables, the
guests help themselves. Sometimes small tables are set up,
and even place cards are arranged for special seating. Unless
she should happen to be incapacitated, a lady should serve
her own plate and not expect an officer to make two trips
around the table. The hostess probably wants you to see her
pretty table and, too, you may not care for such generous
servings as your escort may bring you.

THE COCKTAIL PARTY

Cocktail parties have come into their own! The usual hours are from five to seven. Should you be going on to dinner later, then plan to arrive late, after six, so that you may wear evening clothes. In cities, and on many posts, the ladies wear afternoon dresses or dressy daytime dresses. The officers wear business suits or uniform.

This is one party where you may drop in at any time between the hours mentioned; you are not expected to stay the entire period of time. From thirty minutes to an hour should be long enough.

A thoughtful host and hostess provide tomato juice and nonalcoholic drinks, such as Coca-Cola or ginger ale, for those who don't indulge in stronger beverages. By no means consider yourself a wet blanket just because you don't indulge. Stick by your principles, and remember this: You will be better off if you never drink. This applies both to officers and to their wives. People will respect you for the stand you take, provided you are not rude or critical in regard to the drinking of others, or unfriendly and disapproving in your manner. Cocktail suppers are given from six to eight with necessarily heartier food.

NEW YEAR'S RECEPTION

On New Year's Day all officers and ladies of the command call upon the commanding officer and his wife at an hour and place designated by them, preferably between 11 A.M. and 1 P.M. If the commanding officer's wife is absent, then the officers alone make this call unless the ladies are especially invited.

The ladies wear dressy daytime dresses and hats, of course —something suitable for a luncheon but not quite so elaborate as a tea frock. Officers are in uniform (prescribed) and wear sabers on this occasion.

THE BRIDE ENTERTAINS!

You have finally gotten the rice out of your hair, and suddenly you realize that the day of reckoning is not far distant when you must give your first party. Hospitality accepted from others *should be returned,* just as social calls and all obligations should be repaid. However, this does not mean that the hospitality shown you should be returned exactly in kind. *Junior officers are not expected to entertain on the scale that older officers and their families are able to afford.* As a matter of fact, anyone in the Army who attempts to entertain beyond a scale appropriate to the officer's grade and pay is definitely condemned. Owing to this unwritten law, there is little rivalry among hostesses, and the junior hosts should strive to make their parties as simple, yet as enjoyable, as possible.

The wise bride will keep a social calendar and a record of social engagements. Also, it is a good plan to give a few small parties each month, unless you prefer to "save up" as your obligations pile up and then give one large, wholesale party. The latter method has its advantages, but it is much more sociable and more of a compliment to your guests to entertain them in your own home, if circumstances permit.

Here are a few general hints:

Don't attempt elaborate menus or experiment with new dishes when you have guests. Try out the tempting recipe of a spinach ring on your husband first; then serve it several times before attempting it at a party.

Don't ask too many people. Try to make up congenial guest lists and include at least two good conversationalists, if possible. One other couple at dinner is about all the maidless bride can handle. I know it is hard not to invite the same people every time, because they are your best friends and you enjoy them; but remember, you have social obligations. Confine your first buffet parties to ten or twelve at the outside.

If the party is to be buffet, plan a place where each guest may be seated, with a small table near by if possible. Some hostesses use trays, though it does remind one a bit of cafeteria service. However, a tray or small table is preferable to balancing a plate on a slippery satin lap!

Have plenty of food; in fact, be on the generous side; but your party will be more of a success if you are on the stingy side with liquor. Serve two well-iced strong cocktails or drinks, then have dinner announced.

Keep your menu simple, and above all don't make entertaining a chore and be so worn out by the time the guests arrive that you cannot enjoy them or the party. Plan to have a maid or a cleaning woman in to do the dishes and set your quarters in order, so that the party will be only a pleasant memory to you.

Have one knockout menu, guaranteed to impress any visiting celebrities or relatives, then RELAX!

If you want to get your party off to a good start, seat your guests yourself by arranging place cards. There will be no shy, odd or left over people and this will break the ice.

Your party begins with you! Plan it so that you and your husband will have a good time, and the guests will have the time of their lives. If you feel that it is going to be fun, there will be an infectious gaiety in the air and your husband will fall into the spirit of it. A good book on giving parties is *Entertaining Is Fun*, by Dorothy Draper.

A surprise element in the form of a new and exciting dish may add to your party. The young hostess, however, will feel more at ease if she follows a menu she has tried out many times before. Or the surprise element may be some interesting and new person—a movie celebrity or a new game, a story or a thrilling idea.

The hostess is always in command of the situation. A beautiful table, good food and congenial guests make up the recipe for a successful party, and it needn't cost a lot, either, if carefully planned. Keep everything simple, and plan only food which can be mostly prepared in advance.

YOUR FIRST TEA

If a lovely tea service was among your wedding gifts, then your easiest party will be a tea. The number of guests may be from two to a round dozen or more, and you may choose to serve in the living room before an open fire, or perhaps in the garden, or to convert the dining table into a tea table. Your loveliest cloth will cover the table, and at one end will be the tea service. A pretty flower arrangement will be in the center of the table, flanked by candlesticks or candelabra holding lighted white candles. To carry out certain color schemes, colored candles are often used, but white or ivory tapers are really in better taste. Have all silver shining. If you can't have it gleaming, then don't use it. Substitute crystal or china in its stead. If there is no servant, then prepare everything before hand except boiling the water for the tea.

Near the tea service arrange the required number of cups and saucers and teaspoons, or cups and salad plates. The latter are more satisfactory, as sandwiches may be placed on them. Arrange tea napkins near by.

Place small loaf sugar in the sugar bowl, and provide both cream and lemon. A pitcher of ice water and several goblets may be placed on a serving table or on the buffet.

Trays of sandwiches, cakes, and mints are placed on the

table or passed by one of the younger guests you have asked to assist you. It is customary to ask the commanding officer's wife, or some older person, to pour tea.

Three Suggested Menus for the Informal Tea

Bread-and-butter sandwiches—Cinnamon toast—Tea
Toast or muffins with jam or marmalade—Tea
Water-cress sandwiches—Cookies—Tea

Suggestions for a More Formal Tea

Party sandwiches
Meat sandwiches   *Cakes*
Meat paste of ham   Fancy cakes
Pâté de foie gras   Plain cookies
Chicken or tongue   English muffins
Salad sandwiches   Hot gingerbread
Tuna, sardine, chicken   Layer cakes
Mushroom sandwiches   Chocolate roll
Toasted cheese, onion and   Upside-down pudding
  cream cheese, Roquefort   Tipsy pudding
Cucumber
Open sandwiches: Tomato,
  pimento

Bonbons . . . mints . . . salted nuts . . . preserved ginger . . . stuffed dates.

Elaborate menus are seldom served except at "high tea" or a seated tea, owing to the current fashion in dieting. Few women wish to partake of rich food in the late afternoon. The simpler the food, the better; so, you see, there is no trick to giving a tea! By asking someone to pour, and having one of your younger friends to stand by and assist the person pouring, you will be free to entertain and visit with your guests.

Your First Buffet Supper

Beloved of the maidless for Saturday or Sunday night entertaining, beloved of everyone who enjoys the casual, a buffet supper is a sensible way to entertain a large group with little effort.

Right from the start, you must learn to let other people help you. Don't let all your guests jump up to help. Pick one or two and work them hard. They won't mind and it won't break up the party. There is a simple trick to being the kind of hostess who can turn out a perfect meal with everyone milling around the kitchen, talking, laughing and helping.

By this time your husband may feel that he would like to take a hand in the entertaining and have some of his bachelor friends in; so it is a tossup between a cocktail party and a buffet supper. Both are expensive, as they call for liquor, but the buffet supper is the less expensive of the two. Formal dinners given by ranking officers are often returned by buffet suppers given by junior officers.

Martinis and Manhattans cost less than good Scotch and soda, though it is a waste to make up cocktails ahead of time, as the majority of people prefer highballs. To give a party of this type requires a bit of penny-pinching beforehand on the part of the young hosts.

Serve simple, well-prepared food, plenty of it, and your guests will have a good time. A pretty, colorful table goes a long way. Let your buffet table glow with color and in every way make it the expression of friendly hospitality that it is intended to represent. If the dining room is very small, then greater space can be had by placing the dining table against the wall. Arrange the silver in military precision, with some semblance of balance. Card tables may be set up beforehand if space permits, and the silver arranged at the individual places, or nests of tables may be dispersed while the guests are serving themselves.

For your first buffet supper, limit your guest list to twelve. By this time, if you have really applied yourself to learning to cook, you must have some specialty. Perhaps you are a past mistress at making "country captain," Italian spaghetti, or have brought from home a very fine recipe for baked beans. If you are really proficient, and can turn out a superb product, then serve it over and over again and become famous for it! If your husband is a salad tosser, or one of those male maestros who loves to cook, give him free rein and your party giving will be different, successful and original.

Ten Suggested Menus for Buffet Suppers

Boston baked beans	Italian spaghetti	Creole shrimp
Vegetable salad	Green salad	Rice
Hot apple pie	Frozen dessert	Molded salad
Cheese, coffee	Cheese, coffee	Sherbert-cake
Roast turkey	Baked ham	Chicken à la king in
Wild rice	Brandied peaches	patty shells
Peas	Au gratin potatoes	Asparagus
Salad	String beans	Tomatoes stuffed with
Dessert, coffee	Dessert, coffee	celery
Hot rolls	Hot rolls	Dessert, coffee

Mexican Supper	*Southern Supper*
Chile con carne	Country captain
Mexican rice	or
Frijoles	Southern fried chicken
Enchiladas	Grits or spoon bread
Tomato stuffed with guacamole salad	Asparagus au gratin
Frozen fresh pineapple soaked in rum	Frozen fruit salad or Green salad
Coffee	Coffee

Chinese Supper	Curry
Chop suey	Chicken curry
Rice	Rice
Sweet-sour	Condiments
Spareribs	Salad
Green salad	Dessert
Dessert, coffee	Coffee

Rehearse everything you're going to try on your guests beforehand, from butterballs to sauces. To pep up the menu, try "chicken in the rough." It's crisp fried chicken, and you serve it forth wrapped in damask, like the rolls, in a big wicker basket. It is crispest if you fry for five minutes in very hot fat-and-butter, then reduce to low heat to finish. Another fillip or attractive note to your menu is to serve interesting bread, such as Finnish rye, brioche, French bread, pumpernickel. Italian sesame seed, Swedish bread or bread sticks.

Always set your dinner late so as to allow yourself plenty of time for your last-minute touches. Don't rush through cocktails; it spoils the atmosphere conducive to a leisurely evening of good conversation. Note that the above menus are all of the "supper can wait" type and the *pièce de résistance* will not be spoiled.

Your First Cocktail Party

Unless a large number of guests is expected, it is better to have the cocktails mixed in the pantry and passed on trays. A hostess tray may be filled with celery, small knobs of cauliflower, sliced raw carrots with a bowl of piquant sauce in which to dip them. (See *Entertaining Is Fun*, by Dorothy Draper, page 58.) Should the guest list be large, set the dining table as for a tea, using either an elaborate cloth or a novelty cloth. Appropriate decorations should grace the table. Both the food and refreshment tables may be placed in the garden. One disadvantage of large cocktail parties is that the guests often stay late, and it is the type of party which gets out of hand and over which the hosts have little control. It is a popular but expensive form of entertaining. Always provide tomato-juice cocktails for those who would hesitate to ask for them. Some either do not or cannot indulge in alcoholic beverages.

The first requisite for a cocktail party is good liquor. "Good liquor is not cheap and cheap liquor is not good." Everything for mixing drinks should be set up on one table. The six most popular mixed drinks are: Bacardi cocktails, Daiquiris, dry Martinis, Manhattans, old-fashioned cocktails and whisky sours. Usually, and for even a fairly large party, dry Martinis, with whisky and soda for highballs, sherry, tomato and iced fruit juices, plus milk for those on diets but who like to go to parties just the same, offer something for everyone.

Plain, clear glass is preferable to colored cocktail glasses, and highball glasses with ships, polo ponies, dolphins and flags painted on them seem out of place except on a yacht or in a fraternity house.

Be sure that hot canapés are served very hot. Cold things should be chilled and banked in ice when possible. An old English silver hot dish keeps hot canapés at the proper temperature. Potato chips served hot in wooden bowls are tempting, also hot roasted nuts.

Twenty-five Suggested Appetizers

Sizzling cocktail sausages
Seeded green grapes, split and filled with Gruyère cheese
Oysters wrapped in bacon—broiled
Tamales wrapped in bacon—broiled
Olives wrapped in bacon—broiled
Seasoned cream cheese wrapped in dried-beef funnels

Seasoned cream cheese thinned with mayonnaise for sauce in
  which to dunk cauliflower knobs, carrots, shallots, potato chips
Single spring onion rolled in bread-and-butter sandwich, held
  by toothpick, with green top of onion protruding from one end
Tiny hot biscuit with sautéed mushroom
Tiny hot biscuit with ham
Broiled chicken livers impaled on toothpicks
Extra large head of cabbage, in top of which is a well, hollowed
  out and filled with Thousand Island dressing. Large pink
  shrimps impaled on toothpicks are stuck into the cabbage.
  The leaves which were hollowed out make lovely cabbage
  roses for garnishing the platter
Large pecan halves sandwiched together with anchovy paste
Celery stuffed with Roquefort
Caviar, anchovy, hot cheese canapés
Spiced deviled eggs
Cheese, crackers, cold cuts, olives
Freshly roasted almonds, hot chestnuts
"Hush puppies"—made of waterground meal mixed with finely
  ground bacon and onion. They originated at old-fashioned
  southern fish fries, when a busy cook would hurriedly throw
  a corndodger to the barking hungry hounds that were always
  underfoot. "Hush puppies" (or tiny hot corndodgers) are
  delicious!
Good liquor. Paper cocktail napkins by the dozens, and a good
  supply of glasses, ice and soda.

ENTERTAINING AT BREAKFAST OR BRUNCH

A brunch or breakfast is simply a stand-up luncheon, but
the food is simpler. Breakfast as an entertainment evidently
had its origin in the English hunt breakfast. Provide large
pitchers of orange juice, tomato juice and pineapple juice,
or a large deep silver tray piled with cracked ice in which
pieces of melon, luscious grapes, oranges and other tempting
fruits are kept chilled. The latter makes a pretty centerpiece.

Sausages and waffles; bacon or ham and scrambled eggs; or fried chicken and spoon bread are a few of the combinations you can serve. Have plenty of good hot steaming coffee.

GIVING A LUNCHEON

By this time you may feel experienced enough to attempt a formal luncheon. The buffet luncheon is far easier, unless you have a good servant. If you have a service for eight, then two servants are necessary to keep things going smoothly. In the setting of the luncheon table, the same service should be observed as for an informal dinner except that candles are not used. In the shops today there are so many attractive luncheon sets that the hostess may make her table as elaborate as she chooses. Dainty lace doilies or the lovely hand-painted cellophane mats are beautiful with sparkling silver, crystal and good china.

Service for luncheon is the same in place arrangement as for dinner, except that bread-and-butter plates are used at luncheon. Four courses are usually served: fruit cup or soup, the main course, the salad course and the dessert course. If there is only one maid, and the plates are served in the kitchen to save service, the salad is often placed on the main course plate. However, this places the luncheon in the informal class. At a formal luncheon each dish is served individually, and to make the service move quickly enough, two waiters are necessary for a party of eight.

Setting the Table

Having arranged a low centerpiece of flowers or tempting fruit, place your service plates, if you are using them, in the middle of each place doily. The napkin folded in a picket-shaped point is placed on the left of the service plate. A teaspoon or bouillon spoon should be placed at the right of the luncheon knife, then a luncheon fork for the main course and one for salad at the left of the service plate, and a bread-and-butter knife laid across the bread-and-butter plate at right angles to the other flat silver. The bread-and-butter plate is placed on the left, and the goblet and wineglass at the right. The dessert silver is brought in on the dessert plate with the finger bowl, the fork on the left of the finger bowl, the spoon at the right. A violet, peach blossom, or any small fragrant flower placed in the finger bowl adds charm to the service.

Butterballs add a distinctive note, and may or may not be placed on the butter plate before luncheon is announced. Crystal cocktail glasses filled with crushed ice, holding a small fruit cup, can be made very attractive by tinting the ice with a few drops of crème de menthe. Another touch is to place rose leaves on top of the shaved ice with a luscious black cherry here and there. It gives a Della Robbia effect.

The fruit cocktail glass is placed on a salad plate, then set on the service plate. The idea of a service plate is to have a plate in front of one during the entire meal. The waiter removes the cocktail glass and its attendant salad plate from the right, leaving the service plate in front of the guest. When he returns with the luncheon plate, he removes the service plate from the right and, with practically a sleight-of-hand performance, places the luncheon or dinner plate before the guest from the left. All serving of foods is from the left, and throughout the meal all dishes are removed from the right. The dessert service may be brought in and placed before the guest as the main course plate is removed. The guest removes the doily and finger bowl and places them at the left, where the bread-and-butter plate has previously been. The dessert silver is put on the place doily by the guest.

Wine at lunch is a matter of choice and not at all necessary. If it is served, it should be a light Rhine wine, and in
this case cocktails should not be served before. Or you might
serve a glass of dry sherry before luncheon, but be sure to
have tomato juice or fruit juice for those who do not take
alcohol. Don't mix wines unless you know what you are serving, and please remember that your luncheon may go off
better without any alcoholic beverages at all.

Suggested Luncheon Menus

One hot course at a meal is always a wise procedure, as
many people dislike cold food and it may not agree with
them.

Fruit cup	Hot or jellied con-	Iced melon
Broiled chicken	sommé	Lamp chop
Fresh asparagus	Squab	Spinach ring
Tomato-avocado salad	Peas	Hot rolls
Hot rolls—coffee	Frozen fruit salad	Chocolate pudding
Lime Ice	Hot rolls—coffee	Iced tea

Tomato bouillon	Chicken broth	Tomato stuffed with
Chicken salad	Crabmeat salad served	shrimp salad
Potato chips	in half of an avocado	Layer cake
Asparagus and	Shoestring potatoes	Iced coffee
Almonds au gratin	Hot rolls—coffee	
Hot rolls—coffee	Homemade ice cream	
Pineapple sherbet		

Asparagus soup	Chicken soup with whole-wheat
Broiled mushrooms on toast	wafers
Broccoli with Hollandaise sauce	Cheese soufflé
Honeydew melon filled with lime	Fresh fruit salad with French dress-
sherbet	ing
Coffee	Whole-wheat muffins
	Tea

The food you serve and the way you serve it are just as
revealing of the kind of person you are as the house which
is your background and the clothes you wear. It is fun to

dream up new color combinations both in decorations and in foods. For instance, fancy a dinner of creamed chicken, mashed potatoes, and creamed cauliflower served on a white plate. How deadly dull! Even if the food were perfectly seasoned, it would all taste the same; also, with such an unimaginative hostess I daresay the evening would be equally dull and colorless.

With all the lovely decorations on the market today—all types of accessories, beautiful china, silver, glassware—you can build up a store of interesting and exciting table decorations. Besides these accessories you can develop a line of surface props that will add color to your food . . . simple little things like paprika, pimento, green pepper, parsley, watercress, chives, celery, eggs, tomatoes, sliced fruits and relishes.

Invest in individual pottery casseroles, then three or four large earthenware baking dishes with handles, which may also be used in the oven. Regard each dish, platter or bowl you serve as a still life you are creating.

Early in the game get in the habit of experimenting with condiments, herbs and spices. For instance, add a grating of nutmeg to chicken soup just before serving; a pinch of ginger added to chocolate icing gives a delicious unusual flavor. It has been said that "the discovery of a new dish does more for the happiness of a man than the discovery of a star."

Simplicity in food is the credo of the day, and more and more new canned foods are appearing on the grocery shelves. Excellent vichysoisse can now be bought in jars and needs only complete chilling; delicious canned black-bean soup can be doctored just before serving with sherry and lemon juice; also hot green-turtle soup out of a can needs only a spot of sherry added to it. It can be served thoroughly chilled too from a crystal bowl at table; this goes for borsch which is put up in large jars and can be kept conveniently in the refrigerator. The best madrilene comes in jars and cans. A delectable fruitcake-like garnish for ice cream is aptly named rum-crumbles. Frozen foods are a boon to the housewife, and a great saving in time and labor. The newest culinary gibe about brides is "Can she melt ice?" The latest news on frozen foods is that electric ranges are being designed with food-thawing compartments to unfreeze food in a fraction of the time now required. Frozen coffee is now available. It appears in tiny paper cups, each containing enough concentrated coffee to make six cups of the beverage when added to that quantity of boiling water. Frozen grapefruit sections, cantaloupe balls and seafoods of all kinds in addition to frozen vegetables and meats tend to make cooking problems easier for the brides of today. One suggestion: Do not expect the Army to install stoves with food-thawing compartments, my dear, until the present prewar stoves become so tired and worn out that they have to be "surveyed or scrapped." Exercise your ingenuity, study your cookbooks and the latest recipes in magazines and plan your menus so that there will be a minimum amount of kitchen work at the last moment.

Other good ideas for the table are wicker bread baskets, and why not a real wicker wine-bottle basket to hold the bottle as it is passed at dinner? Straw table mats are practical, and a wooden pepper mill or a silver one filled with fresh peppercorns is a gourmet's delight. Ice buckets more than repay one, and they come in every type and price.

Two other pet ideas of mine: try a few dashes of Angostura bitters on your morning grapefruit or in orange juice or a scant teaspoonful of it in your applesauce; for old-fashioneds (this I learned in Hawaii) keep a can of pineapple sticks and a bottle of cherries on hand. Somehow the long fingers of pineapple seem to give an impression of lavish hospitality!

All social life today is freer and more fun than it used to be. The whole trend of modern life, and particularly in the Army, is toward a more informal and simpler way of doing things. Of course, in Washington and on duty in foreign capitals there will be formal parties, particularly seated dinners, so it is well to know how to plan one, just in case!

GIVING DINNERS, FORMAL AND INFORMAL

For gay little informal dinners to which you invite one or two couples or several bachelor officers the table appointments may be very simple. Candles appear at dinner, and bread-and-butter plates are omitted. Cream soups are used instead of bouillon cups; otherwise, the service is the same as at luncheon. At the informal dinner the host may carve the roast or fowl at table; at the formal dinner the carving is done in the kitchen and all dishes are served by waiters or maids. The use of place doilies for informal dinners is accepted, but regulation-size dinner napkins are preferable to luncheon-size napkins.

Seating Eight at Dinner

The only way to seat eight at dinner and have a lady and gentleman alternate is for the hostess to place the gentleman guest of honor in her place at the opposite end of the table from the host, and for the hostess to take the gentleman guest of honor's rightful seat.

The Formal Dinner

Don't attempt a formal dinner unless you have an experienced cook, a butler and a second maid, or a cook and two serving maids. It is far better to give an informal dinner. At formal dinners the table should be covered with either an elaborate dinner cloth or a faultlessly laundered damask cloth, with a heavy silence cloth underneath. Even the most formal dinners of today consist of no more than five courses, and four are preferred.

1. Soup	1. Soup
2. Roast	2. Fish or entree
3. Salad	3. Roast
4. Dessert	4. Salad
	5. Dessert

Demitasse and liqueurs

The centerpiece of the table, if it is a flower arrangement, should be kept low. There is nothing more annoying than having to play peek-a-boo with a dinner guest across the table. See that the table has been extended enough to give the guests elbow room—twenty inches between places— and that there is enough space for the servants to pass the dishes. The dinner napkin, folded square, should be placed in the middle of the service plate, and if place cards are used, they should be put on top of the napkin. The center decoration, candelabra, compotes holding salted nuts, salts and peppers and individual ash trays are the only extra silver, besides the flat silver, on the table. Salts and peppers should be at every other place at table.

Menu Suggestions for Informal Dinner

Clear soup or	Cream soup	Clear soup
Cream soup	Roast beef—Yorkshire	Roast duck, turkey, goose,
Leg of spring lamb	pudding	chicken
Mint jelly	Franconia potatoes	Dressing, gravy
New potatoes	Cauliflower	Wild rice
English peas	Hot rolls	String beans
Lettuce salad	Iced celery salad,	Currant jelly
Ice cream, cake	French dressing	Hot rolls
Coffee	Sherbet, cake	Endive salad
	Coffee	Mint ice, coffee

Serving the Informal Dinner

One well-known social authority of today speaks of the custom of having the hostess served first as the "Great American Rudeness"! Well, I fear that most Army hostesses when presiding over informal or home dinners are guilty of this "Great American Rudeness." Mrs. Post gives several reasons for the origin of the custom. She says it may be traced back to the dangerous days of the Borgias, when poisoning one's enemies at table was a convenient social usage; or it may go back to the matriarchal system of American tradition wherein the great-grandmother occupied the seat of honor at the head of the table and was deferentially served first; but I believe that the best reason given is that in the frontier days, with untrained help in the kitchen, the well-bred hostess, out of courteous consideration for her guests, wished to try the dish first. If it lacked seasoning or did not have the proper serving pieces accompanying it, then she could make the correction and save both the servant and the guest embarrassment. With complicated dishes, guests often watch the hostess to see just how she manages the service. In Army households, where one is always changing servants unless fortunate enough to carry a family retainer along to various posts, I think the hostess has herself served first at informal dinners for the same reason that the frontier woman did in the old days. She is not sure of her servants!

Several years ago when artichokes were truly a luxury and a great treat, a young officer dined at the home of his commanding officer. Later he laughingly admitted that he had never before seen or tasted the strange-looking object. Very surreptitiously, out of the corner of his eye, he watched his hostess and her manner of approach toward the formal-looking mound of green leaves. The only difficulty was that he did not watch her complete the process of extracting the succulent pulp, then return the leaf to the plate. Instead, he popped the fat juicy leaf into his mouth and started chewing! The more he chewed, the more convinced he was that he was eating a rubber plant, and the more disagreeable and tasteless the spiny leaf became; so he ended by having to swallow the stringy pulp, and from that day to this he declares he has never cared for artichokes . . . not even the hearts!

The one detail that distinguishes a formal dinner from an informal dinner is the question of carving and serving at the table by either host or hostess. If the host carves at the table, it is customary to place the required number of hot plates in front of him, and the maid or waiter carries each plate to the guest, removing the place plate as she serves the meat course. This service is naturally slow, but if a second maid passes the vegetables to each guest served, the food will not grow cold. Another informal custom is for the host to carve at table and serve the dressing and gravy, then for the guests to pass the plate along to the hostess, who serves the vegetables. During this procedure the maid may- pass the rolls, celery and olives. For the salad and dessert courses, if one maid is doing the serving, naturally the service will be slow; but it will not matter, as these foods are served cold. Coffee is generally served in the living room at an informal dinner.

The serving of café brûlot is a charming custom of the old ante-bellum days, and I know of several Army hostesses who, equipped with the necessary accouterments, add a very distinctive touch to their dinner parties by serving this delicious beverage.

Menu Suggestions for the Formal Dinner

Clear soup	Cream soup
Fish Hollandaise	Broiled chicken
Filet mignon	Potato balls
String beans	Peas
Carrots glacé—rolls	Tomato aspic
Aspic salad	Hot rolls
Ice-cream mold	Ice cream, cake
Coffee	Coffee

Liqueurs

The serving of wines at dinner is a chapter by itself, and is of little interest to the younger Army personnel. There are two reasons for this: First, the average junior officer cannot afford this extravagance, and *definitely* it is not expected of him; second, young people are better off without acquiring the "dining with wine" luxury. Youth has enough charm, spontaneity and high spirits without the added urge of alcoholic beverages.

However, to complete the chapter, a brief outline of proper wines to serve at dinner is included:

Sherry is always served from a decanter and at room temperature. It may be served before dinner as an appetizer or as the first wine at dinner. There are special sherry glasses on the market.

White wines: Sauterne, served very cold, accompanies a fish course or an entree. It is the accepted wine served at a women's luncheon. Champagne may be served before dinner, either plain or in a cocktail, or during dinner. It should be served in very thin glasses, and frappéed by putting it into a silver cooler. Since a good quality is quite expensive, it is usually served only at formal dinners, weddings and extra-special occasions.

Claret is served with a meat course.

Burgundy is suitable for a game dinner, and is especially good with duck. It is served at room temperature.

It is proper for the host to be served first, so that he may be sure the wine is good.

Port, cognac and liqueurs, including benedictine, chartreuse, kümmel, crème de menthe, are served after dinner.

Entertaining by Junior Officers and Their Wives

The suggested menus given in this chapter may seem elaborate to the bride, but bear in mind that nothing elaborate or formal is expected of you. A wiener roast, a steak fry, the simplest of picnics or home dinners is greatly enjoyed by older officers and their wives. Further, note that liquor is not expected or necessary, and don't forget that every colonel was a second lieutenant once, and he and his wife understand your problems in entertaining.

HOUSE GUESTS

Every young married couple looks forward to the arrival of their first house guests. They are proud of their own home, even if it is a Quonset, and they want to be hospitable. First of all there is the thrill of anticipation, and getting ready for the guest.

Here are a few tips that may help you in your preparation: If you are fortunate enough to have a guest room, then you and Ted should run a service test on just how comfortable it is by spending one night in it, at least a week before the scheduled arrival of your visitor. If it is a G.I. situation as to beds, there isn't much you can do about it except to hope that your guest likes a hard, solid tamped-down mattress. It is nice if you have soft and inviting beds; provide two pillows for each, one hard and one soft.

On the bedside table, place a small vase of flowers and a tiny silent clock, along with two new and interesting books. Provide a good lamp for reading in bed, one with a high-powered bulb, and a light extra blanket folded at the foot of the bed.

Supply a comfortable lounging chair, or if it is to be a short visit be generous and part with your chaise over the week end. The desk should be equipped with stationery, post cards, several types of stamps, ink and pen. Be sure there is a wastebasket beside the desk.

In the clothes closet, which is entirely cleared, should be plenty of dress hangers, and if you have matched ribbon hangers and closet accessories it will be an attractive touch. An ironing board and a small traveling iron are convenient additions to a guest room cupboard. Line the dresser drawers with book paper in unusual designs, plain white shelf paper or gaily flowered wallpaper. This will give a fiesta gaiety, and it will be fun to open them.

On the dressing table will be fresh powder puffs, hairpins, a pincushion with various kinds of pins, and two needles threaded one with black silk and one with white cotton, just as hotels used to provide.

Luggage racks (wedding presents, we hope) are a great convenience, and in the bathroom all laid out for the guest are plenty of luxurious fleecy towels, bath oil, soap and powder.

A screen is a great convenience in a guest room for those who like to sleep late and are disturbed by sunlight; however, it is easier to place in the drawer of the night table a fresh black sleep shade for the eyes wrapped in cellophane. Eleanor Beard makes some very elaborate and beautiful ones in pastel satin.

For one guest, it is often easy to serve breakfast on a tray taken to the guest room. Your visitor feels flattered, pampered and luxurious; and in the meantime, while she is reading the morning paper and taking a second nap, it gives you a chance to set your house in order and do any chores that are easier to do alone.

The tray is no trouble at all compared to serving breakfast in the dining room, and trays, in their little compass, can be charming. Nothing makes them look more attractive than a flower in a tiny vase, or two varicolored hibiscus—one yellow, one pink or bright scarlet—the kind that grows wild in Hawaii, Florida and California. Even a geranium blossom with two green leaves is most effective. Use your best china, and perhaps, from a wedding check, you may have bought a pretty pastel wicker tray, the stationary kind, with pockets at either end for newspapers and mail. The folding wobbly type can prove disastrous. Dainty breakfast sets come in china and glassware. One trick I learned from a maid I had in Alabama is this: In carrying a tray, look straight ahead where you are walking, forget the tray, and it will remain steady enough for you to arrive with it at its destination, intact.

In this age few hostesses, whether in the Army or not, appreciate surprise guests. There may be exceptions, when your hostess will be so glad to see you (or she may be such a casual person) that she will enjoy having you appear unannounced. In that case, be prepared to take potluck and like it. An Army wife prefers a few hours' notice, at least. Week ends on a post are filled with social affairs ranging from seated dinners and dances to small informal gatherings. It is disconcerting to a hostess to have to plan outside entertainment for unexpected house guests the night she and her husband are invited to the colonel's to an official dinner. The servants are probably off for the evening, and it is foolish for a guest to expect to be asked to a seated dinner that has been planned for some time.

Hostesses at West Point are overworked on this score. Someone's daughter back in Missouri is going to a finishing school in the East, and the mother writes a very enthusiastic letter, saying how "Betty is just dying to see West Point"; and the closing paragraph is so insistent that there is nothing to do but put the finishing touch to Betty's education by giving her a whirl with the cadets, the first free week end. Let us hope that Betty's mother has better sense than to suggest that Betty just go up some week end, uninvited! This sort of thing is what gives Army wives "hostess pains."

As for "Army visitors," that is something else! Service people are accustomed to calls from friends passing through on cross-country jaunts, and these are home folks. If the hosts are invited out, then the guests will know someone else whom they will phone. Or they may be tired and prefer to raid the icebox and go to bed.

On a post, Army people take their social duties toward visiting civilians with a certain amount of formality even though they may be close relatives. They feel that they must include them in everything and entertain them to the best of their ability. This is a hospitable weakness of Army people that is too often imposed on.

If You Are the House Guest

To a young girl: Suppose you have received an enthusiastic invitation to come for a two-weeks' visit to an Army post. Very well, then! You are all set. Arrive as nearly as possible at the time you have given your hostess. Your delayed arrival may upset her plans but early arrivals are even less appreciated. Leave when you are expected to, regardless of the good time you are having.

Don't expect your social whirl to start the moment you get off the train, or feel hurt if your hostess has not been able to provide a new date or some special form of entertainment for each evening. Conditions and circumstances govern these things. At some posts there is a dearth of eligible bachelors. If that is the case, then hide your disappointment and try to appreciate and enjoy the hospitality and good times that are offered. You can always trump up some excuse to cut your visit short, you know!

If your hostess has no maid, then lend a hand when you can. Look the situation over and conform to her wishes. She may prefer to serve you breakfast on a tray, and to have you sleep or stay in your room until she has completed her household duties.

Don't bring in a flock of bachelors after the dance, cook bacon and eggs and make a general mess of the kitchen—unless you are invited to by your hostess. In this case, make the bachelors help you clean up and restore things to order.

Don't expect your hosts to take you to the theater, expensive restaurants and night clubs. They may have very little cash, and are perhaps stretching their budget no end just having you for a visit.

Be particularly thoughtful and gracious to the friends of your hostess who are kind enough to entertain you. In addition to a prompt thank-you note when you return home, it is a nice gesture to send a tiny gift, such as a handkerchief, if you can afford it. A thank-you present of some sort, or a gift when you arrive, is a thoughtful gesture to your hosts. A box of candy or flowers, if your hostess entertains for you, will be acceptable. Children love presents, and the most inexpensive gifts will please them and put you off on the right foot with the juniors.

If you are doubtful about what clothes to take, write beforehand and ask your hostess. She will give you some idea of the parties and entertainments, if any have been planned. Servants should be tipped in proportion to the service they have given you; five dollars would be a suitable tip for you to give a general maid after a two weeks' visit; eight or ten dollars if you are affluent.

To Parents: Army people are usually delighted to have their parents and close relatives visit them, but often the older people aren't so happy over the prospect. The social aspect of Army life is unfamiliar to them, unless they have belonged to the Service or have had prior contacts with Service personnel.

Service people make a special point of being hospitable and courteous to one another's visiting families. On many posts there are groups of mothers who get together and call themselves "The Girls." These old ladies have a fine time over their knitting and at the bridge table, and delight in comparing notes with one another and boasting of their grandbabies.

For the short-time guest, special teas and dinners are planned. An older woman should include one long dress in her wardrobe for evening parties, and an older man should bring dinner clothes. However, a dark business suit is permissible for evening parties. Many older people who have retired from social life have no need for formal evening dress at home, and it would be foolish to invest in a wardrobe of this sort.

If you happen to be a pacifist and dislike everything military—except your son—it might be wise to reserve your opinion. An outburst will only embarrass him. Feel free to ask questions about anything, and if you really want to know about *Post Regulations*, ask for a copy to read.

Don't make suggestions to your daughter-in-law about the management of her house or the children. She may have an Army system of her own—in regard to both—that is absolutely foreign to you. Certain Army regulations will account for her methods of marketing, and of handling the children and the servants. Just be your own natural sweet self, enjoy your family and the entertainment provided, and you will have a happy visit.

To other Visitors: Don't expect fancy accommodations when visiting an Army family. Most guest rooms are equipped with G.I. beds and hard, hard mattresses, accompanied by a pillow that is the all-time low in downy comfort. The guest room will probably turn out to be the attic, and if the quarters are small and there are children, you may expect to share a room with one or more of them. Depending upon the season, you may freeze or swelter, and you will wonder why you ever left a comfortable home equipped with an automatic heating system and air conditioning. Well, this is Army life, and you are perfectly free to return to your comfortable home at any time! Feminine guests have been known to put up with all sorts of inconveniences, and to overstay their welcome, all because of a heart interest.

If you are an energetic male visitor, don't offer to mow the lawn, trim the hedge, or play handyman to government property that may need repairing. You will only embarrass your host. The Quartermaster Department attends to these items and is responsible for the upkeep of government property. Don't offer to repair a leaking faucet or make changes in the electrical, plumbing or heating system. These little items will all be taken care of in time; so save your strength and energy and expend it on your own property when you return home. There are definite orders against making any changes or repairs on government property.

While visiting an officer, refrain from fraternizing with enlisted personnel or civilian employees. It just isn't done!

RANK

During World War II most civilians became familiar with military rank and insignia and a portly colonel with silver eagles on his shoulders was easily distinguished from a slim-waisted young corporal with two chevrons on his sleeve. The military invaded the homes, and the families watched eagerly for promotions of their loved ones and soon learned the proper titles and the distinguishing insignia. So perhaps the following information will be superfluous.

Socially, officers are addressed by their proper titles. For instance: "Good evening, General." . . . "How do you do, Colonel?" . . . "How are you, Major?" . . . "It is so nice to see you again, Captain Smith." . . . "Thank you, Mr. Miles." (Lieutenants were always called Mister, socially, according to old Army standards. Today they may be addressed socially by their official title. No distinction is made between a lieutenant colonel and a colonel; both are called Colonel. The same is true of generals.)

Medical officers in the Army, of the grade of captain and above, are addressed by their title and rank; below the grade of captain they are addressed as "Doctor."

Off the reservation, at civilian parties, ranking officers are not sticklers for military etiquette in seating at small dinners; however, if the party is in any way of an official nature, the guests should be seated according to rank. If puzzled as to rank, call the post adjutant. He will be glad to advise you. Army people enjoy being invited to civilian parties and are always quite flattered when courtesies of this sort are extended.

CALLING

Except in Washington, D.C., it is generally customary
for civilians to make the first call on Army people. The
mayor and his wife, the prominent citizens of a small community, usually call upon the commanding officer and his
family, and perhaps they include several of the other ranking officers; however, many other Army wives appreciate
calls from civilians, too. Each group has something to offer,
and many fine friendships come about because of neighborly
calling.

Evening calling hours and Sunday afternoon are the hours
Army people observe, but they are always glad to conform
to the customs of the community in which they are residing.
If ladies call alone, then afternoon calls between three-thirty
and five-thirty are proper.

Chapter VII

ARMY JUNIORS—TEEN-AGERS TOO!

Here's to the man who wins the cup,[*]
May he be kind and true,
And may he bring "our godson" up,
To don the Army Blue.

—*"Army Blue"*

T HE Army is a wonderful place to bring up children. The nomadic life, with the constant changing of schools and adjustments to varied types of environment at home and abroad, seems to advance rather than to retard the average "Army brat." Children develop a cosmopolitan and gregarious outlook which tends to make them self-reliant the rest of their lives.

In the West Point cadets' slang an "Army child" is described as a cadet whose father is in the Regular Army. Further note, from the West Point *Howitzer*, that "one can always tell these Army children. They ride well, know all the Army answers . . . and outside of being high ranking and wanting Blue Uniforms, they are pretty regular kids."

Today an Army wife is assured of the best in prenatal care by competent medical officers complete hospitalization and excellent medical follow-up and postpartum care of the baby and herself. There is no need for the 'planned parent-

---

[*] The members of the graduating class at West Point contribute their silver napkin rings, out of which a silver loving cup is made. This is presented to the "class baby," or the first son born to a member of the class.

hood' that young couples in civilian life, owing to economic
conditions, sometimes feel necessary. Army juniors early
in their young lives learn to sleep in a dresser drawer, and
like it as well as a downy cradle. It matters little to them
whether their father is a second lieutenant or a major, and
if their parents are equally wise they will have their children
in the early years of their married life.

A childless marriage is always incomplete, no matter how
compatible the couple may be. The woman who goes through
life without a child is robbed of one of life's greatest joys,
and I am strongly in favor of adoption in cases where it is
impossible for a couple to have children. One seldom sees
a man or woman so adamant that he or she cannot learn to
love almost any small child who comes into their home as a
permanent guest. In this postwar era, Europe is teeming with
homeless children; surely there could be no finer work in
the world than for a childless Army family with good security
to adopt one of these underprivileged children.

One point, with young couples planning their families at
some future date—for instance "when Jack is drawing a
captain's pay"—is that sometimes "Man proposes, but God
disposes." The couple may lose the wonderful chance of
fulfillment with which heaven endowed them. I shall remember always the advice of an older Army wife when I was in
the hospital at Fort Sill worrying, needlessly of course, but
just the same worrying as many women do before a first baby
arrives, over how I would ever be able to take care of it.
Very comfortingly she patted my hand and said, "Don't
worry your head, my dear, babies always come with the
directions pinned on."

Just so, you will manage on a second lieutenant's pay even
if you are blessed with twins! It has happened, you know,
and God always provides . . . even to the directions.

JUNIOR IS EXPECTED

Of course you will have the reasonable assurance of your doctor even before you tell your husband and your friends that you are pregnant. Perish the thought of the trite and outworn picture of your husband finding you knitting the proverbial little pink sweater or baby blue bootees, or, what is even worse, the Hollywood version of your fainting dead away, then having the Army medico announce the news!

Be original, think up something pretty special and plan to tell your husband in your own way the wonderful news that will not only linger in his memory but make you infinitely more precious to him. It should be a moment neither of you will ever forget, and one of the most important milestones in your married life.

Your husband will be thrilled and inordinately proud. The waiting period should be filled with plans for the new baby, which you will find pleasure in sharing together. Don't forget it is his child too, and some day when you may not feel too comfortable and your sense of humor is dwindling by all means invest in a copy of *Ladies in Waiting* by Rory Gallagher.

"Bearing a child is a perfectly normal function, and you have nothing to fear but FEAR," says Veronica Dengel, in *Hold Your Man* (Coward-McCann). Pay attention only to your doctor, and discard all superstitions, strange ideas and advice from well-meaning relatives and friends.

You are performing the most important and the most magnificent job of your life, the one for which you were designed. Be grateful that God chose you to be the channel through which to express His love in the perfect baby that you will bring forth. In the last analysis, God is only lending you and your husband the little life which it is your privilege to care for, to tend and to train during this short span we call a lifetime. A child brings a man and woman into a closer understanding, because each has an unselfish interest in its development and welfare; together they work and plan to make of that child a fine man or woman.

THE CHRISTENING

In the Army, a "blessed event" is announced at once from the hospital and the happy news is published in the post daily bulletin. Then telegrams are sent to relatives and intimate friends. The parents may wish to send out engraved announcements, which consist of a calling card, either the mother's or one that reads:

Captain and Mrs. James Theodore Worthing

and at the top of this card a smaller one which reads:

James Theodore Worthing, Jr.
May first

Printed forms of announcements with dainty rosebuds entwining an infant are taboo; only the engraved form given is used. Invitations to the christening are informal, and may be extended verbally or telephoned, since only intimate friends are invited. If the baby's father belongs to a special regiment, battalion or group, it is customary to invite all of the officers and their wives to the christening.

Godparents are chosen only from among one's intimate friends, and, should they live at a distance, proxies may take their places during the ceremony. The idea of godparents is that, if the child should be left alone in the world, the godparents will become its protectors. In Europe, godparents assume great responsibility, but somehow godparents in this country take their obligations more lightly and consider their duty accomplished if they give the infant a silver porringer or a substantial check.

In the Catholic Church, the christening takes place usually before the babe is two weeks old and is always performed in church, if possible. The average christening in the Protestant churches takes place between the ages of two and six months and may be performed at home or in the church.

Arrangements should be made with the post chaplain if he is to perform the ceremony, and he will probably suggest Sunday afternoon as an appropriate time. If the ceremony is held at the chapel, the nurse will take charge of the infant until time to hand it over to the godmother, who holds it during the baptism. It is very necessary that the godmother pronounce the baby's name distinctly, otherwise the child may carry a name through life not intended for it. As soon as the ceremony is over, the godmother hands the baby back to the nurse, who carries it immediately to the waiting car, and she and the baby return home.

The baby is dressed all in white in its best dress. Exquisitely dainty christening robes are sometimes handed down in families, a lovely custom. Even the blanket or carriage robe in which the baby is wrapped should be all white.

It is far easier and prettier to have the christening at home. The baby can be brought downstairs by the nurse at the last moment, which is safer because he is not likely to catch cold. The quarters can be decorated in spring blossoms, and pale pink roses and baby's-breath may be used as a centerpiece on the tea table. I shall describe a christening that took place in Panama several years ago. Dates and names have been changed:

John Morrison Paine 3d, born April 21, 1947, at Colon Hospital, Panama, to Captain and Mrs. John Morrison Paine, was christened at an impressive ceremony at Fort Davis, Gatun, C. Z., on June 20, 1947, in the presence of General and Mrs. Harold Thomas Brinton and the Commanding Officer, officers and ladies of the post.

Garbed in the robe in which its grandfather, the first John Morrison Paine, was christened sixty years ago, and lying beneath the colors of the regiment, the infant was baptized by Chaplain Charles Barrington, with water taken from the Panama Canal. Chaplain F. H. Andreas read the gospel. Mrs. John M. Brown held the baby, and with Mrs. Paine stood proxy for the godmothers, Mrs. William F. Forgy and Mrs. Harrison Barnes. Captain Brown and Captain Steel stood proxy for the godfathers, Mr. Thomas C. Crain and Mr. Thomas C. Crain Jr. of Richmond, Va.

At the conclusion of the ceremony, Col. Matson, with drawn saber held above the infant, fixed its regimental status in the following language: "And now, as Colonel of the 14th Infantry, under an established custom of long standing, and in accordance with the wish of all in the regiment, I do declare John Morrison Paine 3d a son of the 14th Infantry, and I call upon all here present to drink his health, his happiness, and to the hope that he will follow in the footsteps of his father to a distinguished military career." Orange punch was served and all drank to the health of the new son of the 14th Infantry.

The font is always a bowl of silver or crystal and is placed on a small, high table. The table should be covered with a dainty cloth, and everything placed in readiness for the chaplain.

After the ceremony, which is usually held about four or five o'clock, the party resembles an afternoon tea. The mother or the nurse may hold the baby for everyone to admire, but the poor little dear should not be tired out and forced to become restless.

Punch or eggnog is served, and sometimes a loving cup is

passed, from which everyone drinks as he makes a wish for the baby.

If gifts are brought, they may include a silver knife, fork and spoon or silver mug. If wearing apparel is presented, pink is supposed to be for a girl and blue for a boy or vice versa. What difference does it make, anyway, to the modern mother?

A baby can be christened without any festivity at all, of course, but most mothers like to have this opportunity of showing off their "little bundle from heaven" in a pretty way.

EDUCATIONAL INSURANCE

This is a type of insurance that is very popular in the Army, because all parents are interested in a college education for their children. It is also a means of saving, and a convenient way to meet the real educational needs of your children. The premiums on the policies are small if taken out when the child is very young. The plan is that the policy matures when Junior is sixteen, seventeen or eighteen, and there will be ready money to send him either to a good preparatory school, if he plans to enter the Military or the Naval Academy; or to a standard college.

Several years ago there was a young bachelor in the insurance business in an Army town who made a specialty of selling educational policies. He became so proficient in predicting "blessed events" that he gained a wide reputation for his ability to single out prospective customers.

NURSERY SCHOOLS

So little is really known of the wonders accomplished by a good nursery school! However, a poor school with inefficient and inexperienced teachers is worse than no school at all. Up-to-date nursery schools generally have high tuition fees, but if you can possibly afford it, by all means send your child to one.   .

Nursery schools had their origin in England during World War I. They were schools where mothers left their children for the day or portions of the day while they worked. Trained teachers were in attendance, and the results of the training proved so satisfactory that the nursery schools continued after the war and later spread to this country.

Two years of age is not too young for a child to enter nursery school.

The young child is learning constantly, and what he learns may be desirable or undesirable. Character is taking shape, habits are being formed, skills and attitudes are being developed for better or for worse.

The expertly staffed nursery school is designed to enrich the child's day with a wealth of experiences conducive to desirable learnings, and to reduce to a minimum situations fraught with undesirable responses. The shy child learns to greet his companions cheerily. The helpless child acquires self-reliance in donning his play clothes, buttoning, lacing, tying knots and bows and independently selecting his activity materials. The disorderly child discovers the pleasure of opening his locker door on a neat array of personal possessions, play shoes on shoe trees, playsuit on a hanger, art brushes clean, toys and toilet articles in their places, all arranged there by himself the previous day. The retiring child learns to stand up for his rights. The child whose table talk consists of silly noises and giggles is given through educational excursions an incentive to converse and worth-while experiences to discuss. The destructive, the inconsiderate, the selfish, the rude, the crybaby, the unsanitary learn the error of their ways through the anguish of unpopularity with their playmates. The child is exposed to the finest in art, music and literature, thereby developing a taste for richer, fuller living and learning to create beauty himself.

The average busy mother is distracted by many other duties, whereas the child-training specialist becomes mother-teacher, a playfellow, a companion, a storyteller, and to her is accorded this privilege of shaping the lives of the most wonderful of all creatures, little children.

To sum up, a few of the advantages and results of training in a modern nursery school are as follows:

1. Companionship with children near the same age.
2. The development of proper attitudes . . . so very important.
3. The forming of good health habits . . . eating, sleeping, toilet.
4. The sharing of possessions with other children . . . toys, books.
5. Learning to follow directions, take orders, obedience.
6. Learning to live and to play in a group.

After all, one of the most important lessons in life is getting along with our fellow man, and at the age of two years is the best time to start developing the proper attitudes and traits of character.

KINDERGARTENS OR PRESCHOOLS

The word "kindergarten" has become obsolete with the advancement of knowledge about child psychology, health, behavior and mentality. However, to the average parent "kindergarten" still denotes preschool training.

Personally, I feel that if the little child has two years in a good nursery school, where the important habit and attitude foundations of his future are laid, he can skip a year before starting to preschool or kindergarten. At the age of three or four, his mind is open to knowledge. He becomes acquainted with the world through his senses, and he is impelled by them to activity that further educates him. This is the question-asking stage, the imitation period and the imagination stage. His information is increased by the great number of questions he asks. He is a veritable interrogation point, his curiosity knows no bounds; it is a fascinating age. To the mother and to the kindergarten teacher comes the rare privilege of unfolding to this plastic little mind the truths the child is so eager to know. The unhappy concepts some children receive are the result of bungling language used by adults and ugly attitudes toward each other and toward life. Health and happiness should be the first aims in all work with the preschool child.

The average child with the two-year nursery school background seems to get the most out of kindergarten between the ages of five and six. Some parents prefer to wait until their child is three or four years old to send him to nursery school. As you wish, but beware of those important early attitudes and habits, which have their beginnings in the cradle.

In a modern, up-to-date kindergarten the curriculum is well rounded and planned, with special emphasis and freedom given to the child's initiative. Units of work that are related to the child's experience are the basis of his learning. For instance, a kindergarten on a flying field would undoubtedly have a comprehensive unit on aviation. The children would actually build a miniature plane of orange crates with wings of canvas or beaver board; they would visit the hangar line, inspect different types of planes, and the interest would be dynamic, since all children of today are air-minded.

No doubt you have surmised by this time that the kindergarten is my hobby. For fifteen years I have organized and conducted nursery schools and kindergartens at various posts throughout the Army. Like "Mr. Chips," I feel that I have a large family of Army children in whose progress and activities I am always interested. A little child always remembers his first teacher, and vice versa.

Too much cannot be said about poor kindergartens! Beware of them. Unfortunately, kindergartens which really amount to nothing have a way of cropping up in communities. For monetary reasons, and because she "just loves little children," some worthy matron or young girl may open up a private school of this sort, where the little child will learn "to speak pretty pieces as of yore, to sing a few songs, and maybe even to print his name," but what about the habits, the proper attitudes, the trained guidance that your child needs and should have? Schools of this sort are for shiftless, mentally and physically lazy mothers, whose one idea in life is to get rid of their children so that they may pursue their own selfish pleasures uninterrupted. Fortunately, there are few of this type, as the normal mother wishes to give her child the best educational advantages that she can afford.

GETTING JOHNNY INTO THE FIRST GRADE

The bane of my teaching experience was the attitude of young Army parents who insisted on pushing their children. They were all mortally afraid that, because of their moving around in the Army, or because of the poor educational facilities on foreign service, Junior would get behind in his studies and be considered backward. It was their parental pride asserting itself, really!

For some reason Johnny must start school at six. Why? Simply because that was the way his parents did in their youth! What earthly difference does it make whether the child postpones reading and writing until he is six and a half, seven or older! The most important phase of Johnny's life is the first seven years, in which he learns and develops the numberless qualities and habits which go to build his character. For instance, a child who has had his own way, or very nearly his own way, from infancy to the age of seven is so far on the wrong road that he is an almost hopeless problem for his first-grade teacher. Johnny has to unlearn the impossible things that are already fixed habits in order to become a member of the group. At this time, in the transition period, he develops complexes and attitudes that may give him a very distorted and unhappy outlook on life. The child who has attended a good nursery school, where he has learned the rudiments of the formality of the schoolroom, definitely has the edge on poor little Johnny, as you can readily see.

Elementary grade teachers quickly note the difference between children who have had preschool training and those who have not. Educators agree that a delay of six months or so in entering school makes little difference to a child. Many states will not accept a child for the first grade until after his sixth birthday, and in some localities the age requirement is seven. Cheers for the latter!

Medical surveys have shown that the muscles of a little child's eyes are not properly developed for reading until the age of six and a half. His muscles for writing are naturally stronger at seven. We don't need to worry about Johnny; he will learn to read and write, and he will be a stronger student later if he is not pushed. Let us not mistake Johnny's desire to read for brilliance. Reading is perhaps the most important subject in the elementary curriculum, because the child has to read to learn arithmetic, language, history, geography and all other subjects. Poor reading ability often causes failure in the above-mentioned subjects. And why is Johnny a poor reader? Because he started to learn to read before he was physically or mentally developed for this most important learning process.

Mothers often worry because, though Johnny is the same age as Susan, his little next-door neighbor, she is two grades ahead of him. Susan entered the first grade one month before her fifth birthday. Poor little dear! Very well! Watch Susan's progress later. There is nothing sadder than the extra-precocious child who does not fit into the proper age group—who is a misfit with her contemporaries. Far sadder than being a grade behind. A normal child will soon correct the latter situation—his pride will urge him to work harder, and later he may overtake Susan.

Many of the larger posts maintain their own first-class elementary schools through the fifth or sixth grade. It is wise, upon receiving orders to a new station, to write either to the education and recreation officer or to the post adjutant, and make inquiries in regard to the school situation. Explain your particular needs, mention the sex and age of your child and the grade in which you are interested. If you favor private schools, ask for data on this subject. The instruction in public schools is generally good, unless the classes are overcrowded, and Army children seem to need the association with children from all classes of society to round out their education in the give-and-take of life.

In this melting pot in America, which sometimes is near the boiling point, our children, first in the home, then in the school and church, should be taught tolerance and patriotism. Both teachers and parents have a great responsibility in promoting tolerance, in teaching children by their own attitude and example that patriotism is being friendly, hospitable and tolerant to all others who attend our schools and churches and share our way of life. It must be a good way of life, and brought down to the understanding of the youngest child, so that he sees it must be without teasing or quarreling, or making fun of people and calling names, if our country is to be the home of the brave and the land of the free. Children in and from enemy countries must receive tolerance; suggest to the child how he would feel if America had been conquered and occupied by the enemy. Instill into him the idea that name calling, slights or discrimination against those of another race, creed or color is no part of democracy. There should be no slighting remarks about foreigners in the home; children are intuitive and imitative, and they not only repeat but sometimes unintentionally misconstrue the true meaning of a statement.

Owing to the itinerant life an Army child is forced to lead, he misses the feeling of security, in an established permanent home in an established town or community, to which the civilian child is accustomed. In other words, he has no "roots" because his father is constantly being ordered from one station to another. He may have to stop school in the middle of the term to go sailing off to Manila or Tokyo. Of course, it is fun and a fine way to learn geography and history firsthand on the move, but it does not give him a very good feeling of permanency and security.

In the life of children, security is an important factor—in their growth and development. Children have great faith; they feel that their parents are eternal, fixed and unchanging and it is a big responsibility to live up to being a real parent. That sense of safety that they feel in their fathers and mothers is an overwhelming force for their good, and they usually follow in their own lives the example of love and companionship set for them by their parents.

Children thrive on affection and love, and need the security of knowing that they have the love of their parents regardless of what happens. True, a child may have to be disciplined or may be temporarily out of favor, but loved he *must* be always.

Yet he must never be so smothered by love that he is not free to meet his own contemporaries on his own level and in a way the society of his world will tolerate. One sees this in an only child who is more at home in the society of Army adults than with his contemporaries. Fortunately, the cases are rare.

Preparatory Schools

For Army officers' sons who wish to enter the United States Military Academy and follow in the footsteps of their fathers, there are many good preparatory schools.

Millard's, in Washington, D.C., is a popular school for boys who wish special instruction before taking the competitive examinations for West Point. There are many other good ones, known as "tin schools," but the list is too long to publish here.

Severn's at Annapolis is favored by boys who wish to take the competitive examinations for entrance to the Naval Academy, and there are numerous others of good scholastic standing.

A booklet, *Information Relative to the Appointment and Admission of Cadets,* may be secured from the adjutant general of the Army, Washington, D.C., by those who have their hearts set on entering West Point. There are a few basic requirements: The prospective candidate must be at least seventeen years of age, and not more than twenty-two, at the time of admission. He must not be married, nor can he have been married. He must be at least 5 feet 4 inches tall, and not more than 6 feet 6 inches. There is a long list of physical requirements. The standard method of admission is by appointment from a senator or representative in Congress, or by presidential appointment. An appointment is not a guarantee of admission, it is merely a chance to take a very stiff competitive examination.

CHILDREN ON AN ARMY POST

Each post has its own regulations in regard to the deportment of children, but here are a few general rules:

1. Don't fail to acquaint your child with local rules in regard to the swimming pool, golf course, tennis courts, and the officers' club.
2. Don't permit your child to impose upon neighbors . . . discourage frequent calls, picking flowers, teasing pets, playing in driveways and garages.
3. Don't allow vandalism, such as defacing, destroying or injuring government property or private property.
4. Don't permit a child to deface quarters, write on walls, break windows, dig holes in lawns.
5. Don't allow impertinence to soldiers or guards, or tolerate misconduct on school bus.
6. Teach obedience to traffic rules in regard to crossing busy intersections on posts, proper riding of bicycles, scooters, etc.
7. Children or their pets should not be allowed near hangar lines, picket lines, gun sheds or firing ranges.
8. Try to control unnecessary noise, crying or any play that is annoying to neighbors.
9. Teach respect, consideration and courtesy for older people of the garrison.
10. Require strict obedience to rules when government horses are exercised or ridden at will.

TEEN-AGERS

Army teen-agers seem to have come into their own, most of the groups being sponsored by the Women's Clubs on the respective posts. In addition to Brownies and Cubs, junior and senior Boy and Girl Scout groups, special social activities are planned by the teen-agers themselves. Dances, hay rides, wiener roasts, candy pulls, golf and tennis tournaments, picnics are some of the activities enjoyed on various Army posts.

One very active group which is doing fine work is the Barksdale Teen-Age Club. The "Bar-Teens" (Barksdale Field, Louisiana), as they call themselves, have drawn up their own constitution, and members range in age from thirteen to nineteen years inclusive. The motto of this club is: "Better youth makes a better world."

One of the private dining rooms of the Officers' Club is reserved for the teen-agers' dancing classes where instruction in both ballroom and folk dancing is given. In the fall the club attends local football games as a body; in the summer they take a Red Cross lifesaving course. Very definite projects are planned, and the teen-agers are responsible for cleaning their clubhouse before and after their parties. They have their own lending library.

Each club has a counselor, and usually a younger officer and his wife are asked to be sponsors. Dues usually average about fifty cents a month. Such a club gives the adolescents of the post a definite interest in their Army community and makes them feel as if they belong. Their energies are directed and juvenile delinquency is at a minimum. As some very wise counselor said, "The parents are the real delinquents usually, not the children." Throughout the Army, teen-age clubs are being given the interest and co-operation they need to function successfully.

Chapter VIII

CHANGE OF STATION

When we all get down to Shanghai,
Those champagne corks will bang high
Oh! we'll all go down to Shanghai in the fall!
                                        —Army song

O UT OF a clear sky, some morning, you may pick up the
paper and see your husband's orders to service in
Hawaii, or to National Guard duty in Boston, or
perhaps to an O.R.C. unit in Iowa. You gasp, and by that
time your telephone is ringing frantically. Your best friends
are calling either to congratulate you or to sympathize with
you. One point to be made here is this: They are your husband's orders, not "our orders," and if the War Department
has given him no advance notice, simply remember that
you come in the category of a "camp follower," and if you
choose not to accompany your husband to his new station,
that is your own affair.

Before you have been married very long, you will run
across some Army wife who will say, "When we received
orders," and what is even more unpardonable, "When we
get to be majors." She should say, "When my husband receives his orders," or "When Jack is a major." Beware of
that "we." The worst *faux pas* of all, however, is to say,
"When we were in command." Certainly, by the time her
husband has reached the seniority which entitles him to a
command, every Army wife including you, dear, should be

cognizant of the fact that it is a man's army . . . still! Wives have no rank.

It usually takes a few hours, or sometimes a few days, to adjust oneself to orders that involve a change of station. It is unwise to make snap judgments about places where you have never been and to start complaining. Regardless of what you think about the proposed move, don't commit yourself to such an extent that you will be embarrassed at a later date, when perhaps you may have changed your mind. Should the orders come in by radio, or appear in the paper, do not start moving proceedings until your husband actually receives his orders. The quartermaster is not authorized to start packing until the orders have been received by the officer.

Annually, officers submit a "Statement of Preference" report. This applies particularly to the foreign service roster. The officer lists three choices, such as Hawaii, first; Panama, second; and Puerto Rico, third. It is the policy of the War Department in peacetime to consider these preferences, though the needs of the Service must govern selections, always.

PACKING

When orders have been received, the quartermaster arranges for the packing of an officer's household goods. If the distance is not too great, and the transfer company's bid is lower than rail rates, your move may be made by van. This is decidedly the easiest way to move, from the housewife's point of view, though it has several disadvantages.

The transfer company employs experienced packers, and they prefer to do all the packing themselves, even to taking down the pictures and curtains. It facilitates matters for them if, for instance, all of the bric-a-brac is assembled on a table, all of the glassware placed in another space, and your best china segregated. No doubt you will prefer to pack your clothes and personal belongings yourself, and perhaps your flat silver and valuables.

The disadvantages in moving by van are: If at your new station you are to be on commutation, you will have to either place your household goods in storage, which is expensive, or rent a house sight unseen. Often van companies reload household goods to smaller vans in order to comply with certain state traffic laws, and this leads to loss and breakage. Vans have been known to burn up, and to suffer complete loss by accident; but of course, you will be wise enough to protect yourself with insurance. These hazards are simply a possibility in Army moves.

When the move is to be made by rail, the quartermaster lists and tags each article of furniture at the quarters, then removes it to the warehouse for packing and crating. Glassware, dishes and silver are packed at the quarters in barrels, supposedly by experienced packers but sometimes by raw recruits who may be pressed into service in emergencies. Just try not to watch when one of your best Minton cups is tossed across the room from one packer to another. It is easier on the nerves to busy oneself with personal packing in another part of the house.

On permanent change of station the baggage allowance of officers is as follows:

Second lieutenant....................	6,000	pounds
First lieutenant......................	7,500	"
Captain.............................	8,500	"
Lieutenant colonel or major...........	9,500	"
Colonel	11,000	"
Brigadier general....................	12,000	"
Major general.......................	14,500	"

The weights given are gross after packing and crating. You may think you are well within your baggage allowance, but watch out on a southern station if the quartermaster crates your goods in green lumber! Professional books and papers are transported at government expense in addition to the above allowances.

Needless to say, a grand piano and massive pieces of furniture soon run over the baggage allotment, and the expense of additional weight, extra packing and crating must be met by the individual officer.

CLEARING THE POST

Before leaving a post on change of station, an officer must receive various clearances. Having occupied government quarters, it comes within the housewife's realm to see that they are left clean and in good condition. Often a certain sum, usually five dollars, is deposited with the quartermaster, and a corps of cleaning persons cleans the woodwork, windows and floors. However, the housewife herself should inspect the refrigerator, baths and closets to see that they are left in perfect condition. No foodstuffs should be left about, as the quarters may be unoccupied for some time, and food will attract animals and vermin. The final inspection before clearance will be made by the property officer or one of his assistants, when he comes to check the property. Every article of property must be accounted for, from furniture to door mats and electric bulbs.

Army hospitality on such occasions is famous. *Despedidas, alohas* or farewell parties, depending upon the individual's popularity, begin as soon as an officer receives orders. Between the parties and the strain of packing, most Army families leave their station in a sort of daze due to exhaustion. However, it is all fun, and part of Army life.

Farewell calls are made by an Army family when departing from a station. It is customary to call upon members of the regiment, also upon the post commander and friends. The initials "p.p.c." (*pour prendre congé*) are often written in the lower left-hand corner of the visiting card to indicate the nature of the call. "Thank-you notes should be promptly written in return for parties and courtesies extended at your departure.

TRANSPORTATION OF DEPENDENTS

The government pays the cost of transporting legal dependents of officers upon permanent change of station. If the officer prefers to transport his dependents at his own expense (by automobile) he may claim payment after the journey is completed. This payment is determined by the cost of railway fare on the shortest usually traveled route. Or an officer may procure railway transportation prior to making the trip by requesting transportation in kind.

THE NEW STATION

If possible, it is advisable to report at a new station before noon. In any event, one should try to avoid arriving after four in the afternoon. After a few years in the Service you will almost always find friends or at least acquaintances to make you welcome at any new station.

Unless you have arranged to stay with intimate friends, it is best to go into quarters and eat at the mess or stay at a hotel until your household goods arrive. Should there be no hotel facilities near by, and should your quarters not be available at once, you may be forced to accept the proffered hospitality. Accept it graciously, but move into your own quarters at the first opportunity.

Some posts have a guesthouse or an officers' club where the family may stay. At every post there will be new adjustments to make, new friends to meet, and life will be interesting and different. Comparisons are usually odious, and it is well not to start out comparing quarters, social customs and the personnel at your last station with those of your new station. An old saying in the Army asserts that "To some, the last station is always the best, the present one very undesirable, and the future one the most desirable of all." This is just another way of saying, "Distant fields are always greener."

Regardless of how undesirable a station may appear at first, if you look closely enough you will discover some advantages. If you are so fortunate as to draw a good station, enjoy it while you may!

PREPARATION FOR FOREIGN SERVICE

Overseas commanders have established a priority system whereby lists are submitted to the War Department periodically for the movement of dependents. Relative priority is based on longest cumulative overseas service since December 7, 1941.

These lists contain the names of all families of military personnel or War Department civilian employees that the commanding officers can accommodate for the given period. Only personnel who volunteer and are scheduled to remain overseas for a period of one year from the date their families arrive in the theater are eligible for the priority list.

Important to note: Dependents will not be returned to the United States until the individual upon whom they are dependent is returned except in cases of extreme emergency. In other words, homesickness or the fact that you want to have Junior born in the good old U.S.A. will not be an excuse for return passage.

Under no circumstances must you write to the War

Department or to your husband's commanding officer requesting transportation overseas. You might as well save your postage, because the Army doesn't handle the transportation of dependents in this fashion.

The first step is for your husband to make application through his commanding officer or through the proper channels at his station for his dependents to join him. At present, only immediate families are eligible for government transportation: wife, minor children, dependent mother or totally dependent father.

By this time, your Army experience will have taught you not to be surprised if your husband should be ordered to return to the States for the convenience of the government despite his indicated willingness to remain overseas one or two years. Just take it in your stride . . . This is the Army, Mrs. Jones!

NOTIFICATION

Once your orders have been authorized, you will receive a sheaf of travel orders from the War Department. Guard these with care, for you will be required to show or surrender each of the dozen or so copies of the original order. Too, it will make you feel very important and military. This is part of the tape that is known as RED; however, one of the thin carbon sheets will prove an open-sesame when you arrive at your port of embarkation. Should you need more copies for any purpose, you can always have additional true copies reproduced at any Army installation.

By telegram or letter from the Service command nearest your home, you will be advised as to the date, port of embarkation and place where you should report for your transportation overseas. It is well to report promptly on the date specified as checking-in dates and sailing dates are closely correlated. Should illness or some unavoidable circumstance make it impossible for you to report, there are two things to do: (1) Notify the headquarters of the Service command from which you have received instructions, because they are responsible for you. (2) If there is any change in your address, immediately notify the Service command headquarters.

Don't "jump the gun" and report to the embarkation port until you have been notified. In many cases, this waiting will require unlimited patience. I know several wives who have been waiting well over half a year with baggage packed and passport in hand. Most of the delays hinge upon the availability of quarters.

You will be furnished rail transportation between your home and the port of embarkation unless you prefer to drive your own automobile or travel by air. Reimbursement for same will be in accordance with existing law and regulation. Air transportation is authorized only upon express approval of the War Department. Again may I remind you to carry your travel orders with you on the entire journey. Various officials will require copies to authenticate many acts of assistance which dependents will desire.

MEDICAL CERTIFICATES

All persons traveling on Army transports must present medical certificates showing that they have been vaccinated against smallpox, typhoid and paratyphoid (required within twelve months prior to departure). Typhus immunization is also required, and certain additional inoculations, particularly diphtheria and whooping cough, are advisable for children.

Infants under one year of age are exempt from smallpox vaccination. The vaccination requirements can be waived only by the War Department. On South American travel, a medical certificate is required on trachoma, and if one is traveling in the Orient, cholera shots are advised.

The present regulations are that no female dependents who are beyond the sixth month of pregnancy will be transported to any oversea command. No infant dependents are allowed to travel on transports until the age of three months and then only to Hawaii, Panama, the Antilles or Bermuda. Army offspring must be at least six months old before being transported to other oversea commands.

PASSPORTS

The State Department has ruled that all dependents going to Japan and other occupied countries must have passports in their physical possession prior to leaving the United States.

The War Department has arranged that a special section in the State Department will process dependents' passports, and that there should be no undue delay. Ordinarily it takes four weeks or longer to obtain a passport.

Some day when you are looking your best drop in at a photographer's, preferably one who specializes in passport pictures. Snapshots or full-length pictures are not acceptable. Passport pictures are required to be 2½" x 2½" in size or 3" x 3" and should be printed on a light background and signed by the applicant, whose signature must correspond to that on the application form. Two copies of all photos are required.

A birth certificate or a certificate of naturalization is necessary when making application. Children under twelve years of age may be included in the parent's passport. A separate passport is preferable for members of the family twelve years old or over.

PORTS OF EMBARKATION

The principal ports of embarkation for Army transports are Seattle and San Francisco on the west coast and New York on the east coast.

If you are fortunate enough to secure a hotel reservation, you should first check in at the hotel with your hand luggage. An added precaution is to ask for a confirmation in writing or by wire from the hotel management. Do not try to make your hotel reservation through Fort Hamilton.

Fort Hamilton, Brooklyn, is a beautiful Army post located at 95th Street and Marine Avenue. It may be reached by subway from Manhattan (one hour) by taking a BMT *express* train marked "Sea Beach . . . Coney Island," to 59th Street station, Brooklyn, then the Fourth Avenue *local* train from that station to the last stop, which is just a few blocks from Fort Hamilton. Taxi service is expensive.

If you wish to stay at the hostess house either telegraph or telephone Fort Hamilton, Attention: Operations Division, immediately following receipt of the call to the port. Housing facilities are available for a minimum charge of one dollar per day and twenty-five cents per meal. Of course, you may be quartered in a barracks, which will remind you of dormitory days at boarding school, though they do have a special barracks for wives with small children. One large bathroom is shared—first come, first bathe idea! Laundry facilities are available, and you will be glad if you can get to your own electric iron easily.

If the mess at the Officers' Club is not crowded, sometimes arrangements can be made to take your meals there. Hostess houses are not those of prewar days, but they are equipped to handle large numbers and everyone seems to manage.

The telephone number at Fort Hamilton is Shore Road 5-7900.

PACIFIC PORTS OF EMBARKATION

S.F.P.E. (San Francisco port of embarkation) has its headquarters at Fort Mason, San Francisco. It serves dependents embarking for Hawaii, the Marianas, the Ryukyus, the Philippines, Peiping, Nanking-Shanghai, Australia, Kwajalein and, by transshipment, Burma and India.

Dependents embarking for Japan-Korea and Alaska are served by the Seattle port, with Army hostess house accommodations at Fort Lawton.

To do its job the San Francisco port of embarkation has three major installations: Fort Mason, Oakland Army Base and Camp Stoneman in Contra Costa County, forty-four miles from San Francisco.

Fort Mason is the port headquarters, and the fountainhead and nerve center of the port. Oakland Army Base is primarily a base for shipside storage and movement of overseas supplies. It also serves as a disposition center for troops returning from overseas. Here is located the A.P.O. or Army Post Office, through which moves all outbound mail addressed to A.P.O.'s "in care of Postmaster, S.F." Camp Stoneman is mainly a personnel center, designed for both outward and inbound flow of vast numbers of men.

The postwar program calls for using Army-owned transports for movement of troops and military dependents. To accomplish its mission the port has been assigned a fleet of modernized transports, most of them of the Admiral (P-2) and General (C-4) classes. In addition, three hospital ships and a number of freighters will operate in the Pacific under port control.

Fort Mason is rich in historic lore, with almost a century

of Army service. Aside from the dock area, Fort Mason at first glance resembles a typical Army post. There is a chapel, a handsome structure in Spanish style, plus a P.X., a theater, a dispensary, a hostess house, motor pool, utility shops and warehouses.

There is an old saying in the Army that "Time, tide and Army transports wait for no man, and for darn few women." In these days, don't take a chance on any transport waiting for you.

The hostess house is adequately equipped for a short stay. It is Building 257. In the lounge a good library is available. For the children there is a playground in the rear, also a supervised nursery where on the days of individual processing mothers may leave their children in charge of a responsible attendant.

Located in Building 220 are good laundry and dry-cleaning facilities with one-day special service and four-day regular service. In the P.X., Building 251, you will find a beauty shop; there is also a barber shop.

The easiest transportation to downtown San Francisco is to take the "H" car which connects with the "F" carline at Bay Street. The "F" car is the quickest means of public transportation to downtown shopping and the business district. Transportation to the pier on sailing day will be arranged for you.

Seattle will be your embarkation port if you are going to Alaska, Japan or Korea. Fort Lawton is a military reservation in the city of Seattle and is located on a strip of land bordering on Puget Sound. It is about five miles northwest of Seattle's city center.

The hostess house at Fort Lawton has a limited number of rooms. They are adequately but very simply furnished. Each room contains two Army cots, a dresser and a clothes rack.

Boys over seven years of age are quartered in the boys'
dormitory. The charge at the hostess house is seventy-five
cents per person for each day. Meals are obtainable at the
hostess house cafeteria with prices well below those of
commercial dining places. A special nursery and playground
is provided for the children. The hostess house is equipped
with laundry facilities and is near the city bus line.

Overflow dependents are sent to the New Richmond Hotel
in the downtown area of Seattle. Rooms vary from two to
six dollars a day and in addition to a coffee shop in the hotel
there are good restaurants near by. A regular processing
section of the Seattle port of embarkation is installed at the
New Richmond Hotel.

BAGGAGE

A seasoned traveler always travels light, yet you may
wonder how that is possible when you expect to pass through
several climates and the War Department recommends
taking a six months' supply of personal needs and enough
clothing for two years.

It will simplify matters and save repacking at the port of
embarkation if you will separate your baggage and pack with
the idea of cabin baggage and hold baggage. Your cabin
baggage should consist of two pieces of standard luggage
such as suitcases or handbags containing all the articles
necessary during the sea voyage. This is quite an order, but
by careful planning and expert packing, it can be done.

Hold baggage may consist of wardrobe trunks, foot lockers
and boxes but it is limited to 350 pounds for each adult and
175 pounds for each child between the ages of five and twelve
years. In the old days, the hold or trunk room was open
daily except when in port, but don't expect now to even

glimpse the hold or your precious personal baggage until you debark.

It is further recommended that you pack linens, silver and tableware in your personal baggage. Both summer and winter coats must be included since you may be going on trips or you might have to return to the United States on short notice. Coats and warm clothing were at a premium when women and children were evacuated from Hawaii to the mainland in December of 1941.

A good plan is to inventory and to keep lists as you pack; alphabetize or catalogue what is in each trunk and it will prove a great help when you are madly searching for Junior's ear muffs or your electric heating pad. One of the most convenient articles with which you can equip yourself before sailing is an ordinary cretonne shoe bag or, even better, an apron of this sort. There may not even be wall space to which you can thumbtack a shoe bag on a crowded transport, but you can always tie it around your waist. It is ideal for holding toilet articles or manicure equipment and, may serve as a sewing kit. It deserves special mention because it is a standard article of equipment to the experienced Army woman when traveling. Soldiers used the khaki apron idea during the war.

Another indispensable item is a small bag, the knitting bag type. Carried on the arm it will not be considered luggage, even if you are flying. It proves its worth in helping you keep small articles, such as sunglasses, hair nets, scarves, playing cards, bridge scores, books and writing material, with you when on deck.

Standard Army transports are not back in service as yet, but they will be in time. Conditions differ depending upon the type of ship in which you are traveling and the number of passengers aboard. Remember, two pieces of luggage means just that, and no extra hatboxes or last-minute packages. There is no better spot to apply the Golden Rule than on a transport. One inconsiderate, selfish person can ruin the trip for all of those with whom she shares a crowded stateroom or compartment.

HOUSEHOLD GOODS AND AUTOMOBILES

This is a frightening topic but don't worry, the Army will take care of it all for you except getting your car to the embarkation port. Privately owned cars are not shipped to the port at government expense; however, overseas shipment of one privately owned automobile may be made at no expense to the individual if space is available on an Army transport. This is fair enough, and you will probably enjoy the motor trip to the east or west coast.

Should you desire your car to be crated when you reach the port then that expense is borne by you; also, overseas shipment of automobiles may be made by commercial means at the owner's expense.

MAIL AND MONEY

Mail sent to dependents at embarkation ports should be addressed in care of military personnel, using the same A.P.O. number. For instance:

> Mrs. James Worthing
> c/o Captain James T. Worthing
> Hq. & Serv. Group, GHQ AFPAC
> APO 500, c/o Postmaster
> San Francisco, Cal.

In order to avoid confusion, it is advised that all correspondents, including magazine publishers, be advised of the proper address before the departure of dependents from the United States. In time it is hoped that the address system will become less detailed.

It is suggested that banking accounts be maintained in the United States. You should plan to have sufficient funds to pay subsistence charges aboard transports and to cover all expenses while awaiting departure of the transport.

First-class subsistence charges aboard vessels are as follows: Adults and children of eight years or over are charged $1.50 per day, children three years of age and under eight, 75 cents a day, children under three years of age, 25 cents a day. The charges are payable in advance. (The Transport Service takes no chances!)

Not more than fifty dollars in United States currency may be taken to overseas destination by each person. Do not purchase foreign currencies before your departure, since the Army Finance Department has adequate facilities for converting United States currency and dollar instruments into foreign currencies. Of course, additional funds may be carried in the form of Travelers' Checks or United States Postal Money Orders.

Upon your arrival in Japan the United States Army Finance Office will convert all American currencies into Japanese yen. The present rate of exchange is fifteen yen to one American dollar. Only yen currency may be used in Japan by any person. Money orders may be sent to the United States by postal money order.

THE TRANSPORT VOYAGE

General Information

If it is your first trip on an Army transport, you will find a few unique differences from travel on large ocean liners. At present Army transport travel is strictly G.I. Many ships are gradually being reconverted from troopships. Perhaps upon your return voyage things will have shaken down and you can again travel in individual staterooms. Most likely your husband will accompany you. It takes time to get back to normal. Most wives are so thrilled at the opportunity of rejoining their husbands, and so grateful to the War Department for sending them, that they forget creature discomforts and inconveniences.

On the whole, from the "Gallup poll" I have taken, it seems the transports crossing the Pacific have better accommodations than those taking families across the Atlantic. Maybe it is because the Pacific voyage takes many more days, not as many families are going to Japan, Guam, the Philippines owing to lack of housing facilities. Some dependents have traveled as far as Hawaii on the luxury liners of the Matson Line, which have been converted from troopships.

The chief complaint seems to be the crowded conditions, four to fifty persons in a room. There are all types of gripes! One young thing complained because the only fresh fruit available was a bowl of oranges and apples in the center of the table. Another claimed there was no change of linen during the entire trip. A third would have preferred a clean scrubbed table to the food-spotted sheets that served as table linen. (This might be called a legitimate gripe in my estimation!) Some complimented the food; others lost weight. One young bride thought children should be segregated in cabins according to age, as she shared a cabin with eleven little sunbeams and their mothers.

Regardless of the annoyances, make up your mind to this: A transport trip can be a very interesting and a most pleasant experience. The unpleasant features will fade into insignificance twelve hours after you reach your destination.

The first day out is always a trial, and everyone is in everyone else's hair. But after the first few days the passengers relax, settle down and get together. Transport travel differs from the cruises of yesterday, when fine friendships were made at sea only to be casually forgotten as soon as the passengers landed or returned to their homes. Transport friendships have a happy faculty of lasting. There is something very personal and intimate about sitting at table three times a day with a group of people for fifty-six days from New York to Manila. You get to know their idiosyncrasies and their food preferences. Sometimes, perhaps, you get to know too much about them, but you can always skip a meal, you know!

And speaking of meals on Army transports: Unless you are a victim of *mal de mer*, or the old tub gets to romping too much in the waves, you won't want to miss many meals, because the food is exceptionally good. I like one old salt's description of passengers on Army transports. It isn't very refined, but it is expressive. He said that most passengers on his boat suffered from "T.B." One shy young bride looked startled at this remark until he explained "transport belly" as a very common ailment.

Don't expect eleven o'clock bouillon, afternoon tea or cocktails; and should you be more than fifteen minutes late at a meal, you automatically skip that meal. This regulation is strictly enforced. No meals are served in staterooms without special orders from the ship's surgeon. Few passengers are late for meals, and upon the first sound of the large brass chimes carried through the companionways by a Filipino steward there is a mad rush for the dining salon.

On regular transports, deck chairs are provided. You will be wise, however, to take along a folding canvas chair for your own personal use. Standing on deck or running a race to secure a chair can become very tiresome on a long ocean voyage. As one colonel's wife wrote back, "Many's the night

I sat on the steel deck watching the movie between San Francisco and Manila!" Chairs for personal use which cannot be folded are not allowed to be brought aboard. There are no reservations for deck chairs—first come, first served, at any time. A steamer blanket may prove an added comfort, if you care to bother with it. Few passengers carry blankets, as a good warm topcoat usually suffices. If you should want to bring a few small, comfortable pillows, which at the end of the voyage you can throw overboard or give away, it is a smart idea.

Animals are not allowed on passenger transports. No matter how much you love your Scotty or beautiful Persian cat, there is truly no way to smuggle your pet aboard. Don't try it, because it might be a question as to which one of you would be thrown overboard first. Animals are carried on government freight transports, or they may be shipped commercially at the owner's expense.

Laundry facilities are available on the larger transports, and the prices are reasonable. Clothes can be pressed, but there is no dry-cleaning service. Each deck is provided with an electric iron and a small electric washer for the use of passengers. The laundries are the most popular rooms on the boat, and they are a great help to young mothers in solving their infant wear problems. I mean dresses, play suits and rompers! No one bothers with diapers any more, with any of a number of popular utility, sanitary disposable pants for Junior.

Transports no longer furnish soap, so include your favorite supply of facial and bath soap, plus three or four boxes of soap flakes for laundry purposes. Pack your electric iron, with several extra cords, in your stateroom luggage.

As soon as you go aboard, go to your stateroom and get things more or less oriented before the sailing hour. There may be bon voyage gifts awaiting you in your stateroom—perhaps a corsage, and you would like to wear it. But if you have any choice in the matter, tactfully veto flowers. Other than a corsage or so, flowers are a definite nuisance on an Army transport. There will be a perfect dearth of containers, and the cabin stewards are too busy to attend to flowers. To preserve them at all, it is necessary to keep them in an overcrowded refrigerator along with lobsters, crabs and foods that do not help flowers in the slightest.

If you have an idea of placing your gift flowers on your dining table, you will be disappointed. No flowers except the moth-eaten and time-worn little artificial bouquets that have sailed the seven seas time and again are allowed in the dining salon. Your gorgeous flowers will go to waste, and after the third day out, you will wish you could convert them into good detective stories or into some food delicacy of which you are fond.

Despite the attractive offerings in the gift shops, delicatessens and smart stores that make a study of beautiful and useful bon voyage gifts, flowers are still considered the easiest "out" when it comes to "saying IT with something." The only efficient custom that I know of to date—whereby you express your appreciation to the donor by wearing your flower gifts and then show your love for Hawaii and your desire to return—is the custom of throwing the pretty flower leis into the sea as the boat steams by Diamond Head.

Boxes of assorted nuts, crackers, cookies, candy, books, magazines and small baskets of tempting fruit are always appreciated. Baskets containing surprises for children, with written instructions about when they are to be opened, have a great appeal for the small fry. In Honolulu, candy leis made of lollipops or even of miniature toys find great favor with youngsters. Games, puzzles and interesting juvenile stories appeal to mothers as well as to the children, and are wonderful helps for the famous transport quiet hour.

Transport Quiet Hours

Red Cross personnel and a limited number of stewardesses are available usually as playroom supervisors. Cribs, play pens and playrooms are provided for the use of children.

High chairs to attach to mess benches, baby berths, baby toilet seats, baby bathtubs, waterproofed sheeting and limited laundry facilities are available for Army juniors.

Infants under two years of age should be fed in state-rooms. There are stewardesses in attendance; not many, but arrangements can be made for help in regard to children. Also, parents are expected to supervise the eating habits and behavior of their children in the dining salon. Excessive crying and messy food habits are annoying to other passengers. Some transports have a children's dining room, where children are fed before the regular dining hours.

And, speaking of children, did you know that the sacred hours between two and four in the afternoon are reserved? Grownups wish to take their siestas, and they feel that all good children should do likewise. In fact, transport regulations require parents to observe these rules, and if the children do not rest, then they must be kept quiet in the stateroom or taken up on the sun deck, where they will disturb no one.

Fire and Boat Drill

There are very strict regulations in regard to fire and boat drill on Army transports. The commanding officer of troops is required to have a fire and boat drill within twenty-four hours after the ship leaves port. Parents should familiarize themselves with the rules, then instruct their children regarding the adjustment of a life preserver, how to tie it properly and how to report to the designated boat station. The paramount importance of this is obvious. At unexpected intervals throughout the voyage the alarm will sound, and somehow it always seems to occur during the siesta hour! But even though you don't like it, you'd better do something about it before you try for those extra winks.

Ship's Library

Avoid carrying along a lot of books; even people with the best of intentions never read quite as much as they plan to on shipboard. Cheaply bound editions that can be donated to the ship's library or a stack of your favorite magazines that can be read and discarded prove good choices.

The ship's library, on the larger boats, will contain a surprisingly good selection of the most recent fiction, a vast array of murder mysteries and detective stories, and a rather interesting collection of travel books. It also will have many of the popular magazines.

Army transports do not furnish stationery.

Entertainment on Transports

Transports are equipped with motion pictures these days. Sometimes there are fairly recent and good films; at other times you can easily imagine you are living the good old days of the silent movie again. Two performances are given in the evenings.

Amateur boxing bouts staged by enlisted men are enjoyed by all, and often there is sufficient talent among the troops to stage a very successful Amateur Night.

Puppet shows are given and are greatly enjoyed by the children. Birthdays call for individual children's parties, which are conducted in the social hall.

One dance a week is arranged, with an additional costume ball or some type of entertainment, planned by a special committee.

Bridge, backgammon, ping-pong, shuffleboard, bingo and chess have their own devotees.

Religious services are held every Sunday, and on weekdays if so specified on the ship's bulletin.

If there is a gymnasium, it will be open at designated hours to ladies, officers and children.

A beauty parlor and barber shop are also in operation.

Clothes on a Transport

The ever important subject to a woman is: What clothes shall I take? About all the information the government pamphlets give on this subject is: Passengers should take light clothing for use during part of the voyage. Now . . . I ask you!

Let's start out with those intimate underthings! Nylon underwear is a tip to "trippers." Choose a standard make that will not stretch, shrink or run and does not require ironing. Lovely slips, gowns, panties and brassières are on the market today in delicate shades, and in a superior grade of silk jersey. Take along enough lingerie to last for two years, and include enough in your hand luggage so that you will have to do a minimum of laundry while on board ship. The laundry rooms will be crowded, and bending over tub 13 as one crosses the international date line or nears the equator, with the temperature constantly rising and dispositions falling correspondingly short, is not an enviable experience.

Common sense, careful planning and a limited clothes budget govern the average Army woman's wardrobe. Frequent moves make it impossible for her to keep up with fast-changing fashions, but she will be safe if she has a few really good vertebrae in the backbone of her wardrobe. I refer to at least one good tailored suit and a topcoat, or the fur coat that was in her trousseau.

Travel light, but also travel sensibly! You will not need all you think you will. Take few things, wear them often, and relax. On land or sea, at home or abroad, the women who have the most clothes are seldom the best dressed. This is sweet music to the Army wife's ears; she knows that *system* saves just as much money in the wardrobe as it does in her household. Hold on to the really good things in your wardrobe. While, upon first thought, a tweed suit or a fur jacket may seem a foolish thing for one bound for the tropics, don't forget that it is usually cold the first few days out at sea, and San Francisco weather is quite chilly in July and August. Make arrangements to store your furs with some reputable firm at the last port possible. A fur jacket is very welcome in Hawaii during kona weather, despite travel advertisements. A light topcoat is a necessity.

Your clothes probably will be entirely new to your fellow passengers, and a carefully planned old wardrobe can be enlivened with a few smart accessories. Never let the corners of your mouth turn down because you can't afford to invest in a complete new "cruise wardrobe." Simply pinch yourself, and consider how lucky you are to be having this marvelous experience.

Wave good-by in a smart black suit or dress with white accessories, in a print, or in navy blue, the travel classic. If it is blizzarding, go up the gangplank in a tweed suit, covered with a matching topcoat or a fur sports coat, if you own one. An accompanying tweed beret or hat to match the suit is always smart.

Should you be crossing the Atlantic with orders for Germany or Austria, regardless of the time of year, part of the ocean voyage will require woolens. Equip yourself with a

warm topcoat, sweaters, a wool dress or so and slacks. While
most women realize that nature did not design their figures
for slacks, all seem agreed that they are sensible for boat
travel. One wife suggests traveling in one's oldest clothes,
as some of the transports are not too clean. Good dry-cleaning in most foreign countries at present is an unknown
quantity.

From New York to Panama is a six-day trip on an Army
transport, provided there is no intervening port of call. For
the first three days out, you will wear tweeds, or a woolen
dress and topcoat, unless the trip is made in midsummer.
Even then, woolens are often very comfortable on the
Atlantic. On the fourth day at sea, you will begin to get out
that suggested "light clothing." Be sure to include some
jersey or fish-net turbans to wear on deck, and don't forget
your sunglasses.

By the time you reach Panama, it will be hot, hot, hot!
Somehow it always seems hotter at a pier in the tropics than
at any other place. This is due to all the rush and excitement,
no doubt, and to the fact that the boat is not in motion.

A cool mesh dress will be right to wear off the boat, and
white is always good. Perhaps you will be happier if you
have a new, inexpensive dress for this occasion. Dress it up
with smart accessories, a large hat, white purse, shoes and
gloves, or with colored accessories if you prefer. The gloves
you will merely carry, and they should be washable and of
cotton. This outfit will also see you off in Honolulu and in
Manila. Remember, the arrival of a transport is a gala
occasion, and Army women already on the post are always
anxious to see the newest styles from the States.

A smart plaid seersucker evening dress, or a white piqué,
or—you know best what suits you. Anyway, when you go to
the dance at the Union Club on the Pacific side, have one

washable dance frock that will make all of your Army sisters rush to their favorite native dressmaker the next morning.

Aside from your regular wardrobe and the two new washables mentioned, if you can possibly swing it add one of those soft, soft pastel topcoats in your favorite shade.

If you are sailing for the Pacific theater, with Manila, Guam or Okinawa as your destination, take lots of cotton evening dresses. In addition, buy up various washable materials so that you can make dresses or have them made as you need them. In case you do not use all you take with you, be assured you can dispose of it easily to other Army or Navy wives. Also, take the findings for these originals which you will create, as thread, needles, hooks and eyes, snaps and binding tape, also buttons and ribbon, have not found their way as yet to these far-eastern markets. The situation will improve in time, but don't forget, you belong to the postwar pioneering group. Forewarned is forearmed, and may save you some later headaches.

Bon voyage!

Chapter IX

DUTY AT HOME AND ABROAD

U.S., Panama, Puerto Rico, Jamaica, Trinidad, Alaska, Greenland, Newfoundland, Bermuda, Hawaii, China, the Philippines

O F COURSE, every Army wife has visions of the glamorous
life of foreign service. Who doesn't? But in peacetime
there is a good possibility that your husband's orders
may call for duty on this side of the ocean as instructor on
some university campus under one of the Reserve training
programs. This may seem disappointing at first. But remember, although you may think your pot of gold is in some
distant land—perhaps in the southern half of the Caribbean's
periphery—it is very possible that you will find it right here
in the good old U.S.A.

The National Guard

The Regular Army is only one component of the new Army.
Tripled in size and doubled in importance, the National
Guard will be an integral part of the Army of the United
States.

Now, more than ever, the National Guard will conform
to the American concept of minutemen. World Wars I and
II found the National Guard, through no fault of its own,
lacking strength and equipment and, for those reasons, in
need of additional training before it could take the field.
It is planned that the new National Guard will be maintained

at maximum strength, completely equipped and fully trained. Eventually, there will be twenty-seven divisions and many miscellaneous units, and many Regular Army officers will be detailed to National Guard duty as instructors and in administrative fields.

ORGANIZED RESERVE DUTY

Officers' Reserve Corps

The Organized Reserve consist of the Officers' Reserve Corps, the Enlisted Reserve Corps, and the Organized Reserve units. These reserves constitute one of the components of the Army of the United States, the other two being the Regular Army and the National Guard.

In peacetime, reserve officers are not ordered to active duty without their consent, but in times of national emergency the President may order reserve officers to active duty for indefinite periods without their consent.

Officers and enlisted men of the Regular Army are assigned by the War Department for duty with the units of the Organized Reserve.

The same suggestions given to wives whose husbands are on National Guard duty are applicable to Organized Reserve duty.

Every state has its own Organized Reserve units, depending upon the population and the number of reserve officers, and a proportionate number of Regular Army officers are detailed to these units as instructors during peacetime.

The problems of national security are greater than ever, and the role that the Organized Reserve Corps must play, under the leadership of the Officers' Reserve Corps, is one of major importance.

A certain percentage of officers of the Regular Army will be detailed as instructors and will be placed on D.O.L.

(Detached Officers' List). Many Army wives find it a bit
difficult to adjust themselves to college campus or to city life,
but in every way possible they should enter into the social
life of the community and refrain from talking about Army
life. Foolish chatter of this sort often leaves the impression
with civilians that all Army people think about is the social
side of life.

Life in a large city may offer many educational and cultural advantages to an officer and his family. Often officers
find it difficult to live within their pay where there are so
many demands and where they are forced to keep up with
civilians in a much higher salary bracket. When assigned
to small towns, on the other hand, they often find that they
can secure rent within their commutation and are able to
build up a comfortable savings account. For the Army wife,
local conditions will determine her social life. Civilians may
pay social calls, and again they may not. Should they be
courteous enough to call, always return the calls promptly,
within two weeks.

One suggestion: Be very careful about letting your name
be used in sponsoring benefits, especially those in which
the raising of money is the object. Your husband, however,
will know all the answers to this subject.

Also, it is well to avoid social publicity, that is, when
accounts of personal entertaining are involved. Having your
name appear on the guest lists of civilian parties is quite
permissible.

R.O.T.C. Duty

The Reserve Officers' Training Corps was approved by
an act of Congress June 3, 1916, and the system of military
education was established in schools and colleges as we have

it today. The R.O.T.C. has become an important part of our system of national defense.

The main object of the courses of instruction in the R.O.T.C. is to qualify students for positions of leadership in time of national emergency.

The War Department assigns officers of the Regular Army as instructors to various colleges with reference to the officer's particular qualifications. The normal tour of duty is four years. The senior line officer is the head of the Military Department, and is known as the professor of military science and tactics or the "P.M.S.&T." He has the same academic rank which the institution accords the heads of its other departments.

The officers in an R.O.T.C. unit, numbering from one to twenty or more, are considered members of the college faculty, entitled to all the rights and privileges of a faculty member, with responsibilities and obligations similar to those of other instructors. Officers are required to live at or near the institutions to which they are assigned. When on duty they are not allowed to take any courses that the institution may offer unless under exceptional circumstances and with special permission from the War Department; however, an officer's wife or family may study at the institution.

Army families with college-age children find R.O.T.C. duty very attractive, and the average Army wife finds splendid cultural advantages in the social life of the college.

Again, as an Army woman you must make an effort to fit into the community and take part in its civic and social life. Depending upon the size and the geographical location of the institution to which your husband is assigned, social life and social customs will vary. Feel your way around at first, say little and observe everything! Above all, don't say how much you miss the Army and post life. Try to adjust yourself to present conditions, and by the time four years have passed you will probably have made many lifelong friends and can truthfully say that you have enjoyed the detail. It is the old saying, "We get out of life proportionately what we put into it."

Army officers and their wives are sometimes asked to chaperon fraternity dances, picnics and various college activities. Part of your social duty is to participate in faculty and student parties, and if you do so graciously, it will add to your popularity. Don't forget that "unwritten efficiency report."

Faculty members are supposed to set the moral standards in colleges and universities, and social drinking is usually one of the taboos. Fortunately, the pendulum seems to have swung in the right direction in regard to drinking among the younger generation. However, don't be guilty of bringing censure on the Army personnel for excessive drinking or for indebtedness. Officers have been relieved from R.O.T.C. duty for these offenses.

FOREIGN SERVICE

Thou shalt love thy neighbor as thyself.

"Foreign service" is really a misnomer as applied to duty in United States territories, possessions and Lend-Lease air bases. But since it is the Army's way of expressing a tour of duty in Hawaii and Alaska, which are territories, and service in Panama and Puerto Rico, which are possessions, it is probably best to use it. The Department of State also designates any duty outside the continental United States as "foreign service."

In time it is to be hoped that the very word "foreign" may be deleted from our diplomatic and political language. To apply it to a friendly neighboring country might be classed as a provincialism on our part because today we are obliged to live with and among other nations.

After our so-called global war, we need global thinking. On our prewar maps we see the earth divided into two traditional hemispheres, the Eastern and the Western. In the future, geography will probably be taught from globes on which the seven seas separating the continents are all parts of a single encompassing body of water binding the whole world into a geographical unit. On a globe there is no east and west except in relation to an imaginary line set for the convenience of measuring time.

Never in the history of the United States Army have American troops been allocated on such a global basis. Wendell Willkie's idea of *One World* is daily being brought home to us more forcibly. We can no longer close the door on all things "foreign." Whether we like it or not, Des Moines, Iowa, and Moscow, Russia, are on the same aerial beam, and oceans, ports and armies are no real barrier.

During World War II small Army children spoke of their fathers serving on Saipan, Guadalcanal or at Casablanca, as if these bases were near by. And indeed, they are becoming nearer with each speed invention that is perfected.

Especial emphasis is being placed on military bases in the polar regions such as Greenland, Iceland, Newfoundland and Alaska. The flight of the B-29 "Dream Boat" over the arctic wastes proved how vulnerable we might be should another super-Pearl Harbor surprise attack occur. The shortest air distances, as the crow flies, in the Northern Hemisphere, are over the arctic regions. The airplane can come from anywhere and it gets everywhere.

Since World War II, foreign service has been extended to include duty in the occupied countries: Japan, Korea and various islands in the Pacific, Germany, Austria, Italy and the Middle East theater.

In the Western Hemisphere a group of islands in the West Indies has been leased from Great Britain as American Army air bases. These make up the Antilles Department under the Caribbean Defense Command. In addition, military ground and air missions are being set up in most of the Central and South American countries.

Army wives today may expect their husbands to be ordered outside of the continental limits of the United States, and if you have longed always to see other countries, the opportunity is yours, but with this wish go certain responsibilities! Orders may take you to Okinawa, Moscow, Caserta, Rio, Jamaica, Shanghai, Berlin, Vienna, Greenland or to Fairbanks, Alaska, plus a score of other places. If it's "greener fields" for which you are looking—and who isn't?—they say that somewhere over the rainbow troubles melt like lemon drops, and dreams really do come true.

By now, you should know if it's true what they say! If not, then keep on searching.

The Caribbean Defense Command

The principal mission of the Caribbean Defense Command is to defend the Panama Canal. This is of obvious importance to the United States. The Caribbean Defense Command has two major components: U.S. Army, Caribbean and the Caribbean Air Command. U.S. Army, Caribbean with headquarters at Quarry Heights, Canal Zone, has Army jurisdiction in the Canal, Puerto Rico, Virgin Islands and leased Army bases in the West Indies and British Guiana. The Caribbean Air Command with headquarters at Albrook Field, Balboa, Canal Zone, has a fighter wing, with airfields in the Panamanian area, and a composite wing, with headquarters at Borinquen Field, which has bases at Jamaica, Antigua, St. Lucia, Trinidad, British Guiana and Puerto Rico.

PANAMA: A BRIEF HISTORICAL SKETCH

Most Army women want to review their history a bit when their husbands are ordered to stations with an interesting historical background. Panama is rich in its historical setting, and libraries are filled with fascinating stories of early life in the Isthmus, stories of pirates and buccaneers, of the Spanish regime and of the Canal Zone since the American occupation.

Panama was first visited by white men in 1499. Three years later Columbus touched it on his fourth voyage, still seeking a passage to India. Then came the farsighted Balboa, who was the first to discover the Pacific.

Some day take time out to stand on the pile of old stones a few miles out from Panama City, where Balboa is supposed to have taken his stand when he surveyed the turquoise sea and said, "How pacific are your waters!" For poor Balboa himself it turned out to be far from peaceful. His career ended when the governor of Darien caused the explorer to be beheaded for treason.

The Isthmus next became the outfitting base for the exploitation of Peru. Pizarro carried the gold that he had taken from the Incas across Panama by means of horses and slaves. Silver was so plentiful that it is said the horses of the soldiers were shod with it.

Pirates and buccaneers entered the Caribbean and fought with the Spaniards. The depredations reached a climax when Henry Morgan marched his band of twelve hundred followers across the Isthmus, sacked the City of Panama and burned it to the ground. After this onslaught there was a period of inactivity until the California gold rush in '49.

About this time, three enterprising Americans secured a concession to build a railway across the Isthmus. What a feat to undertake! But from this brain child probably grew the Panama Canal of today. At the time, the Isthmus was nothing but a dense jungle and a swamp of the Chagres and Rio Grande rivers.

The attempts by the French government, under the leadership of the great engineer De Lesseps, to build a canal resulted in failure. In 1903 the United States negotiated a treaty with Colombia, and the work on the Panama Canal was begun again. About a dozen years later the Canal was opened.

The Canal Zone is a scant strip of terra firma approximately forty miles long and ten miles wide. It is under the jurisdiction of the Army commander of the department, and he has charge of all activities, both civil and military, during an emergency.

The Panama Canal—The "Big Ditch"

The Panama Canal is as vital as our jugular vein, and it is really a miracle of engineering. The word "canal" suggests a straight-line waterway to the average mind, but the Panama Canal is startlingly unlike a straight-line waterway. It is first a lake, then a river, then a lake again, as it winds its way through the jungle. The banks are bordered with giant ferns and luxurious palms, lazy alligators bask in the brilliant sunshine and launches piled high with green bananas putter back and forth.

Giant ocean liners are lifted from one level to another through the three steps of the Gatun Locks; then they pass through Culebra Cut and on to Pedro Miguel, where they are lowered again through a series of locks to sea level. On a transport it takes about eight hours to pass through the Canal, and it is always a hot and uncomfortable trip. But it is really an interesting day. Children are fascinated by the locks, and they should not miss this educational experience.

It is interesting to remember that the Panama Canal was build by the Army. Colonel George W. Goethals was the engineer in charge; he had to overcome the worst possible sanitary conditions before construction could be completed; on August 3, 1914, the first ship passed through the Canal.

Climate

There are two seasons—the dry season, extending from December through April, and the rainy season from May through November. And how it rains! It rains every day during the wet season, although there will often be sunny mornings. You will become accustomed to it, however, and outside of the trouble of keeping clothes in dry closets, and a few minor discomforts, it is not bad. Since Panama is in the Torrid Zone, and close to the equator, the climate is warm, and humid at times. Generally the nights are cool. Health conditions are good. The *stegomyia* yellow-fever mosquito, easily recognized by the black and white zebra stripes upon its body and legs, is practically unknown in the sanitated areas, and there is little danger for those who observe the health regulations. Children seem to thrive in Panama.

Quarters and Living Conditions

As usual, the housing situation is critical; therefore it is necessary for the head of the family to arrange for quarters before bringing his family to the Canal Zone.

The frame and concrete quarters are designed for the tropics. There are many different types, ranging from vine-covered bungalows on stilts to large rambling two-story frame and concrete structures. Several years ago all of the quarters were equipped with coal ranges, but now most of the officers' quarters have either electric or gas stoves and electric refrigerators. Some government furniture is provided.

Rents in the adjoining cities and towns are high.

The servant problem is ever present.

Schools

The Panama Canal operates a superior school system including a junior college. Elementary and high schools are located on both sides of the Isthmus and are readily accessible to all posts. The junior college is located in Balboa on the Pacific side.

Tuition and books are free through the high school. Tuition for junior college is fifty dollars per year and students are required to furnish their own books. The schools are fully accredited by the Middle States Association of Colleges and Secondary Schools.

The school year begins in September and ends in June. The Superintendent of Schools, Balboa Heights, Canal Zone, or the Superintendent of Documents, U.S. Government Printing Office, Washington 25, D.C., will furnish detailed information upon request.

Transportation and Private Cars

The distance across the Isthmus from Colón to Balboa is forty-seven miles, and the Panama Railroad is the principal means of transportation. All posts except Fort Sherman either are on the railroad or have easy access to it. Strange as it seems, there is no highway. The shuttle trains ply back and forth on schedule, and the one-way trip requires about one hour and forty minutes. There are three trains each way daily.

An automobile is a necessity at all posts except Fort Sherman. A driver's license and license plates are required by both the Canal Zone and the Republic of Panama. The costs are low. Closed cars are recommended because of the additional comfort during the rainy season, though an open car has more resale value. Taxis are not cheap in Panama. It is fun to ride in the old horse-drawn Spanish *carromatas* of yesteryear, and pretend in the romantic moonlight that you are a Spanish queen riding in state or at least a ravishingly beautiful señorita of the old days! But the springs are not too good, and horses have a tendency to forget what they are doing. Yes, a private car is a necessity.

Back to earth, now, and let's talk about

Clothes

Cottons, of course! Or any material that tubs easily and looks better after its bath. Packables, or noncrushable linens, washable silks and cottons will give the most satisfactory service. Velvets, sequin-trimmed dresses or fur-trimmed coats are not for the tropics. An ample supply of shoes of linen, canvas or gabardine should be included. Leather mildews badly, and suede is not cool. By looking over the advertisements in the current magazines or the New York *Times*, you will find that the New York shops will be glad to send you merchandise, and it will reach you by air mail within a week. Good native dressmakers are to be found, and with the lovely materials available in the Oriental shops, stunning evening dresses can be made. A good Chinese tailor can make your linen suits, spectator sports dresses, shorts and slacks, so the clothes problem is reduced to a song, and an inexpensive one at that, if you are a clever singer! If you crave that "States look," you may have to send back to New York for your clothes.

Marketing

The Q.M. operates two large commissaries, one at Fort Gulick for personnel stationed on the Atlantic side and one at the post of Corozal for those stationed on the Pacific side. The commissaries carry a good stock of staple groceries, a fair stock of meat, poultry and dairy products and some fresh fruits and vegetables. The prices are reasonable and in most cases slightly less than prices in the Panama Canal commissaries. There are no charge accounts!

The Panama Railroad operates a number of excellent commissaries which are similar to the so-called general stores. They carry quite a complete stock of staple groceries, fresh meats, poultry and dairy products, fruits and vegetables, some clothing, a very good stock of shoes, a considerable number of the more essential household items and gadgets, a limited stock of imported china, a fair stock of proprietary drugs, cosmetics and tobacco. Electrical household appliances are practically nonexistent at the present time. The prices are reasonable and, in general, below prevailing States prices. Fresh milk is obtained through these commissaries. Officers above the grade of captain may have authorized charge accounts, but those below the captain grade must pay cash.

There are post exchanges at every post, some of which have meat and vegetable departments along with a small stock of imported items.

Some fresh vegetables may be obtained from the Chinese gardens in the Canal Zone. The gardens are under the sanitary supervision of the Health Department. Native fruits are obtainable at native markets and roadside stands.

Medical Care in the Canal Zone

Each post has a dispensary with medical officers available for emergency cases and for handling minor ailments and injuries. The Medical Department operates a general hospital at Fort Clayton and a station hospital at Fort Gulick which are currently providing medical service for the dependents. In addition, these hospitals are operating obstetrical services.

The Panama Canal runs two hospitals which are available to military personnel and their dependents; they are equipped to render complete medical service. The Gorgas Hospital is located at Ancon on the Pacific side, and the Margarita Hospital, which is new, is located on the Atlantic side near Fort Gulick.

Recreation

Officers and their families enjoy various sports in Panama —golf, tennis, riding, hunting, fishing, sailing, swimming. Golf is played all year, in spite of the rain! The golf clubs available are: Gatun Golf Club, located about seven miles from Colón; Pedro Miguel Golf Club, located near Miraflores Locks; Panama Golf Club, four miles from Panama City; Fort Amador Golf Club. Membership dues and other fees are reasonable. The Strangers' Club on the Atlantic side, and the Miramar, Union and Century clubs on the Pacific side are popular with Service personnel.

Cities and Shopping

On the Atlantic side of the Isthmus is old Colón, backed against the new and modern city of Cristobal. These two cities are two different worlds, two different civilizations, and the only boundary that separates them is a white line painted on the asphalt pavement. That is all, yet it is not an imaginary line, like the international date line; it is a real boundary line between the Republic of Panama and the U.S.A. or the Canal Zone.

By day, Colón is noted for its bazaars and shops; then, when night descends, the tawdry night clubs turn on their blazing neon lights, soldiers and sailors in uniform fill the dance halls, and pretty hostesses of various colors settle down to social life as it is lived in the tropics. Army people indulge in seeing this type of night life, but for a steady form of recreation most of the social life is carried on within the circles of the Service personnel on the posts.

The Washington Hotel, in a setting of beautiful palms and hibiscus, with its good swimming pool, is a rendezvous for both Army and civilian parties. The Strangers' Club also is popular on the Atlantic side.

Balboa and Panama are located on the Pacific side. Panama City, with its ruins, is picturesque and has an Old World charm, while Balboa, being a modern city, corresponds to Cristobal. Panama City is spoken of as "the wickedest city" in the world. Could be! But the picture isn't so wicked as one drives by the main street lined with cafés, cabarets and night clubs.

The great national sport of Panama is the lottery, for which everybody buys a ticket. The money taken in by the lottery is used for hospitals and charitable institutions. It creates as much interest in southern climes as the Irish sweepstakes, and I actually knew an Army doctor who won $10,000 once, so you might take a chance!

Religion is important to Panamanians. Even the poorest town has its Catholic church, and the priest is an influential person. Each town and village, too, has its patron saint, for whom a celebration lasting several days takes place every year. Colorful ceremonies and an occasional bullfight mark these holidays.

The national dance of Panama is the *tamborita*. Panamanians, like all Latin Americans, place great value on personal courtesy. Courtesy definitely counts! It is an old Spanish custom for men to throw their arms around each other's shoulders upon meeting. Their native dish is *sancocho*, and consists of a thin soup poured over a mixture of boiled vegetables with beef or chicken. Nothing to write home about!

The word "Panama" means "an Abundance of Fish," and speaking of fishing, be sure to see the fishing fleet anchored below the old sea wall. Then, too, the tarpon fishing at Gatun Spillway is said to be superb.

For sight-seers there are the ruins at old Panama and the Golden Altar in the cathedral there. The shopping by day is good and will be better as soon as trade opens up and the Hindu merchants can restock their shelves. About the best buy you will find today is Panama hats. The best of these come from Monte Cristi, Ecuador. They were erroneously christened in the middle of the nineteenth century by the gold seekers en route to California who, buying the hats in Panama, assumed that they originated there. These hats are made from the fibers of the *toquilla* palm and are said to be woven under water. Get an old-timer to explain how they are woven in circles or rings, and the more rings in the crown of a hat, the more costly it will be.

Some Things to Take to Panama

Flat silver and serving silver
Any reed or wicker furniture you may have

Wrought-iron furniture

Visiting cards

Rain equipment—white or transparent raincoats and umbrellas; or those of light shades are attractive

Inexpensive crystal ware

Some Things Not to Take to Panama

Overstuffed furniture

Antiques

Expensive lamps, curtains or hangings

Fine rugs

Pictures

Valuable books

Furs

Pianos and string instruments

Veneered furniture

Expensive mirrors

Woolen clothing or blankets

Leather equipment

How Service in the Antilles Is Different

Fort Brooke, formerly known as the Post of San Juan, now serves as headquarters of the Antilles Department. It is located in San Juan and occupied by the post commander and his staff. Old stucco quarters stand within the shadow of famous El Morro.

Henry Barracks, at Cayey, forty miles from San Juan, is occupied by infantry and other ground service forces. It is in the mountains and has well-kept lawns and beautifully green-coated hills. The nights are quite cool, and the quarters are equipped with fireplaces. A most desirable station!

Fort Buchanan lies across the bay from San Juan and is occupied by infantry and other ground and service forces. There are 280 sets of government quarters.

Camp O'Reilly is located thirty miles from San Juan, at Caguas.

Losey Field is an ex-Air Force fighter base located eight miles from Ponce, Puerto Rico's second city in size to San Juan. It is now occupied by mechanized cavalry.

Borinquen Air Field is eighty-six miles from San Juan and known locally as the "Cane Patch." Excellent concrete quarters are provided, about 270 sets. It is occupied by Air Force, the 24th Composite Wing.

Vernam Field, Jamaica, B.W.I. (British West Indies), is located forty-five miles west of Kingston, the capital. The base is built on land leased from the British government in 1940. Quarters are temporary but comfortable.

Coolidge Field, Antigua, B.W.I., is located four miles from St. Johns, with comfortable housing for families. Among its attractions is a golf course built on sand, spotted with small white rocks the size of golf balls—a golfers' paradise.

Beane Field is on the island of St. Lucia, about thirty miles from the capital, Castries. There are comfortable quarters, good bathing and wonderful fishing. It is a three-hour trip by motor to Castries over a very poor road.

Waller Field is on Trinidad, B.W.I. There are three military posts on the island. Port-of-Spain is the largest city. Railroads are poor and taxis antiquated. Taxis carry an "H" on their license plates, meaning for "hire." Bicycles are the most common means of transportation.

Atkinson Field is in British Guiana. River boat is the only means of transportation but a road is being built to Georgetown. The auto tax here is high.

The name "Puerto Rico" means, "Gate to Riches"! Judging from its popularity as a mecca for tourists in the past few years, and its importance as a Caribbean military base, it is one of the Army's most important stations. Puerto Rico lies in the path of the trade winds, and the climate is tropical.

Living conditions are good, and the quarters are desirable. The only fly in the ointment is: There aren't nearly enough quarters to go round. If you have to be on commutation status, then enjoy the experience. The exteriors of old Spanish houses are often deceiving. Behind moldy walls that look as if they are about to crumble you may find a charming old Spanish *casa* with a patio of incredible beauty. In Puerto Rico you really have to explore to find an interesting place to live, and exploring may lead you into fascinating avenues of life.

San Juan is the largest city on the island, and it is a wide-awake metropolis, not the sleepy tropical town that might be imagined. Its Casa Blanca or White House, once the official residence of Ponce de Leon, is now occupied by the commanding general of the Antilles Department.

Near by stands La Fortaleza, reputed to be the oldest building under the American flag. It is painted raspberry pink, and is the official residence of Puerto Rico's governor general.

At the entrance of the harbor stands the time-stained and battle-scarred El Morro, a tremendous old Spanish fort whose silent windswept grandeur is overpowering.

In the cathedral lie the bones of the famous explorer, Ponce de Leon, long remembered for the famous "Fountain of Youth," which he sought in Florida in 1513. Puerto Rico reeks of romance and tragedy. Its charm and mystery are intangible, yet beauty and sadness are there. There is also, if one looks for it, plenty of sunshine and pleasant living.

The island of Puerto Rico is about a hundred miles long and thirty-five miles wide and has a population of over two million people. The Puerto Ricans are intensely American. They refer to mainlanders as continentals.

Schools

The public schools are out of the question for American children, but there are twenty private schools in San Juan, including several good Catholic convents. Most of the Army posts have grade school facilities giving instruction from kindergarten through the sixth or ninth grade. The University of Puerto Rico is located at Rio Piedras, and specializes in agriculture and engineering; it also has a graduate school of tropical medicine. The latter is located at San Juan.

Servants

Servants in general throughout the area are mediocre, and most of them are untrained. They are far better in the English colonies than in Puerto Rico. Virgin Island natives are imported to work for Army personnel, and the wage scale varies from five to nine dollars per week. The Puerto Rican servants make very little effort to speak English, and many Army wives find it easier to do their own cooking and to let the servants do the cleaning.

If you can speak Spanish (a language every Army wife should make an effort to learn), it will be a great help in all dealings with Puerto Ricans. We are in *their* country, so we are the ones who should make the greater effort to speak *their* language.

Is a Car a Necessity?

Yes, the posts are large, but you will find a small car with a short wheel base that can be maneuvered on the narrow, winding streets of San Juan much better than a larger automobile. All cars must be licensed and insured to be operated on stations in Puerto Rico. States licenses can be used. The roads are not too good, and no one in his right mind would risk his life in the public cars or *publicos*, as they are called. Their rates are low, about thirty-five cents for a twenty-mile trip, but a conveyance built to hold eight persons usually carries sixteen with all sorts of freight. A passenger may hold a bird in a cage, or a farmer struggling with a live

wriggling young pig whose feet are secured with ropes may
be your seat-mate. The drivers are breathtakingly reckless.
If life should grow monotonous, you might try a trip around
the island in a *publico!*

General Conditions

Whether or not to take furniture? If you do, be sure to
take inexpensive wicker, because termites devour everything except solid native mahogany. Antiques are just their
meat, and you can practically see your favorite pieces vanish
before your eyes.

A sewing machine and a washing machine will prove a
great convenience and worth their weight in gold, while
a long- and short-wave radio will be a real luxury.

There is little to buy at present, except mahogany from
Jamaica and Honduras and native linen from Guatemala.
Drawn-work linen, embroidery, baskets and string rugs will
make their appearance again, later, but at present, prices
are greatly inflated.

Small dinners, buffet suppers, teas and bridge luncheons
are popular, and a great deal of the entertaining is done at
the officers' clubs. There are two important golf clubs: the
Berwind Country Club, with reduced Service dues, and the
El Moro or Army Club. The Conadado Hotel is expensive,
ten dollars a day and up with meals in proportion, but it is
popular with tourists. The Escambron Hotel has a night
club and is famous for its bathing beach and elaborate
cabañas.

The laundry facilities are said to be good, but the dry
cleaning poor. The answer to that is to take plenty of cotton
dresses, both for sports and for evening.

Two recent books about Puerto Rico deal in extremes,
unfortunately; but *Dynamite on Your Doorstep* while em-

phasizing the seamy side, of which there is plenty, also gives the reader an insight into the real character of the Puerto Ricans. *Coconut Suite* goes to the other extreme, but you will find both interesting reading during your tour of duty.

JAMAICA

Vernam Field is one of the most desirable stations in the Antilles Department because the island of Jamaica itself as Christopher Columbus described it "is like a huge hothouse overflowing with rare fruits and beautiful flowers." Jamaica has a colorful history, and there are many points of interest in Kingston.

Gigantic cotton trees, whose seed pods contain a cotton-like fiber for stuffing, coconut palms, banana and bread-fruit trees and ginger plants grow wild throughout the Blue Mountains. In the valleys and glens papayas, guavas, mangoes and purple-skinned star-apples grow profusely.

Jamaica's coastal towns are hot, but it is always refreshingly cool in the hills. Countless rivers and cascades spill down the mountains into the sea. Long-tailed humming-birds with red and green plumage dart among the orchids that cling to the branches of the high trees. Scarlet hibiscus blossoms make a carnival of color with magenta bougain-villaea trailing over terraces and balconies. The streams are filled with tropical fish and fresh-water shrimp.

Kingston itself is a modern city and has several fine hotels and clubs, among them the Myrtle Bank Hotel, the Jamaica Club and the Royal Yacht Club.

On Antigua and St. Lucia there are many scenic points and historical attractions but few hotels and restaurants which are patronized by military personnel.

The climate on all of these islands is similar, and temperatures vary only a few degrees the year round.

TRINIDAD

Trinidad was named by Columbus after the Trinity because as he approached the island he first sighted three mountain peaks. Port-of-Spain is the capital. Trinidad is famous for its Calypso music, which is a weird blend of Oriental and African strains. Fishing for tarpon, kingfish and mackerel and hunting in the equatorial jungles for armadillos and alligators are the chief sports. There is considerable wet weather, the rainy season starting in June and lasting through December.

The Army quarters, 300 tropical-type cottages, are furnished with a limited amount of Q.M. furniture. It is advisable to take wicker or reed furniture, suitable for the tropics, and nothing that will suffer from excessive moisture such as pictures, veneered tables, chairs or other articles in which a large amount of glutinous material is utilized. Pianos and radios deteriorate, but an electric light may be kept burning in the piano, which will help a bit.

Servants are plentiful and reasonable; also, most of them speak English. Few quarters have servants' rooms, although the space beneath the floor of the raised tropical cottages is sometimes used for that purpose.

Several high-standard schools in Port-of-Spain are available. Church-sponsored private schools are among the finest institutions in the West Indies. There are also two excellent colleges. Queens' Royal College offers courses in liberal arts and sciences while the Imperial College of Tropical Agriculture is recognized as one of the finest schools of agricultural engineering in the world.

Hospitals and dispensaries are established on all bases in the Antilles. Prenatal and postpartum care of mother and baby are provided. Maternity wards where wives of officers and enlisted men are attended are provided by each station hospital. Officers' dependents are charged one dollar per day, and enlisted men's dependents are charged the value of one and a half rations a day. Dental clinics are available at every post.

Basic sanitary precautions are important. Personnel is urged to take care of slight chest colds immediately because of the prevalence of tuberculosis. Soil on most of the Caribbean islands is contaminated with hookworm, and Army doctors advise that children wear shoes when playing outside.

ALASKA

Alaska not only is the key to the defense of the United States, but is said to be the most strategical piece of property in our hemispherical defense. Even so, it is sparsely populated and at the last census there were only a few more white people in Alaska than there were people working in the Pentagon in wartime Washington, D.C. As our last geographical frontier, Alaska is destined to be a focal point for world airways and will serve as a vital military and naval base.

Its strategic location and its proximity to Asia caused farseeing General Billy Mitchell many years ago to regard Alaska as "the Achilles' heel of American defense," and now his warning is being heeded. The United States has maintained a small military base in Alaska since 1897, but today the Army has moved in to stay.

There are many popular misconceptions of Alaska. From grammar-school geography, the impression is obtained that it is a land of snow and ice inhabited by polar bears and populated by Eskimos living in geometrical igloos.

The very mention of your husband's orders to Alaska

makes you shiver, doesn't it? Well, that is perhaps because you are not up on your arctic geography! Alaska covers a lot of territory. You may be surprised to know that it is somewhat larger than the combined states of Texas, California and Montana. Also, the climate varies greatly in different sections.

Much of Alaska is mountainous. Anchorage has more snow than Fairbanks. Nevertheless, sometimes the thermometer drops to seventy degrees below at Fairbanks; in summer it rises to a hundred degrees, being generally hotter than either Washington, D.C., or New York. Just to give you an idea, temperature around zero is spoken of as "shirt-sleeve" weather. What a person says when it is a hundred degrees is a matter for his own conscience.

Schools

The public school system on the whole is creditable; but because of the small scattered population and lack of revenue to maintain the schools, many of them are privately supported. While Alaska is rich in natural resources, the greater proportion of its wealth is drained from it. The millions of dollars taken from its mines and fisheries go back to persons who reside in the United States or elsewhere; hence the Alaskan cities are handicapped because of the lack of taxable wealth. Most of the cities have high schools generally comparable to those in the northwestern states. The University of Alaska is located in the Tanana Valley at Fairbanks. It is a federal land-grant college and specializes in courses in agriculture. It is also well known for its school of mines.

There are no servants available, unless you want to try to train an Eskimo. While it can be done, the experience is likely to be an ordeal that will educate you more than it will the servant. Half-breeds or "breeds," as they are called, are inclined to be rather independent and indolent after they have saved up a few dollars. Maybe they are smart, after all. Why should one work puttering around a house if one has enough dried fish for the winter and a good suit of woolies?

Service costs from seventy-five cents an hour up, and laundry work is so expensive it is almost prohibitive. At the newer posts, laundry rooms are completely equipped with stationary tubs, washing machines and mangles.

No, Igloos Are Reserved for the Eskimos

The recent built sets of quarters are small but adequate. Both officers and enlisted men have painted and done most of the repair work themselves on the quarters. On the new posts they have electric stoves, frigidaires and the usual amount of government furniture. By all means, take all of your household goods to Alaska, and lay in an extra supply of useful kitchen articles from the dime store. Furniture is high, owing to the excessive freight rates. Many Army people shop from catalogues, because Alaskan prices are high and the selection is necessarily limited in the stores.

Eskimos are quick to catch on, and once initiated into the charm of gadgets, outboard motors and radios they, too, order from the Flomgommee Ward catalogue, as they pronounce Montgomery Ward. They also take great pride in dancing to the latest jive tunes.

The post exchanges are fairly well equipped, but it is suggested that a supply of paper napkins, paper towels, wax paper and cleansing tissue be taken with you. To make your kitchen work easier, "chore boys" and steel wool will not be amiss.

Inflation hit Alaska during the gold rush, and prices have

been correspondingly high ever since. To give you an idea: a hamburger costs eighty-five cents; ice cream, a dollar a quart.

An automobile is a luxury at an inland station, but in cities you will consider it a necessity, despite the fact that chains are standard winter equipment. There is no network of motor roads or railroads. Owing to the mountains, the climate and the great distances, air transportation has been rapidly developed, and aviation has been a godsend to the back areas. Every year tremendous loads of freight and equipment are handled on the Fairbanks-Nome run, which years ago took over thirty days, and cost an individual over one thousand dollars by dog team. The trip is now made by air in approximately three hours. While still expensive, judged by States standards, air travel in Alaska is by far the most generally practical.

Clothes

In the cities of Nome, Juneau, Sitka, Fairbanks, Anchorage and Haines one sees fashionably dressed women. The cities are very cosmopolitan, and anything can be bought, but luxuries come high. A fur coat is practically a necessity but, strange as it may seem, will be less expensive if bought in the States. Wonderful bargains are to be had in furs, such as reindeer fawn, sealskin, silver fox and ermine, but the cost of making up the furs is something else. It is suggested that lightweight woolens be included in your wardrobe, over which you can wear a very warm coat. Heavy underclothing is a nuisance and a positive danger to health in the well-heated houses. Take a good supply of sweaters and skirts, woolen dresses, afternoon dresses and evening dresses. A pair of lined overshoes or galoshes and a pair of fur-lined carriage boots for evening should be included.

The sportswoman should take along a ski suit (with a wind-breaker) and ice skates.

Equip yourself with plenty of warm slacks, and one warm topcoat with a hood is a *must*. At Adak, the wind blows at times up to a hundred miles per hour, and that is breezy in any language. Most of the time, however, the climate is similar to Washington, D.C. The lowest temperature at Adak is around eighteen degrees above. Oil heat is used.

If you are to be near Sitka or Kodiak, take along plenty of rain gear. A heavy gabardine trench coat with hood will be a joy. Be sure to include galoshes, overshoes and boots. Select cheery, bright-colored raincoats, umbrellas, and ski clothes. You may take a trip into the interior by dog sled or go up to Fairbanks to attend the winter ice carnival.

Don't forget to stock up on your favorite cosmetics, plenty of creams and hand lotions, as the variety and choice are poor in the shops and, I need not add, expensive.

Adak is the new port of debarkation for Alaska instead of Seward, as its harbor can be navigated the year round.

Diversions

Alaska is noted for its beautiful scenery. Its mountains and lakes compare favorably with those of Switzerland, and the nights, bright with the midnight sun (twenty-four hours of sunlight) and the northern lights, indescribable in their ever changing beauty, remind one of Norway.

In the summer, take a trip through the fjords of the famous Inside Passage, where you will see dazzling white glaciers, giant mountain peaks, and valleys strewn with exquisite flowers. Visit Sitka, the old Russian capital; go to Skagway, where you can take a train following the historic trail of '98 passing Rocky Point, Pitchfork Falls, Inspiration Point and Dead Horse Gulch. See the silver fox farms at Carcross and visit the Choutla Indian School located there. Skagway is noted for its flower gardens, curio shops, Reid Falls and "Soapy" Smith's grave.

The small town of Haines, at the head of Portage Cove and adjacent to Chilkoot Barracks, is the headquarters for several Indian tribes. Many of the houses are decorated with totem poles, and the Chilkoot Indians hold their potlatches or big feasts and dances right in the city.

Eskimos may appear slow at first but they are clever. George Allen Ahgupuk, the Eskimo artist, draws on reindeer hide and has made some wonderful carvings of walrus ivory. An Eskimo can take a watch or a motor apart and put it together again so that it works better than ever. But as servants, no!

Fairbanks and Anchorage have two outstanding social events during the winter, the Anchorage Fur Rendezvous and the Fairbanks Ice Carnival.

Don't miss a chance to see Juneau, the capital. Nome is a thriving city, but it is interesting more for its roaring hell-raising past than for its sedate present. It is said that there are only two seasons at Nome—July and winter. However, the seasons are divided into four months of work and eight months of play. With the first break of winter, usually in March, the grand exodus to the hinterland begins. Planes ferry trappers to the beaver marshes for the spring trapping, and following that the planes are busy ferrying miners to the creeks and prospectors to the unexplored areas.

But in the winter, knowing that they will be more or less isolated for the long months of snow, the people of Alaska plan a season of enjoyment and social gaiety. Ski jumping, snowshoeing, tobogganing, hunting, dog and reindeer racing are some of the sports enjoyed. Hunting parties are arranged, and caribou and polar bear hunting is popular. There are also dancing, bridge, badminton, ping-pong and all types of indoor games to while away the short winter days and long nights.

Throughout the year, hunting and fishing are the principal sports. The mountains abound in caribou, mountain goat and sheep, deer and bear. The streams are filled with salmon, halibut and trout. Alaska is the fisherman's paradise and the sportswoman's dream. If you aren't an outdoor girl when you go to Alaska, you are bound to be one when you leave.

Most of the real Alaska is out of doors. Fishing may be said to be the most popular sport, and no license is required. Big-game hunting is so expensive that few can indulge in it. First of all, one must procure a license for hunting, which costs fifty dollars, then engage the services of a registered guide at ten dollars a day in addition to supplies and all the extras that are necessary to the success of this type of sport.

It is not considered wise or safe to start out alone in Alaska. There are miles of rolling tundra, and it is easy to become lost. The dense forests and ice-capped mountains, along with native wild life roaming at large, make mountain climbing and hiking except in arranged parties with an experienced guide a hazardous undertaking.

There are all sorts of stories afloat for the cheechakos or newcomers. Don't fall for the story about white ice-worms that crawl out of the glaciers on sunny days and make a chirping noise.

Alaska is not a frontier country any more, except geographically. It is a very progressive territory, with a small number of people—but people who are self-sufficient, independent and proud, and who have made headway regardless of obstacles. Alaska is tough, and it has been a question of the survival of the fittest. Those who have succeeded are those who could take it.

Air Transport Command . . . Arctic Air Stations

You never dreamed you would go to Halifax, did you? Well, if your husband is stationed at Fort Pepperell, Headquarters Newfoundland Base Command, you will probably travel by the Furness-Withy Line from New York, which takes five days with one day spent in Halifax, or you may make the trip by air which requires some eight hours.

As you approach by boat, you will get a good view of the base. It is situated on the shore of Quidi Vidi Lake, and is ten minutes by motor from the heart of St. John's, the capital. The fine views over the rocky headlands and the ocean are enhanced by the clarity of the atmosphere. The hilly contour of the land, the well-paved streets, the white buildings with their green lawns give an attractive picture.

The climate is not as rigorous as is generally supposed and compares with that of Boston. Winter temperatures are usually between five and thirty-five degrees. There is considerable rain, fog and snow.

The quarters are of permanent construction—exteriors of white asbestos shingle, very attractive modern architecture with strong, horizontal lines and flat roofs. The flat roofs are kept free from snow by the prevailing strong winds. The interiors are attractive, with hardwood floors, living rooms usually painted gray or soft green (unusual for the Army and a change from the usual buff which ranges to O.D.); the bedrooms are in pastel tints; the kitchens are white with red composition counter tops, and the linoleum floor-covering is white, faintly marbled with red.

St. John's is the seat of the government, and the governor and his family reside in Government House. The members of the American Consulate are active participants in the social life of the post. Servants of average ability are available, and the wages are reasonable. The commissary and post exchanges are well stocked, and the base supports its own dairy. Of course, all prices are higher than in the States.

As to clothes: Tailored suits are practical and are much worn by the British women in St. John's. Excellent British woolens are available. A full-length fur coat is almost a must, or a warm coat such as an alpaca pile or one lined with alpaca is necessary. An adequate supply of shoes should be included in your wardrobe, but all types of overshoes can be bought in St. John's.

There are many interesting motor trips, and the Newfoundland Railway connects all the principal towns. The roads are poor, but the scenery is beautiful and the outposts are interesting and picturesque. The air bases in Newfoundland are held under the ninety-nine-year lease arranged by President Franklin D. Roosevelt, and are, to that extent, permanent bases and are being operated as such. At Gander, Newfoundland there is a small Army maintenance detachment.

HARMON FIELD, NEWFOUNDLAND

Harmon Field was named for Lieutenant E. A. Harmon, who was killed in a crash at Dayton, Ohio, in 1929. The post itself is located near the small town of Stephensville, ten miles from the village of Aguathuna and about forty-five miles from the capital of St. John's. The climate is somewhat like that of Maine, though not quite as cold. There is a great deal of snow, and when the wind blows it is bad; otherwise it is fine.

The base is located right on the ocean; you can see the water from the quarters and the mountains beyond . . . truly beautiful scenery at your finger tips. In the summer, with the boat trips available, one is reminded of the fjords and scenery of Norway.

Newfoundland itself is a very poor country. Before the air base was set up, the people around Stephensville earned their livelihood in the woods by chopping down trees and cutting pulp. The additional work at the base gives them more money than they have ever had before, though there is a strict wage scale set up by the Newfoundland government to which the Army must adhere. On the whole, the Newfoundlanders are quite fond of Americans and some of the enlisted men have married native girls.

While the Newfoundlanders speak English as we do, some of their words, phrases and expressions sound strange as, no doubt, ours do to them. For instance, instead of saying, "Where are you going?" they say, "Where you to?" Perhaps it is due to the cold and they like to save their energy instead of expending it on verbs which seem useless to them. Before the Army arrived, these hinterland people had never seen a typewriter, an electric stove or an electric refrigerator. The last-mentioned still intrigues the maids, and they want to place everything in it, including fresh-baked pies, bread etc.

Quarters range from three-room to eight-room abodes and are quite comfortable, even to steam-heated garages. Families pioneering in Stephensville feel that they are putting their ancestors of the gold-rush days to shame. What with carrying water, very little heat (wood stoves) and no refrigeration except the snowbank outside, their life in Newfoundland might be considered pretty grim. Their only consolation is that they are with their husbands, and that they came on their own.

June Williamson, wife of Lieutenant Colonel Walter H. Williamson, writes the following with all the enthusiasm of youth.

Life at Harmon Field is quite gay. You would be surprised at how much we find to do, and how much entertainment there is. Our Women's Club meets weekly, and because there were only two or three wives here when the Club was organized it includes all wives on the Field, also the nurses and Red Cross workers assigned to the Base. The first meeting each month is a luncheon and a business meeting; the second, is a special program with a speaker, entertainment, etc.; the third is a bridge party; the fourth, is work for the nearby civilian hospital which is badly in need of bandages, layettes, Q-tips etc. We also have a monthly project of collecting magazines on the Base for this hospital. If there is a fifth Thursday in the month, we play bingo. Besides this, we have a bowling league; there is a bingo game one night each week at the Club with good prizes and a jack-pot; a tea dance with free cocktail hour; there are movies each night at the theater, and ice skating at the rink on the Base. Skiing is fine here, and in the summer time, the best salmon and other kinds of fishing in the world is in Newfoundland. Other forms of entertainment popular are bridge parties, open houses, "house-warmings," dinner parties, poker parties, afternoon teas, and knitting and embroidery sessions. It is easy to have a party at Harmon Field . . . everyone is so close to everyone else, and all are willing and cooperative.

What You Should Take to Newfoundland

These are important: cosmetics, including plenty of creams and lotions for your skin in the cold wintry weather; soaps of all kinds and soap flakes; linens, as only sheets and pillowcases are furnished.

Include wool slacks and wool shirts and a pair of stadium boots. The boots are a necessity for wear in the ice and snow. Stock up on stationery as the P.X. often runs out. If there is a baby in the family, try to anticipate its needs for a year, and buy things, especially apparel in the correct sizes for a year hence.

The little stores in the village of Stephensville carry very few items of interest or use to Army wives, and what they do have costs about three times as much as in the States owing to the heavy taxes levied by the government.

Take plenty of formals; include some with long sleeves or jackets. One needs more evening clothes on a small garrison than on a larger post because the same people attend the same parties.

Pilots as Shoppers

No bachelor or married pilot ever takes off from Newfoundland for the States without his little "black book" being filled with pages of shopping requests given him by the young matrons at Harmon Field. Of course it is good training for the unmarried men and they will be well broken in by the time they are married. They learn to shop for everything from nylons to baby items such as Q-tips and oleum-percomorphum. They also bring back marshmallows, Ritz Crackers, baby food, canned fruit juices or anything on which the commissary is short or is not stocking.

What to Buy

At the one store in Aguathuna the beautiful handwork made at the Grenfell Missions of Newfoundland and Labrador is for sale. There are wool jackets and parkas with matching mittens, all lavishly embroidered in bright wool thread; snowsuits for children; windbreaker jackets for skiing; bedroom slippers, matching scarves and mittens, and matching mittens and anklets; tapestries, pot holders and carved ivory. The prices are quite reasonable. The post exchange also imports exquisite Madeira linens, place mats and handkerchiefs from the Azores.

Servants are plentiful, willing and may be had for about $7.50 per week.

There are limited facilities now for dependents in the Newfoundland area. Priorities for travel and accommodations are granted by the local commanders. Some dependents granted priorities are sent by ship during the summer months. The remainder of the year they fly in. The ATC is authorized to carry Air Force dependents to this area.

Air Transport Command stations in the North Atlantic Sector also include Goosebay, Labrador and Bluie West One, Greenland, neither of which at the present time has adequate facilities for dependents.

BERMUDA

At Bermuda there are limited accommodations on the base for both officers and enlisted men, but local housing facilities are considered adequate for dependents.

Bermuda is not one island, but some 365 grouped together on the map, only about a dozen of which are of any consequence. Bermuda's beauty is unusual and its basic color scheme of varying greens is different from any other place in the world. Against this background the white and pastel Bermuda houses built of coral shale stand out. Wild nasturtiums, oleander, flowering hibiscus and jasmine blend in with wind-bent cedars.

Hamilton is a town of glaring white coral stone, and Front Street, where the steamers anchor, is the only active place in all Bermuda. The living tempo is that of a sleepy, leisurely, gracious life set long ago by its Spanish discoverers. The main islands abound in golf courses and private tennis courts, and you may be fortunate enough to see the "strange rite of Cricket." The Bermudians give the island its character, and socially they think far from ill of themselves. For years motors were forbidden until their absence became a reasoned asset. Bicycles and horse-drawn carriages are the means of transportation. An older and smaller town than Hamilton is St. George, which has great charm. It is said, "That one unique quality about Bermuda is that it makes old age seem charming and enviable."

ARMY FORCES, MIDDLE PACIFIC (AFMIDPAC)
THE HAWAIIAN DEPARTMENT

Aloha Oe
Its Meanings

It's more than just an easy word for casual good-bye;
It's gayer than a greeting and it's sadder than a sigh;
It has the hurting poignancy, the pathos of a sob;
It's sweeter than a youthful heart's exquisite joyous throb;
It's all the tender messages that words can not convey;
It's tears unshed, and longing for a loved one gone away;
It's welcome to Hawaii and it's lingering farewell;
It's all the dear and silent things that lovers' lips can tell;
It's woven into flower leis and old Hawaiian songs;
It's frailer than a spider web and strong as leather thongs;
It's fresh as dew on ginger blooms and older than the moon;
It's in the little lullabys that native mothers croon;
It's said a hundred different ways, in sadness and in joy;
ALOHA means "I love you." So, I say "Aloha oe."

—Don Blanding

AFMIDPAC or the Hawaiian Department is the important command in the Middle Pacific. Service in Hawaii should definitely not be considered as foreign duty, since the entire territory is part of the United States. Perhaps, in the near future, it may be admitted to statehood, making the forty-ninth state of the Union. You will admit that this is another "foreign service" misnomer! I presume the designation arises from the fact that geographically Hawaii lies beyond the continental limits of the United States, and one has to cross water to reach it. Old-timers or *kamaainas* in Honolulu are inclined to lift their eyebrows in bored tolerance when a newcomer or *malihini* shows his ignorance by referring to Hawaii as a foreign possession.

Neither should service in Hawaii be included with other tropical duty, chiefly because of its climate. Hawaii is as nearly perfect in climate as any spot that has been discovered by man, and rightly deserves its self-awarded title, "The Paradise of the Pacific." There is no definite wet season; yet there is ample rainfall for the luxuriant tropical vegetation that flourishes all the year round. The daily showers are known as "liquid sunshine." Children play undisturbed in this refreshing drizzle that blows down from the cloud-draped hills, and golfers seem to be unaware of the falling drops as they putt through rainbows on the lovely golf courses of Oahu. The normal temperature in Honolulu is seventy-two degrees, with an all-time low of fifty-eight degrees. On the hottest day on record the mercury soared to eighty-eight. (Although it must be admitted that eighty degrees, with the humidity at seventy-five, can be sweaty weather.) Actually the Hawaiians have no word for "weather." It is not in their vocabulary.

All of the large Army and Navy stations are on the island of Oahu, which ranks third in size among the eight principal islands. Hawaii is the largest of the group and gives its name to the entire territory. Colloquially it is spoken of as "The Big Island." Since the territory is part of the United States, United States money is used, United States stamps are stuck on letters, and the English language—with many bizarre inflections and additions—is spoken.

Honolulu, on Oahu, is the largest city and deserves its

reputation as a melting pot for oriental and native peoples, with a heavy infusion of Europeans and Caucasians. The Army and Navy personnel form a floating population, in addition to the thousands of tourists who pour in from all points of the compass.

From the moment Diamond Head is sighted, life takes on an added thrill. The many-fingered harbor itself is a gem, surrounded by purple mountains that seem to rise directly out of the opal sea. At the right, as you approach the harbor entrance, the world-famous Waikiki beach, in the shape of a crescent, gleams beneath its fringing coconut palms. Directly ahead, from the heart of the harbor, rises Aloha Tower, flanked on one side by the pineapple-shaped water tank of the cannery and on the other by the twin stacks of the municipal electric plant. Beauty linked to commerce—that is the keyword of Honolulu.

The harbor itself, with its gorgeous colorings, is at its best in the morning; but should your transport be delayed and your landing be by moonlight, that is something for your memory book. By night the myriads of twinkling lights in the homes on the terraced mountainsides remind one of a giant spreading Christmas tree. Whenever you land, morning or night, it will be wonderful.

All of your friends will be down at the pier to meet you. Or if you do not know anyone, a welcoming committee from the post to which your husband has been assigned will be there to deck you with leis and bid you aloha. The word "aloha" has several different meanings. The first is "love," the second is "farewell," the third is "welcome" and there are dozens of others that can be supplied on occasion.

Smothered in leis of ginger blossoms, *pikake*, spicy carnations, hibiscus, Hilo violets, or even orchids, while the Royal Hawaiian and Army bands play "The Song of the Islands," you will feel something within you that cannot be described. Hawaii is unique in its hospitable custom of greeting visitors to its shores, and in bidding them farewell. It is one of the most endearing things about the islands.

This is the picture of Honolulu and a happy landing before the surprise attack on December 7, 1941, by the Japanese. During the war years, Honolulu was greatly changed. Everything was hustle and bustle, and the easy, leisurely, graceful way of living was changed to a jittery, rushing existence like that of any other overcrowded American defense center.

Today, Hawaii is striving hard to get back into its prewar routine, and again to make Oahu a paradise for the honeymooners and hundreds of visitors who will go to Honolulu when travel is resumed on a wide scale. The war destroyed a great deal of the charm, but the natural beauty remains. War could not destroy the color of the "cup of gold" flower, the songs of the birds of paradise, the beautiful sunrises and sunsets on the Wainaie Mountain Range, the golden shower trees, and the smiles of the Hawaiian lei makers. No, war changed only the people . . . you and me!

Every Army and Navy wife in Hawaii on December 7, 1941, had a different experience and reaction to the actual bombing. Certainly, all are agreed on one point—that the attack came as a complete surprise. My husband was stationed at Hickam Field, and those of us there not only had ringside seats but were actually in the fireworks.

The following account of my own personal experience is taken from *The WACS:*

A War Begins!

The speed of the attack on Pearl Harbor on the morning of December 7 at five minutes of eight o'clock was breathtaking. I know. I was there! Our quarters at Hickam Field overlooked the channel of Pearl Harbor, and that morning before the attack as I sat at my dressing table I was particularly impressed with the beauty of the scene before me. All mornings are beautiful in Hawaii, but this quiet peaceful Sabbath something about the stillness, the silent beauty, made me stop and think: "This is really Paradise; how fortunate we are to be stationed in Honolulu."

As I sat there enjoying the beauty before me, there was a terrific explosion from Pearl Harbor, followed by several more in rapid succession. Bright flames and billows of black smoke shot up from the harbor, and at the same instant the anti-aircraft machine guns went into action.

Down over our quarters came swooping a formation of dive bombers. Their speed was terrifying. My blood ran cold when I saw the Rising Sun insignia on the wings of the mustard gray-green planes. I realized all too well that this was not a practice maneuver—we were being attacked by the Japs.

At first I was stunned. The noise was ear-splitting; tracer bullets made the sky look like a Fourth-of-July celebration; shell splinters rained like hailstones on the tiled roofs. I was alone in the quarters except for a Filipino servant, so together we tried to seek safety. My husband's military duties necessitated his being on the flying line at six o'clock that morning to receive a formation of Flying Fortresses expected in from the mainland.

Of course we had no shelters, basements, or air-raid protection of any kind. Enemy planes diving over us, catching us without even a fox-hole in which to take cover, gave us a very helpless feeling.

Enemy planes came in waves. Attacks lasted from ten to twenty minutes, followed by a breathing spell, or intermission, for what seemed about the same length of time. During the first such lull my Filipino houseboy suggested that we crawl under the house. . . . This we did, but with great difficulty. There was no basement under the *lanai*, or porch, but there was a small

screened window which my servant removed, and I managed
to crawl through. . . .

No sooner was my servant, Aquino, under the house, and both
of us lying low in our improvised foxhole, than the raiders
returned. This time they meant business in our neighborhood.
Fragments of shell flew through the air, again shell splinters
rained on the roofs of the quarters, and as we crawled under
the house to the small windows we could see and hear direct
hits landing on the hangars, on the big barracks, and on the Post
Exchange. Rows of planes were blazing, gasoline tanks exploding,
fire trucks dashing by, and all the time huge demolition bombs
were dropping closer and closer. The heavy guns, the wail of
the sirens, the deep thunder of the anti-aircraft guns, the scream
of the bombs, and the terrific explosions accompanied by violent
reverberations and concussions rocked the house over our heads
to its very foundations. I developed a terrible case of claustro-
phobia, and Aquino and I decided that, rather than be buried
alive, we would seek shelter elsewhere if ever this wave of
attack ended.

It seemed an eternity, but after a while, during a cessation in
the firing, we crawled out and took refuge in the garage. . . . It
was too late to move and there was nothing to do but see this
raid through. It proved to be the most intense, the heaviest and
the longest attack of all. The bombs were dropping dangerously
near—I really felt that if the last bomb missed us, the next one
would have our name and address on it. All this time I did not
know whether or not my husband was flying in combat, whether
or not he was even alive. . . .

At ten-fifteen an officer came around evacuating all women
and children from Hickam Field into Honolulu. He ordered us
to hurry, as a return attack was expected. That ten-mile drive
into Honolulu was perhaps as harrowing as any of the raids.
Planes droned overhead and one did not know whether they
were friendly or enemy. Sirens were shrieking, ambulances were
dashing into town with their staggering loads of wounded and

dying; cars that had been machine-gunned in earlier strafings were off the road with their passengers wounded or dead.

Less than three weeks later, on Christmas Day, 1941, I reccived, along with some fifteen hundred other Service dependents, evacuation orders to the mainland. Our sailing was supposed to be very hush-hush and a military secret. There were three Matson liners converted into government transports, and in the transport on which I sailed there were eight hundred women and children. That five-day crossing of the Pacific as we dodged submarines and possible enemy mines was as grim and wrinkle-provoking as the anxious days in Honolulu following the attack.

No doubt in time the Hawaiian tourist bureaus will use the attack as grist for their advertising mill, and will set out to capitalize on it by showing gullible tourists Pearl Harbor, Ford Island, Hickam Field and, last of all, the thousands of white crosses in Nuuanu Cemetery.

Housing and Living Conditions in Honolulu

The quarters at all of the posts are comfortable and attractive but there are not enough, as usual. Many officers are on commutation status and the rents are high, $75 to $300. The choice is dependent only upon availability and the ability to pay. The houses and apartments, the newer ones, are similar to those on the mainland.

During the war, all of the quarters were used to house the maximum number of officers; consequently the normal allocation of quartermaster furniture was out of the question. To meet the expanded need, the Engineers did a rather ingenious and useful service in setting up an Army furniture factory in which chairs and tables were made.

The normal procedure today is for families going to

Hawaii to have a set of quarters assigned or a place in Honolulu to live before transportation is authorized. Adequate quarters are provided commensurate with the rank or grade of the applicant when available. On some posts or fields the quarters are of stucco, brick or cement or they may be of the low-cost-housing frame type. The houses have from two to six bedrooms.

As to household goods, take everything. The climate is perfect, and you can use anything that you use in the States.

For clothes, take your entire wardrobe. Honolulu women follow the seasons in dress, although they follow at a discreet distance. There are times, even, when a velvet dinner dress is quite welcome and a light fur coat, jacket or furs can be worn very comfortably. Few of the houses have fireplaces or are heated in any way, and when the kona winds blow you will need an extra sweater, jacket or evening wrap. Sleds, skis and ice skates may be left at home, though the small town of Wahiawa boasts a unique ice rink. Sledding is done on *ti* leaves down the steep sides of grassy mountains.

There are good public schools, though many Army people prefer to send their children to private schools. Punahou, the oldest preparatory school west of the Rockies, is the most popular for Service children. Its grades start with the pre-school and go on through high school. The University of Hawaii is an accredited liberal arts institution, and specializes in agriculture and sugar technology. It offers courses leading to the B.A. and M.A. degrees in all standard fields of study. Noncredit courses also are offered in interior decorating, Chinese culture (with conducted tours of Chinese temples in Honolulu), Hawaiian history, the study of the Hawaiian language and other interesting subjects.

The necessity of having an automobile arises as soon as

one lands. There are beautiful motor trips, and the roads are excellent. Taxis are high, in fact, much higher than in New York and Washington or any city on the mainland.

I have referred to Waikiki as being "world-famous"! To the average tourist it is disappointing, because there are so many lesser-known beaches on the island that are much bigger and better than Waikiki. There is an Army-sponsored beach at Bellows Field, and a Navy-sponsored one called Keehi back of John Rodgers Airport. The beach at Fort DeRussey is also popular, and there are some heavenly beaches on the windward side of the island. Kaialua is a delight to those who enjoy surfboarding and sun-bathing on the sloping sands.

Food

The Army has been on the island of Oahu for a long time and facilities compare favorably with those on the mainland. There are two large commissaries, one in Honolulu and one at Schofield Barracks, which are reasonably available to all who wish to use them. Most of the posts provide bus service for those desiring to go to the commissary. Waiting in line is one of the unpleasant features; however, if you will arm yourself with a small magazine or book of the *Reader's Digest* variety, the time will seem to pass more quickly.

Food stocks, in general, are the same as on the mainland. Certain items such as fresh tomatoes and mainland fruits and vegetables are limited in supply. Dependents need bring only enough to satisfy their needs during the five-day ocean voyage.

In Honolulu stores food is necessarily higher than on the mainland. In fact, that goes for almost all commodities except women's apparel. The native markets and curb markets are interesting, with their tempting array of

Hawaiian fruits and vegetables. Delicious sun-kissed pineapples head the list. Then golden papayas and luscious avocados. Avocados sell at five cents each during the season; breadfruit, mangoes, strawberries and home-grown vegetables are in the markets throughout the year.

General Remarks about Life in Honolulu

Visitors and newcomers in Honolulu are referred to as *malihinis*, while old-timers, or people who have not necessarily been born in Honolulu but have lived there a long time, are known as *kamaainas*. In the Army lingo, you are a *kamaaina* after another transport—other than the one you arrived on—brings in a new group.

Social implications of the mixture of races in Hawaii are packed with dynamite, waiting to explode in the face of the careless or unsophisticated newcomer. Be very tactful in your conversation because you seldom know the background of the person you are addressing. Uncomplimentary remarks about the residents of the "Paradise of the Pacific" are better left unsaid.

In Honolulu the following terms are used in speaking of directions: *Mauka* means toward the mountains; *makai* means toward the sea; *waikiki* means toward Koko Head, and *ewa* toward the west or Schofield way.

Although the official language of Hawaii is English, it is an English overlaid with a charming series of Hawaiian, Oriental and Latinate words and inflections. Many of these words will soon work themselves so firmly into your vocabulary that you will be using them without thinking. A *haole* is a person of the white race. A porch or veranda will always be a *lanai*; a woman will inevitably be a *wahine*; you will say *pau* as a utility word for "finished," "ended," "completed" or even "dead"; and everyone but yourself, you'll soon agree, is *pupule,* or crazy!

Swimming, surfing and golf are perhaps the most popular sports. Schofield has a good eighteen-hole course, and Fort Shafter also maintains a good course. Waialae Golf Club offers a fine eighteen-hole course, the distinctive feature about it being that each hole is copied from a famous hole on one of twelve different courses throughout the world.

Oahu Country Club in the Nuuanu Valley is one of Honolulu's social centers and boasts a fine golf course. Tennis finds hundreds of ardent devotees also, and there are dozens of excellent courts available at Army posts and in the city. Horseback riding at Shafter and at Schofield is popular. On the island of Hawaii is the rest camp or recreation center at Kilauea Military Camp. The camp is located in Hawaii National Park, thirty miles from Hilo, at the volcano, and modern two-room cottages are available for officers and their families. There is a central mess.

CHINA

While it is true that the United States has recalled its Army forces and Marines, amounting to some 9,000 men, from China, there is still work to be done there in clearing up United States property.

Our troops were stationed in China as a mediation effort trying to effect a truce between the Nationalists and the Communists. The Chinese now will have to work out their own salvation, and upon the outcome will probably depend the future of United States policy toward China. A handful of American forces will remain on Chinese soil, some 750 officers and men with a military mission in Nanking and probably another in Peiping.

THE PHILIPPINES

The Manila of Yesterday

The Philippines, long called the "Pearl of the Orient," claimed Manila, their capital, as the most Americanized city of the Far East. Manila is located on the west coast of the island of Luzon, and is built around the mouth of the Pasig River on the eastern and inner shore of Manila Bay. Millions of American dollars during the American occupation, lasting from 1898 until the surrender to the Japanese in 1942, went into its building.

Today Manila is a heartbreaking sight. Japanese bombs reduced much of it and the surrounding towns to ruin and rubble.

The air-conditioned Manila Hotel with its swank penthouse (the prewar residence of General and Mrs. MacArthur) was practically destroyed by bombs but it is in the process of being rebuilt.

The fashionable Polo Club, where members of the American colony and those of the international set met on Sunday afternoon for the tea dances, then later stayed on to dine on the velvety grass terrace overlooking the bay, was destroyed. Yes, prewar social life in Manila was pleasant, indeed!

It gives me a nostalgic feeling to know that beautiful Dewey Boulevard with its fine residential section overlooking the bay is no more. Nearly all of the lovely old Spanish homes on Dewey Boulevard and Taft Avenue were burned. Today, the boulevard is a rough road leading to Nichols Field. Of course, in time it will be rebuilt.

The famous Army and Navy Club, used by the Japanese during their occupation as headquarters, has been rebuilt and is carrying on in its old manner.

Nichols Field, located six miles south of Manila, was completely destroyed as it was one of the main military objectives of the enemy. The American Army has rebuilt it, and temporarily Quonset huts and wooden barracks are being used, but they will no doubt be replaced by permanent construction at a later date.

Perhaps the most interesting section of Manila was the "Walled City" or "Intra-Muros" as it was usually called. Only about a mile in length and a half-mile wide, it was the historical, artistic, architectural and ecclesiastical Manila containing the oldest churches, convents, books, bells and gates of the early city. It was the Spanish Manila planned in 1570, surrounded by a picturesque moss-covered wall pierced by five gates. A wide moat formerly surrounded "Intra-Muros," and the Spaniards kept their prisoners in the cells of the thick walls. One means of torture was to place prisoners in the lower cells, so that during the rainy season, when the water in the moat rose, they would have to climb up the walls of the cells until they were finally rescued by their keepers or drowned. In the early days of the American occupation the moat was drained, filled in and used as a municipal golf course.

Everything in the Walled City was typically Spanish and it was supposed to be the finest example of a medieval city in the world. The Americans left it practically untouched. Most of the streets were narrow, so narrow in fact, that two cars could not pass at the same time so one-way streets were necessary. The same was true of two persons passing each other on the narrow cobblestone sidewalks.

The Walled City was also the Oriental shopping district, and a shopper's paradise to Army and Navy wives and feminine tourists. One never went there on a shopping tour if time was of any moment, because in addition to its being a leisurely business it had also something of a social nature. All the Oriental shopkeepers enjoyed their work and time meant nothing. There was no standard price; if one happened to be a good talker, he got the goods usually at his own price. At any rate, it was a custom never to pay more than half of the original asking price. At the Chinese and Indian stores tea was usually served during the sale, and once the sale was completed a gift or *cumsha* was presented by the merchant, its value depending upon the amount of the purchase.

All Oriental shopkeepers are extremely polite, and they will show you everything in the shop, even if they surmise you are only looking. They hope to interest you, and "looking" is usually fatal, because in the prewar days there were so many exquisite things to buy.

The shops were stocked with beautiful linens, laces of all kinds—*point de Venise*, filet, Belgian and Irish—Chinese silks, Japanese kimonos, beautiful cloisonné, fine damascene work from Japan, rare old prints, Ming ware, English china, ginger jars, Chinese rugs and thousands of curios.

"Intra-Muros" was reduced to ashes by the Japanese. This ancient medieval city never can be replaced!

The Escolta still exists as the main street, but it is quite cluttered up with ruins and reminders of bombings. Gradually, modern buildings will be erected, and the Escolta may again become a busy thoroughfare.

The Tondo Market, in prewar days, was the place to see and get acquainted with the native people. It was the largest market and, to the fastidious person, a place of evil smells; however, it was more than that. It was a market place teeming with life—with crafty Japanese merchants applying the "squeeze" in every transaction where they could get away with it; with naked, sprawling babies underfoot everywhere; with parrots squawking, pigs squealing, white-coated Filipino cooks and houseboys buying their daily food supplies for the well-regulated homes of their masters. Sordidness and utter beauty walked hand in hand! The Tondo Market, in fact the entire Tondo section, was bombed on the second day of the Japanese attack on Manila and millions of Filipinos lost their homes. Fire swept the nipa houses of the natives after the bombing and the entire area presents a scorched-earth appearance. Today smaller markets have been set up throughout the city, but the site of the Tondo Market will be a sad reminder for many years to come.

The John Hay Rest Camp at Baguio, 170 miles from Manila, was partially destroyed but is being rebuilt. Nine holes of the golf course have been restored. The town of Baguio was almost wiped out, and the roads were badly used by the enemy. It will take a long time to obliterate the horrors of the fiendishly devised "death march" which cost many American lives on this road.

Corregidor, "the Rock," located thirty miles from Manila across the bay, was, in the old days, considered a very desirable station. Today it, along with Bataan, presents to Americans only reminders of defeat and sad memories. There are still land mines planted there, and no one dares venture on Corregidor unless officially conducted. The Special Services Division arranges tours for Army personnel, but there are no troops stationed on Corregidor. The jungle on many parts of the island is reclaiming its own. Viewed from a crash boat as one circles the island, it still retains its natural beauty.

Clark Field

Old Camp Stotsenburg, located fifty-seven miles north of Manila and formerly used by the Field Artillery and Cavalry as a base, has been taken over by the Air Forces. Its name has been changed to Clark Field. Frame quarters of the bungalow type, and some of stucco construction have been painted and repaired since being occupied by the Japanese. When the enemy withdrew, the quarters were left in bad condition. As one Army wife writes: "There were no doors or windows left on our house . . . probably destroyed or removed by the Japs."

Florida Blanca

About fifteen miles from Clark Field there is a new airfield called Florida Blanca. Two long rows of houses face each other, providing about seventy sets of quarters to date. It is in such a beautiful setting, in a valley surrounded by mountains, that the young people stationed there call it "Shangri-La."

Fort McKinley

Fort McKinley, nine miles from Manila, was formerly the headquarters for the Philippine Division and was occupied by the Infantry and Coast Artillery.

The housing situation is critical; however, the Army is handling the problem efficiently by not allowing transportation to be issued to dependents until the individual desiring his family to join him has facilities assured or the rental of a civilian residence. Temporary accommodations are available at AAATC at Marcelino, Zambales, in a limited quantity.

Pioneering in the Philippines Today

Army life in the Philippines is extremely pleasant despite the heat and the fact that life in a country that has been ravaged by war places the personnel who come in to rebuild on the basis of pioneers. With all of the hardships American morale is high and enthusiastic reports pour back, on the progress that is being made in the rehabilitation program.

The *esprit de corps* is always high in the Air Forces. Call it the enthusiasm of youth or what you will but the wife of the commandant at "Shangri-La" wrote me the following ecstatic report: "We have sixty-one Army wives on our post, and they are the smartest most beauteous bunch I have ever seen (and I am from San Antonio). However, somebody said that was because fighter pilots know how to 'pick and snatch well.' Their beauty as a group is quite famed over here anyway, and corresponds to the beauty of our post."

She also writes that they have no athletic facilities whatever as yet, but that a golf course built entirely by volunteer officer and soldier labor with the help of some Nip prisoners is being completed.

A cement-floored mess hall serves as an officers' club, while the wives have taken over the furnishing of it and of an adjoining guesthouse. Sawali is used and rattan furniture, while bamboo stalks furnish the flower containers and wall vases. All the slip covers were made by the officers' wives. You see these wives are really young pioneers; there is so little to buy that they not only have to be ingenious but have to actually do the work themselves. It is nothing short of wonderful what has been done with the prefab building that serves as a guesthouse. There are bedspreads made out of G.I. sheets and trimmed with scraps of material, ash trays made out of tin cans with the sides cut in strips and curled under, shadow boxes made of sardine cans and shower curtains with matching window curtains dyed chartreuse with atabrine. These wives manage to scrounge materials such as paint and brushes when civilian workers leave them unlocked in a theater or some place where they are working. Of course, they would not think of securing paint for their own quarters in this fashion! It is customary to send to the States and pay for materials used on one's own quarters, and both Army officers and their wives are very scrupulous in this regard. But when it comes to a community project, well . . . that is something else. There is an old Army saying, "God helps those who help themselves: *but* God help those who are caught helping themselves."

The commandant's wife at Clark Field has done a most worth-while job in organizing a post school. It is affiliated with the American School in Manila. The teachers all have teaching certificates, and are wives of officers on the post. Her next project is to organize a nursery school and kindergarten. Materials are very scarce, so when anyone's household goods arrive, Mrs. C.O. stands around and waits, then, as she expresses it, "like a hawk" she makes off with the crates so tables and chairs can be built for the kindergarten. Eventually, the Philippine school system, which in the old days was excellent, will function again.

In Manila there are thirteen private schools in operation, but the Army posts maintain their own schools up to high school level.

Children seem to thrive in the Philippines, though it is a good idea to have an Army surgeon examine a child upon its arrival for physical ailments, as well as for suggestions regarding diet.

Medical care is available and is excellent. A twenty-five-bed hospital is in operation at the AAATC but it is used for emergencies only. The Fourth General Hospital in Manila services all dependent personnel.

Water

Water, either artesian or distilled, is furnished to Army officers upon request made to the utilities officers. Only artesian, distilled or boiled water should be used for drinking or cleansing the teeth. A story is told about an officer and his wife who, upon their arrival in Manila in prewar days, stayed with friends in town. There was the usual round of greeting parties at the Army and Navy Club, and when they reached the home of their hosts, the visiting lady went into the bathroom to brush her teeth. On the shelf there were two bottles of distilled water in transparent liquor bottles. The wife came rushing into the bedroom and whispered to her husband, "Oh, come, look, Harry! Over here they even brush their teeth with gin!"

Servants

One of the joys of service in the Philippines formerly was the ease of obtaining servants, but times have changed. Inflation has almost ruined the islands, and the Army personnel find it difficult to pay the high prices for service. Finally, a fixed salary rate on Army posts was devised, but of course this varies according to the size of the family and the qualifications of the servant.

The servants on the whole are kindly and willing but most of them are inexperienced. Trained servants cost more, naturally. Today, a cook is paid thirty to forty dollars per month, or sixty to eighty pesos; the houseboy, fifteen dollars per month or thirty pesos; and the laundress, or *lavandera*, twenty dollars or forty pesos per month. The amah or nurse receives twenty or thirty pesos a month—ten or fifteen dollars. The laundress comes every day except Sunday and likes to be paid by the week. Chinese servants are slightly higher, but if trained they are usually good.

To an old-timer, it is always amusing to watch newly arrived *Americanos* attempt to hurry the Filipino. Housewives particularly feel that one efficient American servant could do what it takes the cook, the houseboy and the *lavandera,* plus her rise in blood pressure, to accomplish. But after a few weeks in these beautiful, lush islands Americans if they are wise learn to relax.

In the old days only houseboys were employed and they did the work of housemaids, but another change is that young Filipinas are taking their places. The Filipina house-girls cause no end of amusement and sometimes chagrin when they call their mistresses "Mama." Of course, what they are really saying is *"Maniya"* (Mrs.) but the young matrons say it certainly sounds like "Mama" to them.

The servants eat mostly fish and rice with some native fruit.

Transportation and Private Car

A private car is almost a necessity at all the posts. Auto-mobiles should be in first-class condition prior to shipment to Manila. A bicycle or a scooter is a fine thing to include and will more than pay for itself; also, any vehicle can be sold, usually at a profit, when you are ready to leave the islands.

The little horse-drawn *carromatas* and *carretelas,* small carts and buggies drawn by diminutive horses, have disap-peared from the streets and been replaced by the good old Army jeeps. The Filipinos have really gone to great lengths to paint their jeeps every color of the rainbow. Pink, blue and green are the favorite colors. They have also given their mechanical horses fancy names such as "Daisy Jane," "Mae West," "Judy," "the Manila Bombshell" etc. Jeeps are even used for taxis, and while the fares are reasonable often the passenger feels that the reckless chauffeur should pay him for a bad case of jitters or frayed nerves at the end of the ride.

Marketing

Unfortunately, the black market is a thriving organization! Of course, Army personnel use the government sales commissaries, because all food bought outside is ridiculously high. A bunch of grapes weighing about one pound costs one peso; native fruits such as mangoes and avocados are so expensive that American housewives do not buy them any more. Avocados now sell for about twenty cents apiece; before the war, peddlers were glad to get twenty cents a dozen for them. These prices will adjust in time, when things shake down.

There is very little to buy in the way of curios or linens and embroideries, for which the Philippines were once renowned. A few camphor chests and carved wooden articles and some piña cloth might be found, but the prices are out of reason.

Recreation

Most of the entertaining is done at the officers' clubs. Bridge and cocktail parties seem to lead in popularity. Swimming and dancing run a close second. The post movie theaters get fairly current pictures.

However, in the last analysis the social life on an Army post that is more or less isolated depends upon the personnel themselves. Army people have to make their own good times, and the commanding officer of a post and his wife usually set the social pace.

Much credit is due the commanding officer's wife who can efficiently organize executive committees who will attend to the smooth running of a Women's Club. It isn't a hard job if one walks in and inherits a functioning club; it is entirely different to organize a club from scratch!

Again, the wives of officers commanding the newly set-up posts are doing a splendid job, and this is pioneering in its true sense. These wives are young and not too experienced but they are willing and eager to help. Clark Field and Florida Blanca have formally organized Women's Clubs, with a well-drawn-up constitution which provides for all the extracurriculars. They are designed to follow the well-set-up clubs of Fort Leavenworth, Fort Benning and Maxwell Field, with Red Cross activities, reading or book club, flower arrangement classes, bridge, Spanish classes, golf and tennis teams, gin rummy classes or anything that a sufficient number of the group wishes to study.

What to Take to Manila

Be sure to take enough clothing to see you through a two-year tour of duty. This is a large order, but it is absolutely necessary because the natives actually need every piece of cloth or clothing which arrives through commercial channels. The post exchanges will stock some things, such as handkerchiefs, scarves, stockings (I should say the nonessentials). Before the war Manila had many smart dress shops, and they will return when things become more settled. In the meantime, you will be on your own and still pioneering, so go prepared.

Take *plenty* of shoes, and don't depend upon the shoes that the Chinese and Filipino shoemakers will soon start producing. There should be a law against them, because more Army women have ruined their feet by wearing ill-fitting footgear produced in the Orient than Chinese women have bound feet, today! I know from experience, because one of the most embarrassing and painful of all times was when I returned from Manila with a pair of reptile shoes. They were made from a baby python caught in a playful mood in someone's woodbox at Nichols Field. I even had a large envelope purse and belt to match, though I must admit I never carried the purse or touched it with my bare hands without flinching. There was just something too personal between me and that baby python to ever fasten the belt around my waist.

You will understand my feeling, perhaps, when I tell you what happened to the shoes. Apparently, the skin was not treated properly because the first time I wore the slippers in Los Angeles on an extremely hot August day, the python skin started to contract. I was startled, my toes started pinching more and more, then finally the heels and toes looked as if they were bound to meet in their drawing-up process. It reminded me of the story of an Indian girl who "did wrong once" and was sewed up in a snakeskin and left to die out in the Oklahoma sun. With great effort I hobbled into a shoe store, and the salesman could hardly remove the tortuous shoes from my feet. I left the shoes where they lay, and walked out in a pair of good States shoes. You guessed it, the purse contracted too and the belt curled up into a little infant snake. I shudder yet when I think of the python story of the officer on Corregidor and the chance I took with my waistline.

But getting back to shoes. Take all kinds with plenty of the play or sport shoe variety. Serviceable white linen, duck or gabardine shoes that will clean well are preferable to suedes and leather. You want nothing that will mildew, because if it will mildew anywhere, it will in Manila, I assure you. Include a generous stock of white shoe polish, your favorite kind.

You will want the same kind of sports clothes as would be good in Florida or California. Sunback dresses, if you like them, lots of play suits, shorts, slacks and all the cotton evening dresses you can manage. Six will see you through a season if you take a good stock of material along for replenishing. There's something about the tropics that makes you want to get into a long dress every evening for dinner.

Take a variety of rain gear; the rainy season lasts from two to six months of the year sometimes. Be sure to have several colored plastic umbrellas, cellophane, raincoats or capes of bright shades, light in weight and color, but the serviceable kind that won't stick together. Of course you will want several bathing suits, caps and a beach coat or so.

In your household goods include your china, silver and glassware. The last is terribly expensive, even if available. Do not discard any heavy or winter clothes you may have but place them in storage or moth balls. One of these fine days transport service may again be such that you will rate a trip to China or Japan. There, warm clothing and a topcoat are usually welcome most of the year with the exception of the summer months.

In the Philippines clothes do not seem of great importance and little by little, day by day, month by month and year by year you will become less and less interested. Bits will disappear from your costume, depending upon your size, age and occupation. First you may discard your earrings—why wear the silly, cumbersome things in the heat? Next you will decide that stockings are too expensive, and besides you have been told you have Grable legs, and you can see for yourself that your sun tan is perfect. Why all these arguments with yourself, you wonder! Girdles and slips have fallen by the wayside long ago, and finally some morning you will wake up and suddenly decide that you have missed too many boats.

The coolest attire possible is worn during the day, but the government requires even children under seven years of age to wear at least *one* piece of clothing! The mischievous small Tagalog boys choose to wear large Baliwag hats; the Igorot waiters at the rest camp at Camp John Hay in Baguio decide on a G string, and there is a naughty parody on an Army song, something about the "Ladies in Manila," another one about "the men they wear no pants in Baguio." Ask any of your older Army friends, and they will sing it to you, maybe . . . with all the verses!

Tips for the Tropics . . . How to Keep Cool Despite the Thermometer

If it is sizzling outside, try to keep the inside of your quarters cool by keeping them darkened. Have the shutters closed (if you have this blessed protection) or the Venetian blinds or awnings drawn. Insist upon as little furniture as practicable and dispense with useless bric-a-brac. Bare, highly polished floors are preferable to rugs and are much cooler. If you like rugs, use native mats made of grass or *lauhala*, or the white-string pony blankets common in Puerto Rico.

Keep as cool as an ice cube, and cultivate a cool temperament. By that I mean laugh at the thermometer in thin cottons you have brought from the States or feather-light Shantung, provided you can wangle some in from China. Look cool in short hair-dos, use iced cologne and of course, leg make-up instead of stockings if nature hasn't already sun-tanned you. Indulge in large straw hats or carry colorful parasols, the Japanese oiled-paper kind, if you must be abroad in the heat of the day. Make the most of the daily siesta period and relax.

Overstuffed furniture is highly impractical. If you have brought it with you, cover it in white slip covers or some light-colored material. Work out a cool, cool color scheme.

You can't go wrong, ever, on nature's own choice of green and white. Or perhaps you have in mind some cool color combinations such as lemon yellow and gray that are equally effective.

Pianos that are built for the tropics can be rented reasonably at leading music stores. If you are musical and just had to bring your piano, be sure to keep an electric light burning in it.

You won't want pictures, as the dampness and mildew ruin them. In the Philippines blinds, curtains and draperies are not used. The sliding windows, made of small shell squares, are very effective.

Government furniture, such as the dark unattractive steel dining sets, can be brightened by light slip covers made for the chairs, and unattractive bed ends can be slip-covered in some light, cool material.

Pots and boxes of ferns, hanging air plants, cool-looking flowers like gardenias, white gladioli, water lilies, pale pink queen's crown, light yellow hibiscus, delphinium and carnations will strike a cool note. Carnations have a refreshing, spicy perfume. Large containers of dark green leaves look cool.

Dine on the porch or in the garden, if practicable. If the porch is screened, you will enjoy your meals more wherever there is a cool spot and an attractive view. Serve the coolest foods you can imagine. If your appetite deserts you, then the next time you dine at the Manila Hotel, the Candado or the Washington Hotel ask if you may take one of their menus. It will prove a lifesaver on a hot day, and will more than repay you for the embarrassment you may have felt in asking the maître d'hôtel for it. Serve long iced drinks, and skip the cocktails and heat-producing drinks.

Running water—a spray in full play on the garden just

outside your window—will give a cool sound, and should you have a fountain in your garden, turn it on in the morning and evening even if the quartermaster charges you extra for the water.

In the tropics government quarters are usually designed for comfort. Some are equipped with ceiling fans, and almost all include a dry closet. An electric light must be kept burning in a dry closet, but even so, the efficient housewife has the servants air all woolens on sunny days. Mold, moths and mildew are a constant source of annoyance and ruin. Leather goods should be kept polished, and aired often.

Termites will eat the floor right out from under you, believe it or not! And what they won't do to books! Better leave those rare editions in the States, or varnish the pages.

In the Philippines and Hawaii you will have to accustom yourself to white ants and small house lizards from one to three inches in length that play hide-and-seek on the screens and have a field day on the walls of your living and dining room. The little lizards are harmless, and in time you will grow accustomed to them and even become quite fond of them. They eat the mosquitoes, and for that you will be grateful. One family in Manila had a lizard they called Algernon, and he became quite tame; so tame, in fact, that at a dinner party, while he was executing one of his figure eights on the ceiling above the table, he fell into the soup of one of the guests. The hostess was far more distressed at the loss of Algernon than at her guest's misfortune. That is the story, anyway!

The ants are harder to deal with. After an exterminator has done his best, you will still have to put the legs of the stove, refrigerator, tables and beds in small cans of water containing kerosene or some disinfectant.

Wild animals and snakes! You will hear all kinds of hair-raising stories about the python in the Philippines that squeezed a six-foot man into a mass of pulp twenty feet long, and others equally appalling about bushmasters, tarantulas, crocodiles, fierce tigers, sharks and the horrible octopus in Panama. No doubt they are true in a measure, and undoubtedly the jungle and tropical waters are alive with monsters of one kind or another; but generally speaking there is not much danger unless you go looking for it. There are very strict regulations about women riding horseback alone, and few would be so foolhardy as to stray off into the mountains or jungle.

Don't sit around and grumble about the rain or moan about the heat. It won't do one particle of good, and if you keep busy you will forget about the weather. Bridge won't be enough to fill your time, and you will find yourself counting boats pretty soon. Take up the study of Spanish, start collecting something, even if it is only sea shells. Go sightseeing in spite of the rain and learn everything you can about the customs of the place. Do something to keep yourself interested. Cultivate any worth-while civilian contacts that may come your way and, above all, don't be so provincial that you fail to appreciate and recognize the fine qualities of the natives. Make social contacts outside of the Army circles when you can. It is broadening.

A thousand Army wives might spend two years in Honolulu, Panama or Manila and it would be interesting to hear their impressions. Be one of those who can talk about something besides the servant situation, the marvelous Singapore gin slings at the Army and Navy Club, the tea dances at the Strangers' Club and the wonderful Chinese bargains.

Overseas Shopping Service

Mary Naiden, the wife of Colonel Earl Naiden, U.S.A.F., is known throughout the Service for her exquisite taste as a stylist and decorator. She knows the needs of Army wives on foreign assignments; she understands and specializes in planning and assembling smart wardrobes on a budget plan.

Prior to the war, Mrs. Naiden carried on a most successful business by selecting and buying clothes, furs and house decorations, including rugs and draperies, often at a discount from normal prices. She acts as your personal buying agent, and a fee of 10 per cent is charged for executing purchasing commissions.

Shipments are made to foreign countries by diplomatic pouch, A.P.O. or other government transportation whenever possible, in accordance with department regulations for purchasing procedure and shipment of special items overseas.

If you are in a spot and need a very super evening dress for a very special occasion (a formal dinner at the embassy in Stockholm or Budapest) your worries are ended. Simply cable Mary Naiden giving her your size, color and all requirements as to price range etc. Allow plenty of time for delivery. Her address is:

Mary Naiden

Overseas Shopping Service

Cable Address:	P. O. Box 976
Marnaiden	Grand Central Station
Tel. Volunteer 5-1500	New York 17, N. Y.

Chapter X

DUTY IN THE OCCUPIED COUNTRIES

GERMANY, AUSTRIA AND ITALY, JAPAN, KOREA,
ON OKINAWA AND GUAM

> God and a soldier all men adore
> In time of war, and not before
> When war is over and all things righted
> God is forgotten and the soldier slighted.
> —Boston *Gazette*, February 19, 1770

HISTORY is an open book before us! The shooting is over, and the soldier's utility to the nation may appear to be on the wane, but those men on occupation duty have a most important and vital work to accomplish. Today, the war job is only *two-thirds* completed; the *other third* is the efficient and capable handling of the occupation army in Germany, Austria, Italy and Japan.

No one particularly enjoys the job of being an international policeman; but certainly this occupation is the most important part of the postwar program. It is not a job for eighteen-year-old recruits; it is a serious job for well-seasoned officers and soldiers who are accustomed to discipline and who understand how to carry out the policies of their experienced commanding officers.

The Army has little to say as to the political disposition of Germany, whether or not there will be an economic unification with a centralized government or whether there will be a political decentralization. However, it is a known fact that there can never be a peaceful Germany, or a peaceful Europe, unless the individual German knows that his country's living standards can be equal to those in the rest of western Europe. The frontiers imposed upon Germany this time must be defined in a spirit of justice and not in a spirit of greed or revenge. It is a hard task for American Army families to move into a hostile enemy country, and to take up the long-term guidance of the German or Japanese people in their economic, political and social rehabilitation according to democratic principles.

Even before the guns had stopped firing, the Allies had set up local governmental machinery on a provisional basis. Reconstruction in the American zone began immediately. Lines of communication and transportation were put back in operation and a limited industrial production was achieved. However, the German people were primarily engaged with the problems of obtaining food, fuel and adequate housing. They were too apathetic and bewildered to be much concerned with more than their own personal security.

The food ration of 900 calories, palpably a starvation diet, was raised to 1,500 calories a day with substantially more for laborers and expectant and nursing mothers. The lack of four-power agreement on basic financial reforms has impeded the economic recovery of Germany; hence inflation, and so far no plan to place the nation on a sound financial footing. Freedom of thought, discussion and expression have been restored to the German people. The German press is free to publish any material "except Nazi and Militarist propaganda and material constituting a malicious attack on Military Government." The German radio stations have been re-established on a similar basis. The German school system has been partially re-established, and one of the most important milestones is the participation in free elections.

General McNarney says, in the *Army and Navy Journal,* "It may be a long time before Germany has been rehabilitated into a democratic state with a central government subject to the will of the people. *We will not tire.* The road back for the German people will be hard, but it is not the intention of U. S. occupational policy to make it harder."

After the First World War, the returning American Army became that nostalgic lost generation because the soldiers were tired and refused to take on any further world responsibility. Our whole country let down its guard too easily. Germany blamed the war on Kaiser Wilhelm II and the military machine, and we took it for granted that the German people themselves were blameless, and meant well, after all!

Today, the German people are standing by with the hope in their hearts that their dream of world conquest may yet be realized provided the Allies in time grow lax. Germany believes had it not been for American intervention, the super-race would have won. The German youth of today, between the ages of fourteen and twenty-eight, has been carefully and thoroughly educated for world conquest, killing and treachery. No matter how friendly and repentant, how sick the Germans claim they are of the Nazi party, as a nation they have sinned against humanity and they are not to be trusted.

When the Allies marched into Germany in 1945, the Nazis were forced to respect American authority. We held the ball in our hands until the bugle call of "Home to Mother" or "Home by Christmas" sounded. We were the leaders; the British and French would have thankfully ranged themselves behind a firm and vigorous leadership. The Nazi element is calculating that sooner or later the "childish Americans" will get tired of the new game of occupation and pull out altogether.

Public demand forced General Eisenhower to rush into the demilitarization program before the smoke of battle cleared away. American wives and mothers wrote hysterically or telegraphed their congressmen to speed the return of their loved ones. The war was over and they wanted their men home! The Germans emerged slowly from their shell shock and watched all of this American weakness, lack of purpose and lack of political unity and policy. The trained Regular Army moved into the occupied areas and started on the important work of reconstruction.

The Germans today are lost without their law, order and blind obedience to Hitler; consequently, they are sullen and stubborn over the defeat. Gullible G.I.'s return to the United States with tales of German sweetness, good will and innocence. Wishful thinking aside, it wasn't long ago that the corpses of the innocent were stacked like cordwood along the roadsides of Germany, and it has been an even shorter time since our own husbands, brothers and sons were suffering tortures in Japanese prisons.

Lest we forget, I think it would be well if every Army wife might have in her files or scrapbook a copy of W. M. Lawrence's article, "Nazi Murder Factory," which appeared in the New York *Times,* August 30, 1944. It is a description of the German concentration camp at Maidanek, Poland, which was a veritable factory for the production of death. It was a place for highly systematized annihilation, and on November 3, 1943, which was the day the mass killings reached their peak, the Germans executed 20,000 prisoners by shooting, hanging, gassing and other means. It was here that a young Polish woman was bound to an iron stretcher and pushed into the crematorium alive. Barbed-wire fences twelve feet high, charged with electricity, surrounded Maidanek. Inside were more than 200 trim green barracks. Outside the fence were 14 high machine-gun turrets and 200 savage dogs especially trained to pursue escaped prisoners. The shower houses, gas chambers, crematorium and urns were dispersed over the grounds. The ashes were sold to the families of the victims for prices ranging from 2500 marks up.

It has been planned to keep Maidanek just as it now exists, as an exhibition of German cruelty for all posterity to see. Dachau and Buchenwald are similar concentration camps where the wholesale butchery of human victims was carried on throughout the bloody war years.

Germany is a nation of Nazis still, regardless of the fact that the "good Germans" still refuse to believe the horrors of the concentration camps are not their shame or guilt. Germans have no national conscience; they feel that what happens to non-Germans doesn't matter!

If human beings ever learn from experience, it is our duty to make this occupation "stick," to make it a complete success, not to get weary on the job even if it takes fifty years, because it is the only way to keep World War III from becoming more than a potential danger.

As Army wives, our attitude toward all Germans should be that of *fairness, firmness, aloofness* and above all *awareness* so that, as President Lincoln once said "these dead shall not have died in vain."

So You Are Going to Germany

Aboard ship you will be given an "Orientation Outline," the introductory welcome of which reads: "It is a pleasure to welcome you aboard ship. It is our hope that you will have a pleasant journey."

At your debarkation port, which will be Bremerhaven,

Germany, the train is usually boarded directly from the transport. Husbands are not permitted to meet their wives, but here is the pay-off! The Signal Corps boards the incoming ship and sets up telephone connections so that wives may call their husbands (those who have been alerted previously for the call). Approximately 50 per cent of the calls get through, and the connections are said to be particularly good.

An escort officer from each area meets the wives traveling to that area, and is he besieged with questions! All wives agree that the train trip is a dream after their transport voyage. The trains are good, with compartment accommodations and fine diner service. The Red Cross is most efficient and helpful.

Sometimes, owing to the scarcity of passenger rail accommodations, dependents are required to pass a night in Bremen after their arrival by transport. Accommodations are provided on the transport or at hotels.

It is only the river Weser that ties Bremen to the world—this prosaic little ribbon of gray water flowing down toward Bremerhaven. Despite the terrible destruction, Bremen has a certain charm that will be your first impression of Germany.

The time of year you arrive in Bremen will determine the type of clothes in which you should land. The winters in Bremen and Berlin are severe, but the year-round climate is similar to that of Pennsylvania.

In the occupied zones of Germany and Austria, military communities have been established to serve the various military installations. These communities have been set up with due consideration to German housing. The type of house will naturally vary in each community. Adequate heating is provided; for the most part the fuel is coal. The houses are furnished, so that it should be unnecessary for dependents to take household goods overseas. Individuals should, however, consider the desirability of taking such items as bedding, table linen and silverware. Here are some of the practical suggestions offered by wives who are already over there: Include material, bolts of it, for curtains, slip covers and clothes. A hair-dryer is a welcome addition and everyone emphasizes the shortage of soaps—bath, laundry and shampoo! Cleaning materials, such as Dutch Cleanser and Sani-Flush, and disinfectants are scarce. Take a medical kit or first-aid supplies for home use. One wife suggests bringing paint; she does not add the type or amount, so you can figure that one out for yourself. Take studio couch covers, standard slip covers and hangings if you do not care to make them yourself. These come in sets, and while considered rather mediocre in the States, they will look attractive and smart in Germany or Austria. Take a supply of curtain rods and fixtures.

Rugs are among "the critical items not currently available," so you might include a few chenille or string scatter rugs. Shower curtains, towel racks, mirrors, bolts of shelf edging for linen closets and shelf paper may give your German home a lift.

The stoves and refrigerators available in the area should be adequate, although they will not be as modern as those used in the States. If you should take your own electric range or icebox, be sure to take a transformer to permit their utilization with 220-volt current. Include a good supply of electric light bulbs, cords and plugs.

It is planned to make the military communities as much like Army posts in the United States as possible. Quarters are assigned on the basis of rank or civilian classification and size of families. The following items are for issue on memorandum receipt:

Furniture	Household Furnishings
G.I. beds, mattresses	China, set for 6
Pillows	Silver, set for 6
Divans	Glassware
Armchairs	Kitchen knives, forks, spoons
Dining chairs	Potato mashers
Desks	Can openers
Dining, kitchen, coffee and end tables	Frying pans and griddles
	Meat grinders
Chiffoniers, bureaus and wardrobes	Canister sets
	Pans, for muffins, cakes, roasting
Table and floor lamps	
Mirrors	Rolling pins
Bookshelves	Flour sifters
(Items not currently available: rugs, refrigerators, ranges, table linen, sheets, pillowcases.)	Tea kettles, sauce pans

You will be smart to take along your favorite cooking utensils, egg beater, sieves, strainers, rare condiments and spices, a bolt of cheesecloth for dustcloths, stacks of paper napkins and your favorite electrical equipment for the kitchen. You will find the commissaries and post exchanges exceptionally well stocked, and as time goes on they should get better.

Quarters

Most Army wives are pleasantly surprised in the billets or quarters awaiting them. If your husband wears stars you may live in the home of a baron, a count or some member of the nobility. Enjoy it while you may! Lieutenants through

captains are permitted three bedrooms, one bathroom, while
enlisted men draw living room, dining room, kitchen, two
bedrooms, one storeroom, one bath. On the whole, however,
quarters are assigned according to the size and needs of
families; consequently, a sergeant with a wife and four
children may be assigned a much larger house than a major
who has only one dependent, his wife.

In Frankfort, for the most part, families live in small
houses and apartments.

Servants

This is one of the subjects about which it is not tactful
to write home in a bragging manner! By now you have heard
of the Trading with the Enemy Act. In the occupied zones
of Germany and Austria, servants are provided for families
through employment offices supervised by the Army and
the military government. They are paid by the local burgo-
master, as an item of occupation cost, the sum of twelve
dollars per month for a fourteen hour day if it is required.
This is the only method by which help can be obtained at
the present time. The number of servants depends, of course,
on the type of house occupied and the local needs. In other
areas than the occupied zones the hiring of servants is a
matter for the individual concerned.

There are various reports on the servants: One is that
they are not very dependable, especially the English-speak-
ing ones, who have a superior attitude and take too many
things for granted. The same Army wife who reported this
says that most of the servants seem to have a mania for
washing everything in sight, and on one occasion washed
her husband's "pink breeches." Such energy!

A general's wife reports that on the whole the servants
are good, but that it is like the Orient—each does only his

own job! For instance, cooks cook, but they won't wash dishes or clean the kitchen. They consider themselves artists.

A major's wife from Vienna writes: "Occasionally here, one does find a hard working servant who is eager to please, but naturally the difference in language is a barrier. They are most interested in getting fed, and there have been several examples of a theft of food so a close watch has to be kept on supplies."

Schools

Comprehensive plans have been forwarded to the War Department for approval concerning the education of children from the first grade through high school in Germany.

There will be no civilian schools in the occupied zones; informational and advisory service will be provided to aid parents and students in selecting colleges in the near-by countries of Europe. Present plans provide for schools which will be representative of the American standards.

General Notes

There is not very much entertaining owing to the fact that each member of the family is restricted to food rations totaling thirty-five dollars per month. At present there is no fresh milk. Later, when freight planes are in operation, milk will probably be flown in from Denmark and Holland. The post exchanges handle condensed milk and other milk products.

Production of civilian clothing is limited at present, and even this is rationed. It is suggested that dependents bring with them sufficient clothing for at least one year. This situation, too, will improve in time. Laundry, dry cleaning, shoe repair and similar services are provided by the Army exchange facilities.

If you own an automobile that is in good condition, by all means take it. Motoring is one of the finest ways to see Europe, and you will enjoy it. Army wives write that they are greatly depressed at the first glimpse of the bomb-leveled cities. The destruction in Berlin and Munich is horrible, while Cologne was one of the hardest-hit cities. Keep a stern grip on your emotions and sympathy; always remember that the Germans brought this upon themselves and had the Allies not stopped them, America would have been next.

ARMY LIFE IN VIENNA, AUSTRIA

Should you be fortunate enough to have a tour of duty in the Vienna Area Command, by all means enjoy it, because in the near future the four great powers will probably recognize Austria's independence and withdraw their occupation troops. The city of Vienna is occupied jointly by military forces of Great Britain, France, Russia and the United States. Each of the occupying powers has assumed supervision of a section of the city, using existing *Bozirk* (district or ward) boundaries. Bozirk Number 1 is international.

Housing

American Army families live in the United States zone and are assigned quarters in requisitioned houses, apartments or hotels formerly occupied by Austrians. Many of the houses have beautiful gardens, both floral and utility. Although it is up to the individual occupant, the Austrian owners are usually allowed to harvest their gardens owing to the critical food shortages in Vienna.

Shopping Center

Food, fuel, clothing and other necessary as well as luxury items are strictly rationed in Austria. Army personnel do their shopping at the United States Army stores, consisting of sales store, post exchange and beverage store located in the Community Shopping Center.

On opening a family mess account there is an allowance of seventy-five dollars for the initial stockage of staple articles. All sales are on a credit basis.

Identification

A special identification card for residents of Vienna, known as "The Four Powers Pass" written in three languages, is recognized by all four occupying powers and should be carried at all times. Holders of this pass may travel throughout the twenty-one *Bozirks* of Vienna and along the Vienna Tulln Road.

Health

The water supply of Vienna is good; however, tests indicate that it does not meet the Army standard in chlorine content. It is recommended that the water be boiled.

Army medical facilities are available at the 110th Station Hospital.

Government Motor Transportation

Here in Vienna is one time in the Army that you are allowed to ride in United States government vehicles when accompanied by the "head of the household" or his designated representative. However, dependents are not authorized to drive government cars.

There is bus service to the Community Shopping Center. While Vienna transportation systems were badly damaged during the war, most of the streetcar lines are now operating. The cars are smaller and older than our American trolleys, but they still run and will transport you safely to your destination.

Recreation

In Vienna there is a varied program of year-round activities: music, art, entertainment, tours and sports. There are two American motion-picture theaters which show the latest films. Within the United States zone of Austria there has been established a fairyland of vacation spots for weekend excursions or holiday leaves. Untouched by the war, these rest resorts have been selected for their scenic beauty, comforts and seasonal activities. Picturesque hotels high on snow-capped mountains, others on shores of large lakes, locations world famous for skiing, boating, hunting, fishing and mountain climbing are available to Army families.

Schools

There are four categories of schools established in Vienna for the education of American children: nursery, kindergarten, elementary and high school. The school building is located at 85 Gymnasiumstrasso.

An exceptionally well-qualified staff of American teachers is in charge. Teachers of foreign languages and of arts and crafts are qualified Austrian professors. The tuition charges are extremely low.

German Translation

Mrs. Tobin, wife of Lieutenant Colonel James L. Tobin, M.C., of Vienna has made up a most interesting booklet in English and German containing useful household words and phrases, the names of cooking utensils, household items and a Q.M. sales store food list. This should prove helpful equally to the housewife and to the servants in her employ.

For instance, the colonel's lady wishes to tell Gretchen to bake the potatoes. She consults her "La Tobin Booklet." English: Bake the potatoes. German: *Backen sie die Kartoffel.*

She can consult Section II and find that a rolling pin is a *Nudelwalker* in German; that a dining-room table is a *Spoisozimmer-Tisch.* She will also find the list most helpful in making up her commissary order.

German is a guttural language, and not pretty! But learn to speak it.

The Mediterranean Theater

Dependents going to Rome, Leghorn or Caserta, Italy, are required to have passports and the proper visas. Caserta is the headquarters of the United States forces in the Mediterranean theater. It is in the southern part of Italy, about eighteen kilometers north of Naples. The headquarters is located in the winter castle of the former Italian king. Caserta is on two good highways, one of which runs from Rome to Naples, the other to the famous Pontine Marshes (Anzio). It is perfectly situated from the standpoint of being near enough to the mountains for skiing in the winter and near enough to Capri and beautiful beaches in the summer. A week-end visit to Rome is a pleasant diversion. You will enjoy the small Italian villages with their little open-air markets, built around the main square.

At Caserta there will be a representation of all types of troops of the United States occupation forces.

Housing

Italy is having a housing shortage too, so in most cases quarters will be furnished in buildings requisitioned from the Italian government such as furnished hotels, apartments and villas. Whenever the geographic location permits, families will eat in central Army messes. This is necessary because of lack of quarters with kitchens and dining-room facilities.

Laundry of the G.I. type can be done, but articles requiring special starching and ironing had best be done at home. Army wives should equip themselves with washboards, irons etc. The electric current is different, so include a transformer.

Keeping in Touch!

The Army operates five radio stations in Italy, all of which broadcast a variety of American programs. Also, three Army newspapers are available, which provide an adequate coverage of topics of local interest.

Time magazine and *Newsweek* can be obtained in most countries and should be read each week to get news from home that might not appear in the Army papers.

Medical and Dental Service

The Army has adequate medical facilities for taking care of dependents requiring attention. It is suggested, however, that all possible dental treatment be accomplished prior to departure from the United States as some difficulty may be encountered in obtaining new dentures in this theater. It is also suggested that any special medicine not normally available from Army sources be brought.

Here are a few items which either are not available or are hard to obtain in Italy: bridge chairs and tables, lamps, baby beds and carriages, hot-water bottles, cosmetics, special baby foods, books for children, cameras, radios, athletic equipment, clocks, rugs, mirrors, table linen, silver, needles, thread, findings.

The American Red Cross recommends additionally the following:

At least 6 pairs of shoes, mostly walking

1 pair formal shoes

2 pairs dress shoes

1 pair overshoes

Shoelaces

Formal or evening dress . . . jersey preferably

Flannel nightgowns or pajamas

Stockings, anklets

Slacks, play suits

Washable gloves

Suits (more practical)

Blouses and changes of accessories

Cardigans or other sleeved sweaters

Short-sleeved sweaters

Bathing suits and caps

Housecoat to double for beach robe

Fur coat, or warm wool coat

Reversible sport coat

Raincoats

Umbrellas

Lingerie

6 months' supply personal items

Costume jewelry

Electric iron

Coffee maker

Electric hot plate

Can opener and corkscrew

Bluing, Clorox, starch

Clothespins

Skirt hangers

Coat hangers

Sheet music

Army Tours and Trips

Now we are ready for the icing on the cake. Army personnel and their dependents, after they have been in the European theater six months, are eligible to take any or all of the seven special leave tours arranged by the Theater Special Services.

These include trips to Paris, the French Riviera, Rome, Switzerland, Denmark, Holland and the United Kingdom. In addition to the advantage of seeing these fascinating places at a greatly reduced travel rate, the tours are also offered with the idea of promoting Allied good will and of paving the way to an enduring peace.

It is only through direct contact that we can come to a friendly appreciation of other peoples and understand their ways of living. The tours are devised to give the maximum in pleasure and enjoyment to those fortunate enough to avail themselves of this wonderful privilege.

A Few Travel Tips

1. The more knowledge you take to a foreign land, the more you will be able to appreciate the beauties of the country and its people.
2. Know in advance what arts, shrines and landmarks are worth seeing, and learn the stories related to them.
3. Armed with knowledge, you will have an intelligent viewpoint, which is an unmistakable sign of a seasoned traveler. Don't transport only your body from place to place, but travel with your mind.
4. An understanding of the language will open all sorts of doors to you. You will find a foreign-phrase book with four or six languages in parallel rows a valuable help.
5. To take the children costs little more and Darwin says, "Travel changes places from names on maps to pictures in the mind." The plastic minds and memories of childhood retain impressions a lifetime.
6. American boisterousness conceals from others their finer qualities.
7. Foolish spending leaves a trail of inflation. Americans have given the idea that everyone is a millionaire and also in some instances have earned the dreaded phrase, "those horrible American tourists."
8. Have respect for the European or Asiatic in whose country you are traveling. Americans have a tendency to order everyone around in high-pitched voices.

9. Watch not only your thought but your language in speaking of your hosts. Uncomplimentary or derogatory terms are naturally resented. Avoid calling Italians "Wops" or "Dagoes;" Germans "Krauts" or "Heinies;" Chinese "Chinks;" English "Limeys;" Japanese "Nips;" Filipinos "Flips;" Negroes "Niggers." Respect the dignity of man regardless of color, creed or religion.

10. Don't sound off about the superiority of everything American; making constant comparisons is crude. Travel with the idea of promoting a better understanding, and of making other nations respect and like Americans.

American Express Tours

American Express, or AMEX, as it is popularly known in travel lingo, arranges Army tours to Paris, the Riviera and the United Kingdom. This agency, under the supervision of the Theater Special Services, arranges every detail from transportation to hotel accommodations with tips, including the organized tour itinerary and program.

If you are new to European travel, these conducted Army tours under the wing of an intelligent and witty conductor will give you a wonderful bird's-eye view of Europe, which is all you can expect on a first trip. Then, the next trip, go back and concentrate on the Alps, the château country or the section that appeals most to you. The only way to really know a country is to spend some time living there, mingling with the people, not rushing through on a tour.

On a conducted trip you see more for your money, and at a great saving in time. The itinerary is carefully worked out as to train and bus connections. The ideal way, of course, is to be completely independent and to travel vagabond style;

but this is only for the seasoned traveler, who knows the world rather well and considers it his oyster to explore.

Eight Days in Paris!

On the Paris tour, four hundred persons are allowed at a time and the cost ranges between thirty-five and thirty-eight dollars. The price of the tour includes hotel accommodations and meals in Paris, rail transportation, gratuities to hotel servants for rooms and meals, taxi service to and from railway station to hotel and sight-seeing tours of Paris and Versailles with guide lecturers. Military personnel are granted the military rate at a 75-per-cent discount, but civilians must pay the full fare on French railroads. Also, tourists must pay for meals en route on trains or at stations and expenses of a personal nature, such as laundry service, entertainment etc. A minimum of baggage is recommended as porters are still scarce and not always available.

Imagine eight days in Paris! Of course, in that time one can only get a bird's-eye view but the value in taking a conducted tour lies in the fact that you are able to see much more in a limited time and that later you may be able to return and see the sights more leisurely. Somebody once said that "to study Paris is to gain a window that opens out onto the history of Europe."

Just walking through Paris is a very exciting thing. Nostalgically, my mind runs back over past days there . . . to the gay, painted shutters . . . lilacs in bloom in the Bois de Boulogne . . . the lacelike shaft of the Eiffel Tower . . . the bookstalls along the Seine . . . crêpes suzette at the Café de la Paix . . . mass at Notre Dame, an afternoon at Versailles.

Spend every waking moment in Paris seeing all you can. There is no city in the world quite like it.

To the Riviera!

The twelve-day tour of the Riviera leaves from Paris and includes stopovers at fabulous places like Nice, Cannes and Monte Carlo. The Riviera is often spoken of as the paradise of millionaires. Well, the government has generously made this tour available for Army personnel at the low charge of $51.50 and for civilian tourists at $83.50.

Cannes, located eighty-five miles east of Marseille and seventeen miles south of Nice, is one of the oldest and most aristocratic resorts along the Riviera. For over a century it has been a fashionable vacation spot for generations of international society. In its early history it was a small fishing village. In 1834, Lord Brougham, Lord Chancellor of England, was on his way to Nice, and at Cannes he was refused permission to cross the frontier because of a cholera epidemic. He decided to wait at Cannes and liked it so well that he built a villa there. The modern city is built on a broad sweeping curve of the coast, and in peacetime the blue, blue harbor is filled with pleasure yachts from all countries. The streets are lined with palm trees and beautiful hotels.

Be sure to see the old fort built by Richelieu and the bare cell in which the Man in the Iron Mask was imprisoned by Louis XIV for eleven years. His identity is as obscure as that of the Unknown Soldier, though there are various theories. Some of them are that he was the illegitimate son or the twin brother of Louis XIV or the son of Cromwell. In any case, the story goes, his mask was not iron at all, but silk or velvet.

Nice is more on the commercial side, but it has interesting casinos and a beautiful location overlooking the blue Mediterranean. Antibes is more exclusive as a resort than either Nice or Cannes. Here you will find orange groves, acres of olive trees, snow-capped mountain peaks and a profusion of flowers.

Near-by Grasse, about twelve miles from Cannes, is a woman's paradise. It contains over thirty perfume factories, but you will be wise to inquire about duty and taxes before buying. Here you will find about 50,000 acres of violets, jonquils, tuberoses, jasmine, spicy carnations and mignonette. Grasse has another specialty: flowers and fruits crystallized in sugar.

The climate in Monte Carlo is the best thing about it. It is noted for its former gambling casino, its elegant hotels and beautiful surroundings.

The United Kingdom

The seven-day tour of the United Kingdom concentrates on London with organized sight-seeing, then side trips to Windsor, Eton, Stoke Poges, and three days of free time. The tour starts from Paris, and the crossing of the Channel is made by the Dieppe boat, which sails approximately three times a week. The tour price is $83.50 for military personnel and $93.75 for civilians, which includes the transportation, hotel accommodations and other items already noted in the other tours.

While in the United Kingdom, visitors will be under the British food rationing system; also, only ten pounds sterling may be taken into the United Kingdom.

A week is too short a time to acquire a thorough knowledge of English habits and customs but you will soon learn that a drugstore is called a chemist's shop; sodas are sold in milk bars; a saloon is a pub and each pub has its ladies' lounge. No ladies drink at the bar in England. In the theaters, orchestra seats are called stalls, and unreserved seats at the back are in "the pit." Lyons tea shops are good and well dispersed throughout London. It is customary to tip generously.

London covers seven hundred square miles. The West End contains all the theaters, the principal hotels and stores.

In the center is Piccadilly Circus, similar to New York's Times Square. It is the gay center of London and got its name from a house whose owner made foppish trimmings, collars and doublets which were known as "pecadilloes."

Switzerland Tour

The Theater Special Services operates the Switzerland tour on the basis of 400 permitted participation daily. There are fourteen different itineraries and all processing is done at Mulhouse, France. The basic cost of this tour is thirty-six dollars. Two hundred Swiss francs may be spent (approximately forty-six dollars in Switzerland) on watches, music boxes, Swiss embroideries, pastries, wines and other tempting products. Any attempt to acquire additional funds is illegal and violators are subject to disciplinary action.

You will be enchanted with the little Swiss chalets perched on the mountainsides, the long avenues of poplar trees and the fields laid out in little blocks. The valleys all look fertile and well cultivated. It is worth getting up early to see the Jungfrau at sunrise, and perhaps your itinerary will include luncheon at the Rhone Glacier.

A Visit to Denmark

An increased quota in the eight-day Denmark tour now permits 300 personnel to start weekly from Bremen for a trip to the medieval castles and the well-stocked shops of Denmark. The tour includes six full days in Copenhagen. The tour price is forty dollars.

Denmark is the land of the vikings, and it is one of the countries of Europe which seems to have been untouched by the war. You will enjoy the quaint costumes of the people and the tantalizing mixture of Old-World charm and modern progress. Try their wonderful pastry.

Holland Tour

Through the co-operation of the Dutch-Allied Goodwill Committee the Holland seven-day tour has been arranged. Twenty-five persons daily start from Bremen and make sight-seeing trips to Amsterdam, Volendam, The Hague and other important cities. A sail on Lake Westeinderplassen is included along with a trip through Asscher's diamond factory.

The tour price is forty-four dollars paid in Dutch guilders. You can swim in summer at Scheveningen, and it is fun to see the "bathing wagons" drawn by horses. The bathers ride out into the sea, undressing as they go, then dress upon their return. On the streets everybody, young and old, rides bicycles.

You can take a boat through the canals of Amsterdam and see the magical purple windows on the houses along the Heerengrachte; you can see the Volendam fishermen and sail over the Zuider Zee to Marken, the home of wooden shoes and stiff lace caps. There are stiffly starched lace curtains in every window, houseboats anchored along the canals, gorgeous flowers—beautiful geraniums and tulips—in every yard. In Leyden, where the Pilgrim Fathers lived, you will find quaint little houses with dormer windows. You will see swans serenely floating along the canals, that are filled with water lilies. Gaily painted windmills are in evidence. Wagons of flowers line the roadside. Poppies grow wild and at the Aalsmeer Flower Auction you can buy great armloads of roses, tulips, sweet peas, chrysanthemums in season for practically nothing at all. In the beautiful landscaped parks garlands of pink creeper roses swing between the posts.

At the Holland Club you will meet pretty Dutch hostesses, and perhaps you might ask one of them to help you buy old copper, silver, Delft plates or Dutch tiles to take home as souvenirs.

Visit the famous cheese mart in Alkmaar, and don't miss having a cup of the most delicious hot chocolate in the world.

The Rome Tour

Processing for the Rome tour starts at Mulhouse, France, and the basic tour cost is twenty-four dollars. There are additional charges on this tour as much time is spent traveling before one arrives in southern Italy. Four and a half days are spent in Rome proper, which again only gives the sight-seer a mere glimpse.

St. Peter's, of course, will be one of the *musts* of your tour, along with the Coliseum. If possible, you should arrange to drive out to the Villa de Este, famous for its gardens, and no doubt, having come this far south, you will arrange to visit Naples and the ruins of Pompeii, and take the famous Amalfi Drive, including a visit to Capri.

Tours in Austria and Bavaria

The Special Services has also arranged special tours with Munich the central point: boat trips on the Rhine and the Danube, one-day tours to Berchtesgaden, to Oberammergau; half-day sight-seeing tours to Dachau Concentration Camp, Ettal Monastery; trips to the Bavaria wonderland of winter sports; to Salzburg, famous for its music festivals; to the beautiful Austrian lake resort region.

For Army wives fortunate enough to spend a year or two in the European theater, unlimited opportunities are offered in travel. Switzerland has splendid schools for the Army juniors; the Sorbonne in Paris presents special courses; for Army personnel stationed in Heidelberg, Berlin or Vienna each in its own field offers specific advantages whether it be languages, music, ballet or art.

This type of duty offers a "university afloat," a Rhodes scholarship and the cultural advantages of a foreign finishing school all rolled into one on a G.I. basis. Early in the game learn the *plus* values of life by carefully evaluating your money and time.

Cultivate the art of looking for beauty and of enjoying whatever your present station offers. Many Army women make a habit of rushing through life, then reminiscing on "remember what a good time we used to have in Shanghai." Enjoy the present; it is all one can ever be sure of, really.

When I mention the art of looking for beauty, I mean the little things in life. It may be a snow scene, a bird darting by or a sleeping baby. A light in a window bespeaks life and drama. Maybe you are buying tulips in Amsterdam, violets in Paris or oranges at a market in Naples. Whether you buy or not, you have the capacity and privilege of taking away with you the months of sunshine stored up in the scarlet of the tulips, the blue of the violets and the gold of the oranges. The look in the eyes of the man or woman who proudly harvested them can be carried along, too; and the look of admiration in your eyes will make the merchant happy and bring back the romance inherent in his business. If we want more out of life, we must give thanks and applaud it!

FAR EAST COMMAND—ARMY LIFE IN JAPAN, KOREA,
ON GUAM AND OKINAWA

In the short period of occupation in Japan, the Americans
under General Douglas MacArthur have made great strides.
To transform Japan, the most militaristic nation on earth,
into a democracy and a peace-loving nation requires more
than the provision of the new Japanese Constitution re-
nouncing arms as an instrument of policy. It means taking
away the power from those who waged Japan's last war and
keeping it away from those who might want to start a new
one. It means so educating the younger Japanese that they
will not want to risk defeat a second time, like the stubborn Germans after World War I. It means teaching the
younger Japanese to appreciate their new advantages so
thoroughly that they will never again respond to military
propaganda.

In January of 1946 General MacArthur severed the connection between Shintoism and the state, and at that time
the emperor renounced his claims to divinity. It is hoped
that this will eventually serve as the moral basis for political
democracy in Japan.

In addition to the right of freedom of worship, the Japanese women have been given the right of suffrage. In 1946
they voted for the first time in history. Further reforms
are in store, the net result of which will be to take the whole
provincial government out of the hands of the national
government and to put it in the hands of the people.

THE FAR EAST COMMAND

The Far East Command consists of ground, sea and air
forces in Japan, Korea, the Philippines, the Ryukyus, Mari-

anas, Bonins and Volcanos. Supreme headquarters is located in Tokyo, the capital of Japan. The headquarters of the Eighth Army is located in Yokohama; the I Corps is stationed in Kyoto, the IX Corps at Sendai and the XXIV Corps in Seoul, Korea. There is a base command at Kobe, and a Korea base command in Jinsen.

The Air Forces now operate under the new title of Far East Air Forces (FEAF), replacing the former designation of Pacific Air Command (PACUSA). The Fifth Air Force is stationed at Nagoya, Japan; the Seventh Air Force at Hickam Field, Hawaii; the Thirteenth Air Force at Clark Field, Philippine Islands; the Twentieth Air Force at Guam; and the 1st Air Division at Okinawa, Ryukyus. (Of course, the forces and stations mentioned at the present time are subject to change; but this is the present setup.)

Housing Conditions

Dependents were first allowed to go to Japan in July of 1946. Both officers and enlisted men worked faithfully and hard repairing and redecorating—in some instances building—quarters for their families. In every bulletin sent out, General MacArthur made it clear that "personnel must agree to accept such abodes as may be made available to them." In other words, he warned that conditions were rugged and that Army wives should be prepared to do a bit of pioneering when necessary. All housing units at present are of low-cost frame structure and owing to the limitation on material and labor are below the standards of such housing in the United States.

The permanent housing phase of the dependents' housing program is getting under way. The apartment in the future will be of two-story construction with kitchen, living and dining rooms on the first floor and the bedrooms and bath upstairs. Each unit is to be completely furnished with all of the essentials including refrigeration, heat, dishes, rugs, linen and curtains.

Apartments, hotels and in some cases private residences have been taken over by the government. However, at this early date it is not fair to set much store by this temporary housing condition. In time conditions will change; regular Army compounds or posts with permanent quarters may be built, so take it all in your stride. Some type of home has been planned for you, otherwise you would not be given transportation; so make the best of it, and should you draw a typical Japanese home with sliding doors and windows of paper, enjoy it. By the law of averages, a miniature Japanese garden may go along with it and such a garden can be incredibly lovely.

The water supply in Japan varies with the locality. Water for drinking and cooking purposes must be chlorinated before using. Army personnel is allowed to buy food only through Army sources. Powdered and evaporated milk are available, and in time the commissaries and post exchanges will provide special baby foods. Except for "fancy groceries" the commissaries carry almost everything.

Medical Care

Adequate hospital installations and facilities are to be maintained in Japan to provide medical care for civilian dependents. Certain hospitals will have out-patient service and be equipped to give dental and optical repair service. Such hospitals will also be staffed with personnel qualified in obstetrics, gynecology and pediatrics. Medicines will be available at Army dispensaries but particular brands of household remedies or many well-known proprietary medicines such as laxatives etc., should be brought along. The post exchanges are not allowed to handle such items, and there are no American-style drugstores in Japan to date.

Make arrangements to have certain special items that may be needed shipped to Tokyo or to your station. It generally takes ten to fifteen days to get a letter to the States, and at least one month for a package from the States to reach Japan.

Immunization against smallpox, typhoid, typhus and tetanus are required within twelve months prior to departure for Japan; children should also receive immunization against diphtheria and whooping cough. Additional requirements are cholera shots within six months of going to Okinawa, Guam, the Philippines, China and Japan.

"Plague vaccination is not a pre-requisite to travel but may be given to all one year of age and over, upon arrival at destination at discretion of command concerned."

"If travel by air is indicated, a written certificate from a medical officer must be obtained verifying that the individual has been properly immunized, is free of lice, is not suffering from a communicable disease, and is not likely to introduce disease as a result of his travel."

Schools

No Japanese schools are suitable for the education of American children. The few parochial schools that existed have had their plants damaged or destroyed and their instructors removed. It is planned to establish the first eight grades of school in each large community by civilians suitably trained. High schools will be organized in a similar manner.

There are available, through various schools in the United States, correspondence courses which will enable parents to teach their own children or hire tutors to do so.

Climate and Clothing

The climate of Japan is similar to the central section of the United States. During five months of the year heavy overcoats, ski clothes for children, and fur coats will be comfortable. During the spring months, which incidentally are lovely, suits, both winter and lightweight types, will be practical. Cotton and lightweight summer clothes will be useful the rest of the year. In the long periods of rain and dampness in the fall you will need raincoats, galoshes and boots.

Inflation has hit Japan, too, and prices are about ten times as high as before the war. There is little to buy, unless one wishes to patronize the black markets, and then the quality is poor. Take plenty of shoes with you, as Army wives in Japan say the thin-soled ones seem to wear out very quickly. Several pairs of good heavy walking shoes for shopping or walking around town will save your better ones for dress occasions. The Japanese have done an amazing job of clearing away the debris and rubble, but walking is still pretty rough in spots.

Recreation

Recreation facilities abound in Japan. Within easy motor or train distance there are mountain, lake and seashore resorts where the Army operates hotels. There are also golf courses and tennis courts; be sure to take plenty of sports equipment with you. Fishing (both salt and fresh water) is good, boating, mountain climbing and skiing are popular.

Army movies and stage shows are scheduled, and sym-

phony concerts are held weekly. The service libraries are
well stocked with recent fiction and nonfiction books.

Japanese train service is good; the trains are modern and
include day coaches and Pullman cars. Some of them have
been taken over by the Army and include regularly scheduled
military trains operating between all important cities
throughout the islands of Honshu and Hokkaido with access
to many resorts. This transportation is available to dependents.

Try to visit Nikko, famous for its shrines, Nagoya, Nara
and Kyoto, the old capital. If the cherry-blossom festival is
revived, it is a beautiful pageant you should not miss seeing,
in April.

As for entertaining, the ever present cocktail party comes
first. Small seated dinners, large ones, too, for those in the
upper official brackets, are popular. Teas, morning coffees
and Coca-Cola parties, plus bridge luncheons, seem to take
one round the clock.

Private Automobiles

The roads in Japan are generally poor; however, short
trips to near-by ocean and mountain areas can be made from
the larger cities. The streets in the cities are narrow and
rough, and present a problem to driving civilian-type
vehicles. However, a car in good condition will be a joy.
Maintenance is the big problem because at the present time
there are no garages.

Surplus jeeps may be bought, and "it is said" that they can
be made quite comfortable. I have yet to see a comfortable
one, regardless of cushions, side curtains and paint jobs!
They do provide transportation, however, and are more
easily maintained in operation than other private vehicles.

What to Take to Japan

Chintz or drapery material	Candles
Lamps	Assorted household tacks
Washable rugs	Silverware
Cocktail glasses	Linen
After-dinner coffees	Picture wire, hooks
Electric icebox	Laundry starch
Electric iron	Clothes hangers
Electric toaster	Silver polish
Small radio, extra tubes	Wax paper
Beds	Paper napkins
Springs	Kitchen utensils
Mattresses	Kitchen toweling
Uniforms for servants	

Electric clocks and large radio and victrola combination machines are too much for the electric current of 100 volts and 50 cycles.

There are no storage facilities in Tokyo, so check and double-check on your list of household goods. In time all quarters will be adequately furnished so it is suggested that only a minimum amount of household goods be shipped to Japan.

Servants

Most of the servants are untrained, but they are quick to learn and if properly instructed develop into wonderful cooks, maids and laundresses. Each one does his own assigned task, so it is necessary to have several in a well-staffed household. They are most courteous, and there is much smiling and bowing from the waist. Army wives in dealing with servants should be careful to modulate their voices and to speak in low tones. Americans are prone to raise their voices in the effort to make themselves understood . . . the same idea as screaming during a long-distance telephone call. Loud voices are considered bad form in Japan as in other civilized countries, so a servant loses respect for his mistress if she shouts her commands. The wages are approximately ten dollars a month and up for each servant. Owing to the rate of exchange of the yen, Army wives may find the prices of wages high.

Korea

For those dependents proceeding on to Korea, most of the above information is applicable except that the food situation in Korea is critical, and only food that is furnished by the Q.M. is available. There is ice only in limited quantities. Certain leaf vegetables, fresh fish and some fruit may be purchased from local civilian markets at inflated prices.

Dependents are requested to bring a twelve months' supply of toilet preparations, cosmetics, perfumes, personal items.

Houses and apartments are very scarce, and an effort is made to locate dependents as near as practicable to Army installations where Servicemen are on duty. However, some installations are located in areas where there is no available housing for dependents. This is a temporary condition, and in the near future it is hoped that housing conditions will improve when plans for bases are more permanent. I am only recording the score as it is today, in the early days of the occupation, so don't become too discouraged.

There is also, at the present, a very limited amount of household furnishings provided by the Army. Here is what the Q.M. can issue: canvas cots, folding chairs, folding tables, O.D. wool blankets. (If you have never slept under them you have something to learn! There is little warmth in them unless you tuck yourself in between four or six, and then the weight of the blankets will make you so tired by morning that you will not wish to rise and shine. By all means, take your own woolly blankets, and a down comforter or two if you can manage.) There are no cookstoves nor refrigerators available at present, but don't worry about this because the Q.M. has a way of rustling up the essentials. You may get a homemade ice chest made by an enterprising soldier carpenter, but it will answer the purpose. And from some place, someone will also requisition a stove, you will find!

It is advised that electric, gasoline or kerosene cooking stoves, also refrigerators, be brought by individuals if possible. It is not practical to take a gas stove.

Expensive furniture should not be taken to Korea because of the damage inflicted in transporting. There are no household furnishings available in Korea for sale, which brings it down to where you will be expected to carry your second best with you, provided you have acquired several grades of furniture in your short career! Of course, no one would want to risk a Steinway grand piano or valuable antiques on a detail of this sort, but personally I always like my furniture and household goods around me wherever I live. Most Army families completely refurnish and replenish about every ten years anyway, so perhaps you may as well use the best you have and enjoy it.

Take all of your clothes, both old and new, and plan on enough to see you through your entire stay.

It doesn't sound too promising for taking a car owing to the lack of good roads, lack of servicing facilities, lack of garage and storage space. Just to make it harder, gasoline is rationed. Let your conscience be your guide, but if I wanted to take my own automobile I would, and hope for better roads, a garage and unrationed gas. They will all come

in time. There *are* movies libraries and parks and play-
grounds are promised later. The Red Cross conducts sight-
seeing tours; so you are assured there is really something to
see, after all!

Personal Business Arrangements

Only yen currency may be used in Japan, so upon arrival
you can exchange your States dollars for Japanese yen. The
present rate of exchange is fifteen yen to the American
dollar.

It is suggested that banking accounts be maintained in
the United States.

All adult persons before their departure for overseas duty
should set their affairs in order. In view of the difference in
state laws, and the present difficulties to be encountered
in finding persons in Japan who are authorized to administer
oaths required on legal documents in compliance with state
laws, these matters should not be postponed until arrival in
Tokyo.

1. Power of attorney: Numerous circumstances may arise
   while dependents are absent from the United States in
   which it will be necessary for someone to act for them.
   Under such circumstances personal affairs can usually be
   conducted to the best advantage by an agent or attorney
   acting in your name and behalf. The authority to so act
   may be granted conveniently through a power of attorney
   to a member of the family remaining in the States or to
   any other person of legal age or capacity.
2. Important papers: All important papers, such as insurance
   policies, should be assembled and placed in a safe-deposit
   box in a conveniently located bank.
3. Wills: Both husband and wife should make wills. Consideration should be given to the making of a will dispos-

ing of estates in accordance with personal wishes and the laws of legal residence.

4. Debts and obligations: Satisfactory arrangements should be made for payments or the receipt of payments during your absence.

5. Income tax: You should familiarize yourself with obligations concerning tax returns and payments.

6. Insurance: All policies should be analyzed to see that the protection desired is provided for. This includes property insurance.

Personal Observations in Japan

I had the good fortune to visit Japan twice before the war, and it is a country that always has interested me. My first visit was in the autumn when the hillsides were aglow with yellow, bronze and golden chrysanthemums. However, my most wonderful remembrance of the beauty of Japan is the springtime, when I had the privilege of attending the cherry-blossom festival held in Kyoto.

The cherry is to the Japanese what the rose is to Americans. "It is the subject of innumerable poems, and every year vast crowds make excursions to the more famous plantations. The cherry blossom is said to typify the Japanese view of life. It is a blaze of glory while it lasts; but its life is short. It does not fade gradually, its end is sudden, like that of a soldier killed in battle. It inspires a gaiety tinged with sadness, the sentiment dominant in the Japanese character." (From *Traveler from Tokyo*, by John Morris, New York, Sheridan House, 1944.)

Customs

The Japanese set great store by ceremony and the avoidance of giving offense. That the more intelligent Japanese actually regarded the emperor as a divinity is questionable; however, the leaders of Japan in the expansion of nationalist feeling exploited the idea to gain their own ends. The outward signs by which the emperor's divinity was proclaimed were many and various. For instance, no one was allowed to look down upon His Highness from a higher level. As a result, when he was due to pass along certain streets, the police ordered the lowering of all blinds on upper windows.

When the emperor appeared in public, onlookers were supposed to avert their gaze; also, it was customary to remove one's overcoat regardless of the weather. "Every school in Japan had a photograph of the 'Son of Heaven,' and in a fire, earthquake or any other calamity his portrait had to be saved at all costs." There are cases on record of a school principal losing his life in an attempt to save the imperial photograph, or having failed, committing suicide.

The Japanese marriage customs are unique; marriage is more a family affair than a personal one. A go-between or matchmaker makes all the arrangements and the strictest formalities are observed. Adoption is prevalent, especially where there are no male heirs. Also, if a man wishes to divorce his wife and is anxious to show the world that he bears her no ill will, often he adopts her as his daughter. The Japanese do not connect love with marriage, though sometimes it develops. The object of marriage to them is procreation, the overwhelming desire for the continuance of the family, which is all intertwined with ancestor worship. Most married men, if they can afford it, keep a mistress. Sometimes the mistress comes to live under the same roof with the wife; quite often it is said the women become good friends (oftener not, I imagine).

The geisha is a subject of great interest to Americans. She is not, as popularly supposed, always a prostitute, although many geishas have special admirers with whom they live. The chief requisite is that they be pretty, and as early as the age of seven they are taught to exploit their charms. Their primary object in life is to entertain the male. You will have to get your further information on geishas from your husband, as they do not appear at any party at which ladies are present.

The formal Japanese hairdress is intriguing. When a girl marries, she has her hair dressed in the traditional manner. Should she have short hair, she wears a wig. The make-up that accompanies this style of headdress is the painting of the face and neck with a dead-white liquid; only the lower lip is rouged. The traditional style of hairdressing is very laborious, and to keep the hair from becoming disarranged requires one's sleeping on a wooden pillow, which looks more like a little wooden neck rest. (I prefer mine made of satin and stuffed with kapok.) The wooden pillow is quite restful, however, but I am afraid, in time, might present the problem of a dowager's hump at the base of the neck.

During the war, women's patriotic societies picketed the streets remonstrating with any well-dressed women who happened to wander by. There was a government regulation against wearing expensive and richly embroidered kimonos, and any display or ostentation of wealth was decidedly frowned upon. Permanent waves were also forbidden during the war.

John Morris says, in *Traveler from Tokyo*, "Japanese babies are usually carried papoose fashion on the mother's or the nurse's back . . . their legs straddling the waist of the person carrying them. The result is that most Japanese, to some extent, are bow-legged. Of course, squatting on the floor is not conducive to well-shaped legs. The Japanese realize this and have an expression which means 'legs like a giant radish'."

Naturally, Japanese women are at a distinct disadvantage in short skirts, so they walk with tiny mincing steps trying to keep the knees together, which in turn makes them walk pigeon-toed. It is said that geishas are trained to walk in this way by holding a thin piece of paper between their knees.

The Japanese have a passion for Occidental clothing, which really is not becoming to them. The men affect morning clothes, striped trousers, cutaway coats; even the humblest official possesses the formal outfit. The higher officials wear top hats; others don anything in the way of headgear that happens to be convenient—a soft cap, beret or straw sailor. Again, the government officials usually wear sparkling patent-leather shoes, but the lesser fry would just as soon wear tennis shoes with a morning coat.

Bowler hats are also popular, but for some reason they are worn only with kimonos, not with Western dress. The Japanese wear their shoes many sizes too large for them because it is the custom to remove shoes before entering a home. This is one reason why Japanese housewives have such clean matting floors.

Nothing arouses any comment in the way of styles or clothing worn in Japan except a foreigner in a kimono. Then the Japanese are most critical. Have a care as to the material you choose and the size of the pattern and its color. This applies to both men and women. Usage demands that the older the wearer the smaller the pattern and the more drab the color of the material. The Japanese kimono is most comfortable as a lounging robe during the humid Japanese summers.

The Japanese are omnivorous readers, particularly of magazines. Often they will line up in a news agent's shop and read them for nothing. Also, when they buy a magazine, they do not seem to mind if it is dirty, and almost torn to pieces from reading and handling.

Mr. Morris makes the comment: "It is said the Japanese language is about as hard to conquer as Mt. Everest." But it is not too hard to learn to speak it. Americans have difficulty in acquiring a completely monotonous voice, which is one of the prime requisites. To learn to read and write the Japanese language is something else again. It is made up of some five or six thousands of ideographs, and there are no fixed rules as to whether the writing shall be in horizontal lines or in vertical columns. Many Japanese, even, give up in despair and claim that the constant looking at the dancing and swimming ideographs impairs their eyesight. Well, certainly the Japanese are the most bespectacled nation in the world, but they are proud of it "because they claimed before the war to be the biggest manufacturers of spectacles in the world."

Baseball, boxing and mountain climbing are their most popular sports. Again, they like to copy everything European, so they have their Japanese Alps, on a small scale, of course. The Japanese people have a great appreciation of art and beauty, and nowhere can nature be so well appreciated as in the mountains. No doubt you will climb Mount Fuji, Japan's highest and most widely advertised mountain.

You will be surprised at the flimsy structure of Japanese houses. They have no solid foundations, and the partitions are of paper screens which make it possible to arrange rooms as one wishes. The floors are covered with mats about three inches thick which fit into slots in the wooden floors. There is little or no furniture except low tables; these are brought in when required. There are no pictures except a scroll or painting in one corner of the room which forms an alcove. A beautiful vase with a flower arrangement, or a work of art in bronze is placed in front of the scroll.

Modern Japanese usually have one room furnished with European furniture to prove to foreigners that they are modern. It is closed off. In their living quarters, they have no beds but lay their bedding on the floor at night and keep it stored in wall cupboards by day.

The Japanese are very clean, and there are thousands of public baths which men and women use at the same time. Many of their restaurants are named after famous eating places in the States; for instance, the Rainbow Room, far from commanding a view of the city, is situated underground. There is a regular chain of "southern" kitchens which specialize in our famous American dishes such as fried chicken, waffles, strawberry shortcake, but everything is a pale and sickly copy of the original. One or two experiences will convince you. The Japanese admire the looks of food, the beauty of the containers in which it is served and the decoration of the room much more than the taste of the food.

Sukiyaki is the only Japanese dish I ever learned to like. It is made of strips of beef cooked with vegetables over a small brazier; the guests take turns in stirring it and attending to the cooking. At the last, two raw eggs are broken over the top of the mixture, both of which could be dispensed with to suit my taste. Eels are a great delicacy, and the Japanese eat great quantities of seaweed.

"Another popular dish is *Tempura* and it is made of various kinds of shellfish, lobsters, shrimp fried in batter and served very hot. A bit on the greasy, heavy side!" says Mr. Morris.

We stayed at the Imperial Hotel in Tokyo, and from the moment we docked at Nagasaki, I felt as if we were under surveillance. Although everyone was extremely polite, I am sure our every move was watched. We had to check our camera, which was amusing to me in view of the fact that many Japanese in America went about armed with a Leica and binoculars for twenty-five years before Pearl Harbor.

The Imperial Hotel was built by Frank Lloyd Wright. It was one of the first buildings in Tokyo to be built on earth-quake-proof principles. It rests on a bed of semi-liquid mud instead of being built on a solid foundation, and it is said that even in a slight quake the Imperial may shake like jelly, but it does not fall down. If I lived in Tokyo, I would dash to the Imperial at the first tremor!

I shall always remember the beautiful pink, white and coral azaleas and the Japanese miniature trees that decorated the lobby of the hotel. You should make it a point to visit Tanaka's Garden in Tokyo and invest in one of the lovely "tray gardens."

ARMY LIFE ON OKINAWA SHIMA

With good weather, it takes a little less than two weeks by boat from Hawaii to Okinawa. On this voyage you will have the thrill of crossing the international date line. In addition, depending upon the time of year and the prevailing monsoons, a small typhoon may be encountered to relieve the tedium of the journey.

When your ship docks at Buckner Bay, you will have your first glimpse of the beautiful tropical island, the lush green of the lowlands, the mountains and the blue-greens of the water. The beaches are still strewn with wrecked ships, tanks and supplies left from the invasion and some from disastrous typhoons. The Army has cleaned up a great part of it, but one can still get some idea of how it must have looked during the war.

Typhoons are prevalent in this part of the Pacific, and they are given girls' names. The first alphabet has been exhausted and letter B of the second alphabet is up. In October of 1945 it was the typhoon "Louise" which did such terrific damage. Army tent cities, Quonset towns and pre-fab communities dot the island now.

The climate and scenery of Okinawa is similar to that of Florida. The lovely cool nights are comparable to those in San Francisco, and it stays cool as long as the sun is hidden. The summers are very hot but pleasant with the near-by beaches. The rainy season is similar to that of the Philippines.

Hookworm in the soil makes it dangerous to eat anything grown underground, and most native children have the disease from going barefooted. There are native tombs called *haka* all over Okinawa. During the war they provided the Japanese with almost invulnerable gun emplacements. They are square, boxlike tombs, and the more expensive ones are turtle-back shaped. The Okinawan may live in a modest home, but he will spend ten times the cost of it on his tomb. The Okinawans are pleasant and friendly. They make much of each transport of newly arrived Army personnel. The native children line the roadsides to call the one English word they know: "Hello." All of their English words end in "o"; for instance, when they master the word "nice" it is "nice-o." Our government is gradually repatriating the natives, aiding them in building new villages or helping them in rebuilding old ones.

The natives have two kinds of homes, the Japanese type or the more affluent home with a red-tiled roof. The wooden, Japanese type of home usually has a thatched room. The interior is furnished with grass mats on the floor, low tables with tea and sake or wine sets, shrine niches for religious moments and and sliding bamboo screens which can be opened to the outdoors or closed against the typhoons and cold weather. Everyone has a small garden, perhaps on the side of the mountain, terraced to retain the water.

Army families are limited as to the use of water and electricity. The electric lights flicker and fade at the most inopportune times—ironing is interrupted, cooking simply stops at times and the story persists about the Army wife who baked her Thanksgiving turkey over a candle.

Money resembles cigarette coupons and is military currency. The natives are paid in Japanese yen, and there is no bank or even a notary public, so no legal business can be accomplished. As Peggy Lindsay, to whom I am indebted for her letter to the *Air Force Woman's Magazine*, writes, "It is a rare experience to have money mean so little, and to have no place to spend it."

Army wives should take several bolts of cretonne, chintz or other material from which to make slip covers and curtains. The following electrical equipment will prove a convenience when the current is on: an electric toaster, electric hot plate, electric mixmaster and electric iron. Take two old-fashioned flatirons if you can find the latter in your mother's attic or in a secondhand store.

There are no stores on Okinawa, and your shopping is limited to the commissary and post exchange. There are no cosmetics to be had, so lay in a good supply of your favorite soaps, powders and perfumes.

Outside of salt and pepper there is a dearth of condiments; so stock up on spices, herbs and condiments that give zest to your cooking. Another good suggestion is to visit a good dime store and stock up on essentials like thumbtacks, curtain rods, picture wire, clothes pins and the hundred and one things you need in settling a house.

Take sturdy walking shoes, plenty of slacks and play clothes and as many evening gowns as you can manage. There are three officers' clubs, and dances are held on Wednesday and Saturday nights and on Sunday afternoon.

There is a movie every night, a bridge club which meets twice a month, swimming from the beach and deep-sea fishing for those who enjoy this type of sport.

There is a Night Watchman's Committee composed of G.I. sitters who consider it a privilege to watch babies for fifty cents an hour. A well-organized and enthusiastic Women's Club is in progress whose members work with the Red Cross and in the Thrift Shop. A grade school has been organized with Army officers and their wives forming the school board. The Calvert and California State School System is their guide. The University of Okinawa is run by the Army.

The Thrift Shop is really a Woman's Exchange because here articles one doesn't use are sold to someone else who needs them. Okinawan maids are available, and though untrained they are eager to learn and anxious to please.

Each month ships bring new dependents to "Okie," and it is a gala day when a ship docks. Everyone turns out to meet the ship in gaiety and celebration.

ARMY LIFE ON GUAM

Guam is the largest and the most beautiful island of the Mariana group. It was first discovered by Magellan in 1565. Three years later Miguel de Lopez Legaspi took possession of the archipelago in the name of the crown of Spain. It was under Spanish rule until 1898, when Spain ceded it to the United States. Since that time it has been used as a naval station presided over by a chief executive, an officer of the United States Navy with the title of governor who is appointed by the President.

The island is only 30 miles long and 6 miles wide and covers an area of 226 square miles. It has a healthy and agreeable climate with a rainy season comparable to that of the Philippines. When the monsoon winds blow, typhoons often follow and Guam has suffered some severe earthquakes.

The natives are called Chamorros and can be trained to be good servants. They speak a Malay dialect interwoven with Tagalog. Sword grass abounds, part of the island is jungle and the finest coconut trees in the world grow on Guam. Breadfruit trees are plentiful, and the ilang-ilang trees which are famous for their perfume. The chief exports are coconut oil and copra. There are no snakes on the island, but plenty of nonpoisonous scorpions and centipedes.

Chapter XI

ILLNESS AND ARMY HOSPITALIZATION

Officers are entitled to the medical services provided by agencies of the Army. Whenever practicable, the wife, dependent children, and servants of officers, and dependent members of the family when residing with an officer, are likewise furnished medical service without cost to the officer.

—Army Regulations

H OSPITALIZATION and medical and dental attention, while not classed as pay or as an allowance, are definite emoluments to which an officer is entitled. At a large Army post there is always a station hospital, and smaller garrisons are equipped with a dispensary, at least. During an emergency, it is impossible for the Medical Department to administer to personnel other than enlisted men and commissioned officers, except in cases demanding immediate attention.

The ranking medical officer or post surgeon is assisted by a staff of doctors and an especially trained staff. There is always an O.D. or medical officer of the day who is on call or on the alert at all times. The post surgeon has certain calling hours, and these hours should be respected except in cases of immediate danger, emergency or a definite relapse in a patient's condition. For instance, if Junior has been running a slight temperature all day, do not wait until ten o'clock at night to phone the hospital to send an O.D. "at

329

once." Doctors, even though they are O.D.'s appreciate consideration; however, should something serious develop, such as convulsions, by all means telephone for the O.D. Medical officers are more than willing to serve, and they regard legitimate calls not only as part of their duty but as an opportunity to serve their fellow man.

If a patient is at all able, he should go or be taken to the hospital during outpatient clinic hours, which vary on different posts, though the usual hours are from nine to twelve in the forenoon or from one to three in the afternoon. This information will be covered in *Post Regulations.* Light, cheery waiting rooms, equipped with magazines and current newspapers, are usually available. Upon entering the Outpatient Service, give your name and the required medical data or case history to the orderly or nurse in attendance. Then wait your turn and, except in emergency cases, never try to get special service or earlier attention. Everyone in the waiting room is probably as anxious as you are to get away to other tasks and duties. "Pulling rank" for special service causes decidedly unfavorable comment.

Infants and small children who need scheduled medical attention should be placed in the hands of a good civilian pediatrician if you can possibly afford it. Army doctors are entirely too busy to attend to weighing babies, changing formulas and the hundred and one needs that infants and small children seem to require. If you go regularly to a good pediatrician, you will feel free to call upon him for advice or service at any hour of the day or night. Please do not misunderstand or misconstrue this suggestion! Army doctors can and will render pediatric service, if time and their duties permit; but, remember again, except in cases of sudden illness or extreme emergency, women and children still come in the category of "camp followers" and should not expect service from busy Army doctors. Dependents must necessarily be cared for only after the needs of the enlisted and officer personnel have been administered to, as soldiers rank first service. It is decidedly unethical to go to a civilian doctor during the day and then call an Army doctor at night. It looks as if you were pitting the skill of one doctor against that of the other, which is very unfair.

Note: Most Army hospitals have qualified pediatricians available today.

Dental officers cannot find enough hours in the day to take care of the molars of Uncle Sam's fighting men, let alone take time out to straighten Johnny's teeth or do the intricate and time-taking work required for fillings, bridgework and inlays. If an emergency arises, however, Army dentists are willing to give service. Since the war, the Army provides competent dental care for dependents when facilities are available. If they are not, consult a good dentist in town, not the most expensive, but a reputable one with whom you can arrange to make monthly payments if there is to be a long-drawn-out piece of work, such as putting bands on Johnny's teeth. If you were in civilian life, you most assuredly would expect to pay for this service, and so it is in the Army. Of course, you may be fortunate enough to be stationed at a small garrison not overcrowded with troops; in such case often the Medical Department will administer to all types and kinds of requests; so accept their services and be thankful.

ARMY NURSES

The Army Nurse Corps of the Medical Department is composed of graduate nurses who have the same relative rank as commissioned officers in the Army. Having passed a satisfactory examination to determine her efficiency, the

Army nurse is appointed to the corps and is commissioned as a second lieutenant.

She is accorded the same obedience from enlisted men and patients in and about military hospitals as is accorded commissioned officers of grades corresponding to their relative rank.

While Army Nurses are not eligible as members of courts-martial, they may prefer charges against any member of the military service. They are entitled to the same privileges and allowances, except mileage, as are prescribed for commissioned officers of grades corresponding to their relative rank.

—*Army Regulations.*

An Army nurse enters the Service as a second lieutenant, and the requirements are, in addition to being a registered nurse, that she be between twenty-two and thirty years of age, a graduate of an accredited high school, unmarried and a citizen of the United States. The highest office in the corps is that of superintendent, which position carries with it the rank of colonel, and the superintendent of the Army Nurse Corps is appointed by the Secretary of War. All other appointments are made by the Surgeon General with the approval of the Secretary of War. The superintendent has six assistants with the rank of major. Chief nurses have the rank of major and captain, and below this grade the nurses are first and second lieutenants depending upon their length of service.

The reason for quoting regulations in regard to the status of Army nurses is this: Many Army wives do not know that Army nurses are commissioned officers of the Army, and these fine women deserve all the consideration and respect that is their just due. Army wives, who receive the best of care in the hospitals, are sometimes not too thoughtful or courteous to the Army nurses outside in the social circles of the post. They are definitely a most important part of the

Army, and should be included in the social life of the post. I am sure this attitude is not intentional, but since it is one of thoughtlessness and ingratitude, it should be corrected.

The Army Nurse Corps established a magnificent record by its heroic services in World Wars I and II. The top strength of the corps was 57,000 nurses, and over 1,400 nurses received military decorations in World War II. Seventeen nurses were killed in action. Five hospital ships have been named for nurses, and one general hospital bears a nurse's name.

ARMY HOSPITALS

Army hospitals necessarily have a set of regulations as long as a Canal Search Warrant, but a few general tips will suffice to acquaint the Army wife with the general requirements. The general hospitals are:

Walter Reed	Washington, D. C.
Brooke General	Fort Sam Houston, Texas
Army and Navy Hospital	Hot Springs, Arkansas
Fitzsimmons	Denver, Colorado
Letterman	San Francisco, California
William Beaumont	El Paso, Texas
Madigan	Tacoma, Washington
McCornack	Pasadena, California
Murphy	Waltham, Massachusetts
Oliver	Augusta, Georgia
Percy Jones	Fort Custer, Michigan
Pratt	Coral Gables, Florida
Tilton	Fort Dix, New Jersey
Valley Forge	Phoenixville, Pennsylvania
Tripler	Honolulu, Territory of Hawaii

Each large command or post has its own station hospital, and each small post has a dispensary or clinic, with medical officers in attendance.

If you are to be a patient in an Army hospital, there are several things you should know before entering. Should you not be a bed patient, and are able, you may be asked to make your own bed. This is no hardship, yet some Army women object strenuously, even when they can see that the busy nurses need a helping hand. The meals are served at the most unusual hours; in fact, after a week's sojourn in the average Army hospital, you will find yourself losing all track of time. Breakfast varies, but it is early enough to remind you of your convent boarding-school days; dinner follows the natural hour of midday, and you will receive the light collation called "supper" any time between four and the usual cocktail or tea hour. Large hospitals employ expert dietitians. The cost of food varies from $1.00 to $1.25 per day; so, naturally, on this limited amount a patient cannot expect anything very individual, special or fancy to tempt his appetite. The food is wholesome, well cooked and nicely served, though inclined to be on the heavy side.

With obstetrical cases or surgical cases, each patient should provide her own special nurse if she can possibly afford it. With one nurse to a ward, it is impossible for a really sick patient to receive the attention she may need. In obstetrical cases, the special nurse should be engaged in advance, and many young mothers arrange to take the nurse home with them from the hospital. This is wise, because if the hospital is crowded, obstetrical patients are often sent home at the end of five or ten days, and certainly the services of a qualified nurse are needed at this time.

As a patient, your general attitude toward hospitals, doctors and nurses is important. If you "hate" hospitals, are "afraid" of doctors and nurses, "dread" anesthesia, "can't take" medicines, you have two strikes against you! Sounds infantile, but intelligent people often have such phobias, which are hangovers from a badly conditioned childhood.

If there is an operation on your calendar, one of the planned kind and not an emergency, it's smart to ask your doctor what you can do before and afterwards, to get well speedily. Once you are in the hospital, and out of anesthesia, there are many specific ways of speeding your recovery. Your doctor will tell you after he has finished your particular piece of tatting and embroidery.

Remember that food is therapeutic, and don't think you are being dainty and delicate when you pick at the food on your tray or ignore it. Of course, I'll admit the soup may taste like diluted library paste at first, and the solids may resemble sawdust but nevertheless, it's part of your recovery and being a good soldier to eat your rations . . . so tuck it away.

Drink the water the nurse brings you while it is fresh, and don't feel you are doing her a favor. It's your health, not hers. That goes for all fruit juices, too.

As soon as possible, put on make-up, particularly lipstick; and it will improve your morale to wear a ribbon in your hair. Reading is one of the best ways to keep your mind off discomforts; the less you dwell on the pain, the better off you will be. If you make up your mind you are going to be the sickest woman in the Northern Hemisphere, you'll probably come close to that unhappy state. This is what is known as "the law of expectancy" and it seldom fails.

Enlisted men in the Medical Department are called corpsmen, orderlies or ward attendants. They assist the nurses and do most of the cleaning and the menial work connected with the hospital; so don't be surprised when a sprightly young soldier enters your sickroom with your tray or comes in to sweep and dust. Don't ring for the nurse unless it is absolutely necessary for you to call her. She is a busy person.

It is a gracious thing to give the nurse or nurses who have given you special care a small gift though, of course, this is not expected. Some patients prefer to wait until they return home, then invite the nurses to dinner or to some social affair later. Nurses appreciate these little courtesies, as their social life is limited at best, because of their strenuous hours and arduous duties. Why not make the effort to know the nurses on duty at your post? Patients who receive an abundance of flowers usually ask that some be sent to other patients or to the various wards, and this is often done when a patient is leaving a hospital.

Visiting Army Hospitals

There are very definite hours for visiting patients in Army hospitals, and visitors are required to observe the regulations. Morning visits are seldom allowed, owing to the fact that the doctors are making their calls and inspections and the nurses are occupied with changing dressings, giving baths and attending to the general care of the patients. The visiting hours are usually from two to four o'clock in the afternoon and from seven to eight in the evening. In corridors you will see signs requesting "Quiet . . . No Loud Talking," and you are required to observe these rules.

Either send in your name or ask the nurse if it is convenient for you to see the patient, and under no circumstances barge into a sickroom unannounced, as Army people are wont to do sometimes in Army hospitals. Confine your visit to only a few minutes. Doctors prefer that the visitors do most of the talking but keep the conversation in a light, cheery vein. Patients who are recovering from operations, however, often like to relate the grim and gory details as they imagine them; so if you must, listen sympathetically. Avoid launching into a long dissertation on an operation that *you* once had. If the patient is bent on talking about her operation, give in gracefully and listen! After all, she fancies herself the martyr and heroine, and let her enjoy her moment.

It is unwise to ask a patient, "How do you feel?" If she looks well, she will probably resent being told so, and if she looks ghastly, you should be too tactful to tell her so.

If you take flowers, it is well to have the florist arrange them in an inexpensive container, because Army hospitals do not go in for charming flower receptacles, nor do the nurses have time for flower arrangement. Small blooming potted plants are preferable, but even they require care and someone has to water them and set them out of the sickroom at night.

An amusing book, or the best seller of the moment, provided it is not morbid or terribly exacting, would be an acceptable gift to one convalescing. Several of the latest magazines, or a box of sweets or a tempting basket of fruit similar to a bon voyage basket might be welcome. Attractive small jars of jams, marmalades and jellies often give an invalid a lift. Any little novelty, or any gift that shows a kind thought, will be appreciated.

Army hospitals have strict rules concerning visiting maternity patients. Don't ask to have the baby brought in unless the mother and nurse suggest it. It is quite all right to take gifts to the hospital, but if many arrive, something may be lost in the confusion, and it is better to wait until the mother and infant return home. Common sense should warn you never to visit anyone who is ill if you have a cold or are recovering from one.

EMERGENCIES

On the first page of all Army telephone books there is a section listed "EMERGENCY CALLS." . . . "To report a *fire*, call the operator." On a flying field, "*crash*" is listed following *fire*. Call either the operator or the control tower. Next, *crash boat crew*. Surgeon emergency is listed; then follow the numbers for the guard house, plumbers and electricians. Some time when you are waiting for a call, familiarize yourself with these numbers and this information, just in case an emergency should arise.

WILLS

The mentioning of a "last will and testament" is a very ticklish proposition in some families, and yet every well-advised officer should talk over these important matters with his wife. Many wives also make wills—a wise precaution if they have certain bequests they desire to make. Personally, I think that every Army wife should make a will, no matter how little of this world's goods she may have to bequeath. At the time of death, and in the stress and strain of readjustment, often a husband will dispose of, by selling or giving away, valuable possessions that the deceased would wish to be given to particular friends or to members of her own family.

In addition to discussing wills—while it is not a very cheery subject—officers and wives should discuss and come to some decision as to where they wish to be buried. If there are children, family burial plots should be considered. An officer should decide where he wishes to be buried and leave written instructions to this effect. He may make one of three choices, subject to local health laws and sanitary regulations: (a) at the place of his death; (b) at his home;

(c) in a national cemetery. In cases where death of an officer occurs suddenly, it is difficult for his widow to make important decisions when stunned by grief. This extra hardship can be averted if the husband has been thoughtful enough to discuss these important matters during his lifetime.

A will sounds like a formidable instrument, when really it is nothing more than a legal document whereby a person disposes of his property in the manner he wishes.

A *testator* is the person who makes and leaves a will in force at his death. A *codicil* is a postscript or an addition to a will that must be executed with the same legal formalities as the will itself. An *executor* or *executrix* is the person designated by the testator to carry out the provisions of the will. The wife may be chosen as the executrix of the husband's will or vice versa.

The *probating of a will* consists of presenting the will to the office of the registrar of wills in the county where the deceased had his legal residence.

It is well to consult an attorney for the preparation of a will, and if this is not possible, then *never* try to make any but a very simple will without the advice of a lawyer. *A will must be in writing.* The law in most states requires at least three witnesses to a will. The purpose of the subscribing witnesses is that someone will be available who can testify to the authenticity of the testator's signature. Consequently if the persons who have witnessed the will are not available at the time of the testator's death, difficulty will be experienced in probating the will. Should a witness die or be transferred, say, to foreign service, and not be available, the officer should destroy this will and prepare a new one. Since the authenticity of the signatures of the witnesses must be proved in court at the time of probating the will, care should be exercised in selecting witnesses who will be available to simplify this legal requirement. A will which in its execution does not completely conform to the provisions of the statute law of the state in which it is to be probated is invalid, notwithstanding the intention of the testator.

Short Form of a Simple Will

All my estate I devise and bequeath to my wife, for her own use and benefit forever, and I hereby appoint her my executrix, without bond, with full power to sell, mortgage, lease or in any other manner dispose of the whole or any part of my estate.

JAMES THEODORE WORTHING

Dated July 1, 1947

Subscribed, sealed, published and declared by James Theodore Worthing, testator above named, as and for his last will in the presence of each of us, who at his request and in his presence, in the presence of each other, at the same time, have hereto subscribed our names as witnesses this July 1, 1947, at the city of Montgomery, Alabama.

....
Witness   Address
....
Witness   Address
....
Witness   Address

The *marriage* of a man and the *birth of his child*, subsequent to the making of a will by him, have the effect of revoking such a will in many states. A new will must be made.

Joint bank accounts were mentioned in Chapter V. If cash is deposited in the bank in the husband's name only, his wife cannot draw it out of the bank until the will is probated, even though he left it to her by will.

Chapter XII

DEATH AND MILITARY FUNERALS

*May we find a soldier's resting place beneath a
soldier's blow,
With room enough beside our graves, for Benny
Havens, Oh!*

— "Benny Havens"

When the death of a Regular Army officer occurs at or near his
station, or in an Army hospital, the local quartermaster will take
entire charge and arrange for local burial or shipment of the
body (*all*) at government expense.

ARMY people are like one big family, and in times of
sorrow and stress they draw even closer together
and prove themselves wonderful friends. Upon the
death of an officer at an Army post, every consideration is
shown his widow and family, though there is little outward
show of mourning and grief. The commanding officer or
his representative assists in making funeral arrangements,
supervises the conduct of the funeral and takes care of all
official reports. To be relieved of all these trying details
means much to one in sorrow.

Should an officer die under unusual circumstances, such
as in a train wreck, an automobile accident or an airplane
crash outside an Army post or hospital, his widow should
send radiograms or telegrams immediately, as follows:

1. Telegraph the deceased officer's Commanding Officer, stating
   the details and requesting instructions.

341

2. Telegraph the Adjutant General of the Army, War Department, Washington, D.C., giving the deceased's full name, rank and branch of service; date, place and cause of death; cemetery where burial is desired; and request instructions as to burial arrangements.

3. If burial is to be in a national cemetery, the widow should apply by telegraph to the Quartermaster General, War Department, Washington, D.C., for a burial lot in the national cemetery desired.*

Excited though she inevitably is, she should be careful to *give definitely the address where the reply will reach her!*

Should the widow be living on a post, all of these items will be taken care of by either the commanding officer or the post adjutant. On the death of an officer at a military post, the flag is displayed at half-staff and so remains between reveille and retreat, until the last salvo is fired over the grave.

Army Etiquette Toward Persons in Grief

In Army circles, when death occurs, there is no outward display of mourning except in the observance of the military customs of the Service. There are no drawn shades, crepe-hung doors, muffled bells or hushed voices, despite the deep sorrow of the family of the deceased. There is a certain *esprit!* Death is accepted as an inevitable happening, and while everything possible is done to show consideration to the bereaved family, post life goes on in an uninterrupted manner except during the actual funeral services.

Calls

If death is sudden and unexpected, as happens on occasion in the Air Force, then usually a medical officer, accom-

* Reprinted from *The Officers' Guide,* Military Service Publishing Company.

panied by the post chaplain and the commanding officer's wife, or the widow's most intimate friend, go to break the sad news. It is wise for a doctor to be in attendance in case the shock should prove so great that the bereaved wife needs medical attention. No one, except the most intimate friends, should call at a time like this, and even intimate friends should not call unless they can be calm and collected. Acquaintances on a post usually send in a note of sympathy, or some flowers from their garden with a note of sympathy, or simply leave cards. Should you know the bereaved family well, you might offer your services in a note or offer to call, if and when they would like to see you. If there are young children, kind friends often ask if they may take care of them. A very intimate friend might send over tempting food. Persons in deep grief usually feel that food is not for them, yet it is better for them to eat, otherwise physical weakness only adds to their general depression.

A close friend or a servant should be at the door to receive callers, to accept cards and to take messages. Under no circumstances should the bereaved person be expected to carry on a telephone conversation. Army women are so schooled in being practical that when bereaved they often purposely busy themselves with their personal affairs as soon as possible. It is unwise to be alone with one's thoughts at a time like this, and immediately they begin to make necessary adjustments and to work out future plans.

A house funeral or a funeral at the quarters is something that is entirely unheard of in the Army. Whether there are any regulations on this subject I have not been able to find out, but the lying-in-state is always at a funeral establishment, or special arrangements are made for the body to be taken to the post chapel for a short time before the ceremony if that is the wish of the family. Sitting up with the dead is no longer an essential tribute of veneration, unless the lying-in-state is a public ceremony for a deceased personage.

Funeral Directors

The director in charge of a military funeral is one who has obtained a yearly contract with the government; in other words, he has been able to secure the contract by making the lowest bid. Once in a while an unscrupulous racketeer type of director will secure the government contract, and this type of individual is crafty. He will find out to the penny exactly how much insurance the widow will have at her disposal; then he tries to work on her sympathy, and encourages her to invest in the most elaborate and expensive funeral possible. By omitting to give an itemized list of costs, which he knows no one wants to bother with at a time like this, he will order his own automobiles for the funeral procession; he will prevail upon the family to invest an unreasonable amount in a casket (money that, in later years, the poor Army widow may need desperately) and in every way possible increase the expenditures of the funeral. Someone who knows the widow's taste and circumstances, preferably an officer's wife, should go personally to the funeral establishment with the officer in charge and make all arrangements and plans. It is not a pleasant errand, but one that is very necessary. I am glad to say that funeral directors of the type here mentioned are few.

Mourning Clothes

Mourning clothes to be worn to the funeral do not receive the regard and formality of past years. An Army widow looks through her wardrobe, and usually has on hand a plain black dress, suit or coat. If there is any colored trimming, it can be removed. Stores and all dressmaking establishments will always give precedence to mourning orders and will often

open their shops on holidays and after hours to accommodate a customer. Nearly always friends or acquaintances
will offer to lend wraps and veils.

It is a matter of choice and taste whether or not the widow
wishes to wear mourning after the funeral; however, in the
first throes of grief, she should avoid disposing of her entire
wardrobe. If she decides to wear mourning, then many
articles of wearing apparel may be dyed successfully.

Mourning or the emblem of black gives a woman certain
protection when she is in the depths of real sorrow. On the
other hand, a person in mourning should observe all mourning conventions. Conspicuous attire, exaggerated fashion and
boisterous manners are highly inconsistent for one in sorrow.

An officer in mourning may, if he wishes, wear a crepe
sleeve band of from three and a half to four and a half inches
in width on his uniforms and civilian clothes.

CERTIFICATES OF DEATH

A widow should obtain from the doctor in attendance on her
husband at his last illness a *Certificate of Death*. A copy of this
certificate must accompany various claims, including settlement
of commercial insurance policies. She should also ask two officers
who intimately knew her husband, to identify his remains before
the casket is closed. They will then be prepared to furnish the
affidavit required by commercial insurance companies to be
filed with the claim for insurance due.*

MILITARY FUNERALS

Military funerals are divided into four classes, as follows:*

1. With chapel service
2. Without chapel service
3. With graveside service only
4. With ceremony prior to shipment of remains

* Reprinted from *The Officers' Guide*, Military Service Publishing Company.

A full military funeral consists of the following elements, and the procession is formed in the following order:

1. Band
2. Escort appropriate to the grade of the deceased, including bugler and firing party
3. Colors
4. Clergy
5. Caisson and casket bearers
6. Caparisoned horse (if the deceased was mounted)
7. Honorary pallbearers
8. Family
9. Patriotic or fraternal organizations
10. Friends

The selection of honorary pallbearers, if they are desired, is made by the family of the deceased, or its representatives, or the commanding officer. When the procession has been formed, the band and escort are put in march by the commander of the escort. The procession marches slowly to solemn music.

Before the beginning of the service, the funeral escort is formed in lines opposite each other and facing the chapel. Members of the immediate family, relatives and friends of the deceased enter the church before the casket is brought in. The members of the family occupy front seats on the right of the chapel.

If the casket is brought to the church on a caisson, at the proper time the commander of the escort will bring the escort to

ATTENTION . . . and command
1. Present
2. ARMS

At the command the band plays suitable music, the casket is removed from the conveyance by the active pallbearers or casket bearers and carried between the ranks of honorary pallbearers into the chapel. After the casket has been carried into the church, the band ceases playing.

The honorary pallbearers form in two ranks facing each other, and make an aisle from the conveyance to the entrance of the chapel. They occupy front seats on the left of the chapel.

At the completion of the service, the honorary pallbearers follow the chaplain in column of twos as the casket is removed to the entrance of the church. They again form an aisle from the entrance of the chapel to the caisson or hearse. When the casket is placed on the caisson, they, if marching, form a column of files on each side of the caisson, the leading member of each column opposite the front wheels of the caisson. If riding, they enter their automobiles at this time.

When the caisson is halted, the honorary pallbearers form in two columns, facing each other in a line that extends from the caisson to the grave. The six active pallbearers carry the casket between the lines of honorary pallbearers to the grave, and place it on the lowering device. Next, they raise the American flag that has covered the casket, and hold it in a horizontal position, waist high, until the conclusion of taps. The flag is then folded as prescribed in *Army Regulations*, care being taken that it does not touch the ground.

As the casket bearers remove the casket from the caisson, the commander of the escort commands:

1 . . . . Present
2 . . . . ARMS

At the command "Arms," the band plays an appropriate air. When the casket has been placed over the grave, the band ceases playing, and the commander of the escort then commands:

1 . . . Parade
2 . . . REST

The escort executes parade rest with officer and men inclining their heads. At this point the chaplain conducts the graveside service. At the conclusion of the benediction, he moves two steps to the side or rear.

The commander of the escort then commands:

1. Escort, less firing party
2. Present
3. ARMS
4. Firing party
5. FIRE THREE VOLLEYS

The firing party then fires three volleys of blank cartridges, assumes the position of ready, and remains in this position until the conclusion of taps. At the command of "Arms," the bugler takes his position at the head of the grave and sounds taps immediately following the last volley. The entire escort is then brought to order, the band and escort are put in march in quick time by the commander of the escort.

And I mean "quick." The band marches off playing a lively air . . . in the old days something like "For He Was a Jolly Good Fellow"! After all the pomp and ceremony, this may sound disrespectful, but it isn't meant to be in the slightest . . . it is merely a custom of the Service.

The national flag is used to cover the casket at a military funeral, and it is placed lengthwise on the casket with the union at the head and over the left shoulder of the deceased. The flag is never lowered into the grave.

Branch Customs of the Service at Military Funerals

The Cavalry Drill Regulations require that at the funeral of a mounted officer or enlisted man, his horse, in mourning caparison, shall follow the hearse. It is sometimes customary for the boots of the deceased officer to be slung across the saddle, heels to the front, thus signifying that his march is ended. Spurs are put on the boots, hoods to the rear. Sometimes the saber of the deceased is also fastened to the saddle.

At the funeral of an Air Force officer, an escort of planes is timed to fly over the funeral procession. During the graveside services the hum of their motors can be heard as they drone overhead. A V, or five-plane formation, usually has one position unoccupied, signifying the place of their former comrade. This is their salute and farewell to their fellow officer.

At the funeral for all branches except the Air Force, the three volleys are fired from rifles.

Origin of Certain Customs at Military Funerals*

Firing Three Volleys at Military Funerals: In the funeral rites of the Romans, the casting of the earth *three* times upon the coffin constituted the burial. It was also customary among the Romans to call the dead *three* times by name, which ended the funeral ceremony, after which the friends and relatives of the deceased pronounced the word *"Vale"* (farewell) *three times* as they departed from the tomb. Today, when a squad of soldiers fires *three volleys* over a grave, they are, in accordance with this old Roman custom, bidding their dead comrade *Farewell, Three Times!*

* Reprinted from *The Officers' Manual,* by Colonel James A. Moss, George Banta Publishing Company.

Taps

This practice involves a deep-felt sentiment. . . . "Rest in Peace." In the daily life of the soldier the sounding of taps at eleven o'clock at night, signifying "Lights Out," announces the end of the day, implying that the cares and labors of the soldier are ended for that day. So does the sounding of taps at his funeral signify the end of his day . . . his "Rest in peace!" There is no other call so beautiful, no other call that arouses so much sentiment, so many emotions in the soul of the soldier as the sounding of TAPS.

> *Fades the light;*
> *And afar*
> *Goeth day,*
> *Cometh night;*
> *And a star*
> *Leadeth all*
> *To their rest.*

MILITARY FUNERAL WITHOUT CHAPEL SERVICE*

When the services at a chapel are omitted, the escort for a military funeral forms at or near the entrance of the cemetery. The officer in command supervises the transfer of the casket from the hearse to the caisson. During the transfer of the casket, the family and friends remain in their automobiles until the funeral procession is formed. The funeral services proceed then as outlined above.

Graveside Service

All military elements participating in a graveside service should be in position prior to the arrival of the remains. Should troops not be available, or should the family wish to eliminate any military elements, the following will suffice:

* From *The Officers' Guide*, Military Service Publishing Company.

1. Clergy
2. Pallbearers or casket bearers
3. Firing Party
4. Bugler

Ceremony Prior to Shipment of Remains

In cases where the remains of a deceased officer or soldier are moved to a railway station or other point of shipment to a distant place for interment or final disposition, funeral services, modified as necessary, may be carried out. If no further military honors are anticipated at the place of interment, the volleys of musketry may be fired and TAPS sounded at the discretion of the Command Officer and dependent upon local conditions.

Often a military service is held at the funeral establishment, before the body is shipped to its destination. If military honors are anticipated at the place of the final disposition, the firing of volleys and the sounding of taps is omitted.

Cremation Services

In cases where the remains are conducted to a cemetery and the ashes are to be interred with military honors at a later time, the ceremony will consist only of the escort to the crematory. Arms are presented as the remains are borne into the crematory. The firing of volleys and sounding of TAPS are omitted.

In case the funeral ceremony is held at the crematory, and no further military honors anticipated, the volleys may be fired and TAPS may be sounded at the discretion of the Commanding Officer and dependent upon local conditions.

In all phases of the funeral where the cremated remains are carried by hand, one enlisted man will be detailed to carry the receptacle holding the ashes. Four enlisted men will also be detailed as flag bearers. When the receptacle has been placed on the stand before the chancel of the chapel or when placed in the conveyance, the flag will be folded and placed beside the receptacle. Remains are cremated only on written request from relatives.

FLOWERS

In the absence of a funeral director, the officer in charge of the funeral sees to the arrangement of the flowers at the chapel and at the grave. He appoints someone to remove the cards from the floral tributes, with a brief description and a record of each offering. This list is turned over to the family of the deceased after the completion of the funeral.

EXPENSES OF BURIAL . . . MONUMENT OR MARKER

Should circumstances be such that a widow might have to employ a local undertaker, then she should obtain an itemized bill to support proof of expenditures. The limit of reimbursement in the case of a Regular Army officer varies between $85 and $150, depending upon the circumstances. In case of the death of an officer of the National Guard or a Reserve Officer, the amount does not exceed $100 for both burial expenses and transportation.

If the widow or family does not provide a private monument in a national cemetery, the Government erects a white marker headstone of regulation pattern inscribed with the rank, name and branch of the deceased. The widow or family should not contract for a private monument until both the design, material and subscription have been submitted to, and approved by, the Quartermaster General.

FUNERAL ESCORT

Army Regulation 30-920 provides—"that transportation, including return when required, may be issued to a relative or friend, to accompany remains to the home of the deceased or to a national cemetery for interment, when the relative or friend is at the place of death and desires to accompany the remains." With an unmarried officer, a brother officer is usually asked to escort the remains to the home of the deceased, but in the case of a married officer, it is customary for the widow and children to act as an escort to the place of burial.

BREAKING UP THE ARMY HOME

Circumstances determine how long an Army widow may occupy quarters after the death of her husband, but a generous allowance is from two weeks to a month, if the commanding officer of the post approves. Two weeks is usually long enough in which to pack household goods, make adjustments and attend to all official business before clearing a post. However, on foreign service a family may have to wait for a transport or, as the other extreme, a widow may wish to close her affairs, pack and clear the post before leaving for the funeral.

Whatever the circumstance, it is one of the most difficult of undertakings! She feels now that her life with the Army is over. Friends of long standing, years of service together . . . how she will miss them! She will probably find upon going back to the home of her girlhood that she has lost contact with the friends of her youth. Her interests are different, and she finds it very difficult to adjust herself to her home surroundings and environment. This is why so many Army widows settle in Washington, San Antonio and San Diego. Their contemporaries usually retire in or near one of these Army cities, and they long for Service companionship.

If affluent, which few are, the Army widow should travel a bit before deciding on a permanent home. The quartermaster will store a deceased officer's household goods for one year, and in this time she should be able to make a decision. If she is able and capable, her salvation will lie in finding some suitable work. If she has not been trained for a profession, then there is no time like the present for her to equip herself whereby she can make her own livelihood. A special talent of any kind, no matter what, should be developed.

If the desire to be connected with Army personnel is still strong, she can perhaps make herself valuable in some capacity. Today there seem to be more opportunities than ever before. Army hostesses are in demand, and the remuneration is good. All types of positions are available in the civil service field, and the nursing corps is crying for Army and Navy nurses. The widow answers that all positions mentioned here require special training. True, but what worth-while position today doesn't? The Army widow should be in a position, financially, to take courses and work to equip herself. Of course, where there are small children who need a mother's care, that is a different matter. But nature has partially solved the problem here, as the mother must keep so busy that she has little time to think of herself and her loneliness.

After the first break with friends at the last post is made, things should be easier, though there will be days of heartbreak and loneliness when she will long for the companionship of Army friends who sympathize and understand. She should try to interest herself in some worth-while work as quickly as possible, and avoid feeling sorry for herself.

ARMY MUTUAL AID ASSOCIATION

If an officer belongs to the Army Mutual Aid Association, his widow or dependents will need no outside legal help in the filing of necessary claims. Upon official notification of a member's death, benefits are paid without awaiting request;

also papers and instructions regarding other claims are sent out by the association's office. Practically all widows have to ask help in filing and securing their various claims, if they do not receive it from the Army Mutual Aid Association.

Benefits for Widows and Dependents*

Six months' gratuity: This payment is a lump sum equal to six months' base pay, including longevity, flight pay and pay for qualification in the use of arms. Payable to widows and children under 21 years of age and unmarried or otherwise to designated dependent relatives.

Write . . . Finance Office, Army Pay and Mileage Branch, Washington, D.C.

Government Insurance: Not over $10,000 . . . must have affidavits in support of insurance claim (in duplicate).

Write . . . The Director of Insurance, Veterans' Administration, Washington, D.C.

Arrears in Pay: Any unpaid pay and allowances remaining to credit of deceased; to legal heirs, whether dependent or not. Application Standard Form 1055 for officers on active duty. Letters testamentary if claim is filed by executor of estate. Receipted itemized undertaker's bill, if claiming reimbursement of funeral expenses.

Write . . . Claims Division, General Accounting Office, Fifth St. and Judiciary Square, N.W., Washington, D.C.

Pension: Explanations too lengthy and involved to list here.
Write . . . Director, Dependents Claims Service, Veterans' Administration, Washington, D.C.

* From *The Officers' Guide*, Military Service Publishing Company.

In Regard to Pensions:

1. Write in for information in regard to pension claim as soon as possible after an officer's death. Payments do not begin until after all necessary papers to substantiate claim are filed and approved.
2. Death certificate is necessary.
3. Certified copy of public or church record of marriage or other acceptable proof.
4. Birth or baptismal certificate or other acceptable proof of widow or children under 18 years of age.

There are several other benefits and compensations to which widows and dependents of Army officers may be eligible, such as world war bonus or adjusted compensation, aid from the American Legion, aid from United Spanish War Veterans, etc. Information in regard to these compensations will be furnished upon writing to Administrator of Veterans' Affairs, Washington, D.C. Should he not have the information available, he will refer you to the proper authorities.

LETTERS OF CONDOLENCE AND THEIR ANSWERS

There is no set form for a letter of condolence, and some regard it as the most difficult of all letters to write. It should not be, because in it you should say exactly what you feel, regardless of expression. It may be ungrammatical, poorly worded, but so long as it is truly sincere, it will be appreciated. Letters which show admiration of a person's character or fine traits, and express genuine affection, are the most acceptable ones. If you cannot say anything of this nature, don't give false praise to the dead, but write an honest word of sympathy to the bereaved ones. Write as simply as possible, and make it brief. Avoid quoting the Bible or writing platitudes. A person in grief does not feel like reading a long philosophical dissertation! A simple letter of friendship, or a telegram expressing genuine sentiment, showing admiration for the good qualities of the loved one who has gone to the great beyond, is about the greatest comfort that we can offer. A sincere handclasp, without an uttered word, can sometimes speak volumes to a broken heart.

Letters and telegrams of condolence, and floral tributes, should always be answered with a personal note, unless the grief-stricken person is prostrated or for some reason is unable to write a note showing appreciation. In that case, some member of the family should perform this service. Only a line is necessary, and there is no immediate rush about answering. A personal card, with "Thank you for your kind sympathy" written across it, is preferable to the engraved form. This is another type of letter whose message must be sincere and genuine.

Chapter XIII

SERVICE IN WASHINGTON

In the Army there's sobriety
Promotion's very slow—
—"Benny Havens"

SERVICE in Washington carries with it definite rules and regulations in regard to official and social life. Knowledge and observance of even trifling rules of etiquette become vitally necessary there. Army wives, as a rule, look forward to their husbands' having a tour of duty in the nation's capital, regardless of the fact that living conditions may be difficult there. Rents are high, and servantless "cliffdwelling" or apartment life has little appeal; but, to offset this, the Army woman considers the cultural advantages—the theater, concerts and musicales, art groups, interesting lecture courses—that are an integral part of life in Washington.

THE HOUSING SITUATION

How to get a place to live in Washington is the concern of every Army officer ordered to duty in the nation's capital. The Army has set up a Housing Section of the Officers Service Center in the Pentagon Building. It is necessary to register here in order to get a certification of membership in the armed forces, which is necessary in order to place an application for quarters in one of the government housing units.

As these places have long lists of applications, it is usually necessary to wait from three to six months before your name finally reaches the top of the list.

Your next best chance is to contact every housing unit, apartment house and real estate office possible, placing your name on the waiting lists or making periodic calls if they do not have waiting lists. After all, personal contacts are the surest way of obtaining living quarters. At the Sandoz Real Estate Agency ask for Mrs. M. Finn, an Air Force widow, who will be glad to help you with your housing problem.

Keep an eye on the extensive classified ad sections of the Washington *Post* and the *Evening Star*. It is even advisable to insert an ad yourself, as some owners who do not advertise go through the "Apartments and Houses Wanted" section, then select a likely prospect.

It is suggested that officers reporting for duty in the capital arrive with the idea of locating adequate quarters before moving their families or shipping their household goods.

For family accommodations, the two hotels popular with the Army that can be contacted in advance for reservations are the Brighton Hotel at 2133 California Avenue, N.W. and the Martinique Hotel at 1211 16th Street, N.W. Other leading hotels in Washington are the Mayflower, Connecticut Avenue; the Statler, at 16th and K streets; the Shoreham, 2500 Calvert Street; and the Wardman Park, 2660 Woodley Road.

Washington is a city of apartment hotels. The Westchester, at 4000 Cathedral Avenue, and the Kennedy Warren, on Connecticut Avenue, house so many Army personnel that they should have an underground connection with the Pentagon. If you have never seen the famous Pentagon, you have something to which you should look forward. Set aside a day, wear a comfortable pair of shoes, have a definite goal, get a guide and be on your way. If you do not have a destination in mind in the building, then you will walk miles in the enormous labyrinth and will probably backtrack. Multiply this with endless yards of red tape in the way of passes, guards, guides, and interminable delays and you have a picture of the Pentagon during the hush-hush war period.

CALLING

In diplomatic Washington, as in prewar Europe, it is the newcomer's place to make the first call. Army officers should ask for official information in regard to the calling policy in effect. The calling hours are from four to six in the afternoon. In the Army Sunday, unless otherwise specified, is the accepted calling day. Evening calls are not made except between intimate friends or friends of long standing. An afternoon or daytime dress with light gloves is proper attire for the Army woman, while an officer wears dark civil clothes unless otherwise directed. The first social call is made upon the chief of the branch to which your husband belongs. If your branch is large and well represented in Washington, a reception may be given which will take the place of personal calls. For instance, at the first of the fall season, the Air Force gives an evening reception at the Bolling Field Officers' Club which takes the place of calling. Should you arrive after a reception of this kind has taken place, the customary call is made upon the chief of the branch to which your husband belongs.

At an official reception of this sort, the officers wear either the blue dress uniform or special evening dress uniform. However, effective July 20, 1940, the War Department issued Circular 75 to the effect that the wearing of blue and white dress uniforms would be optional. "For the duration of the present emergency," it says, "the wearing of either blue or white dress uniforms is not required of officers serving within continental limits of the United States, including Alaska, except as required for wear at the White House." Officers of the National Guard and the Officers' Reserve Corps are authorized to wear the dress uniforms but are not required to do so.

When an officer is in full evening dress, his lady wears formal evening dress. I need not suggest to you that you should make an effort to look your best at a social function of this sort. Your clothes and the way you wear them create that all-important first impression. You are being introduced into a world of smart society. Owing to the present emergency and the order above quoted, civil evening dress or the field service uniform may be worn on these occasions, except to social functions at the White House. The former or civil evening dress with white tie is quite correct to wear to the White House.

Your second call is upon the Army Chief of Staff, who resides at Fort Myer. The calling days or "at homes" will be announced in the Washington papers, so watch for the announcement and call on the specified day.

Calling at the White House is merely a form of respect, as neither the President nor the President's wife returns the call, or seldom if ever sees the callers.

An amusing story is told about a group of officers who called at the White House. No doubt their respective wives, after vain efforts to prod their husbands to perform their social duties, had given up the idea of calling at the White House. One enterprising officer suggested to three others with whom he was playing golf at the Army and Navy Country Club that they stop by the White House on their way home, and "drop cards." So, in their golf clothes, and armed with the necessary cards, they drew up under the porte-cochere, and one officer alighted from the car to present their cards. It just happened that the First Lady happened to be passing by the entrance, and she insisted that the foursome come in for a chat. Needless to say, they were very much chagrined over their attire and appearance, but with her usual charm and tact, the President's wife rose to the occasion and saved the day for them.

Calls at the White House may be made at the regular calling hours from four to six in the afternoon, but visiting cards may be left at any time. Two of the officer's visiting cards are left, and one of your own. Always write your address on each card. A card index is kept on file. Should your mother be visiting you or living with you, on her visiting card should be written the address, and underneath, "Mother-in-law of Capt. J. T. Worthing" or "Mother of Capt. Worthing." Invitations to the annual Army and Navy reception do not include house guests and are seldom sent to officers below the grade of lieutenant colonel. The annual White House call should be made in the fall.

If calls are made by reserve officers serving on active duty, they should indicate their status by writing "Active Duty" on their cards. It is wise to watch the announcements in the social columns of the various Washington papers so that you do not plan to call on an afternoon when the President's wife might be entertaining at tea.

Calling at the various embassies is optional, but touring the embassies is definitely not in good taste. However, if you have connections, it is quite proper to call. For instance, if you are of direct Swedish descent, you will be welcome at the Swedish Embassy. Calling at the embassies consists of leaving cards, after which you will receive an invitation to tea or to a reception. Friday is the official "day at home" for diplomats. During the season (January until Lent) they receive between four-thirty and seven o'clock.

A nice custom for Army wives is to call on the wives of the chiefs of branches, but this is not required. If your home ties warrant, you might call on the senator and congressman from your home state. A social call now may prove very helpful a few years hence when Junior is trying to get an Academy appointment.

WASHINGTON SOCIETY EDITORS

There is a very definite Army regulation in regard to social items in newspapers. No accounts of social entertainments or parties involving Army personnel are allowed to be given to newspapers. Announcements of engagements and weddings are exceptions, but be very careful and refuse to give a society editor any news regarding parties or social functions. "Arrivals and departures" or "personals," however, are permissible.

INVITATIONS

The President of the United States holds four special receptions every winter. The first, to the diplomatic corps; the second, to the judiciary; the third, to the Army and Navy, and the fourth, to Congress.

The diplomatic reception is said to represent the court society of America and is the most brilliant; but the Army and Navy reception is very colorful and picturesque, with the officers of the Service resplendent in their full-dress uniforms. At the Army and Navy reception you will detect a strange, familiar odor pervading the air, but upon the second whiff you will recognize homely moth balls. Some of the blues are out for their yearly airing. Gold braid is everywhere, there are colorful Service badges and war medals without end, and each branch of the Service is represented by its own colors. Spectacular indeed is the scarlet-lined military cape of the Artillery officer; the Infantry officer's cape lined with sky blue; the Cavalry officer's choice of deep yellow; and the Air Force officer's cape of ultramarine and orange. Each branch of the Service has its own colors, insignia and epaulets to distinguish it. The Naval officers in their full-dress uniforms add to the splendor of the gathering. The Army and Navy wives in formal evening dress are a pleasing addition to the beautiful setting. At an official reception, the officer precedes his lady in going through the receiving line.

If you have left cards at the White House and your husband is above the grade of major, you will receive an engraved invitation asking you to attend this official reception. In the left-hand corner of the invitation will be written "White Tie," meaning formal evening dress, and the full-dress uniform is in order. Should an invitation read "Black Tie," then a tuxedo or blue dress uniform is correct. However, the Army-Navy reception will be strictly formal, and the full-dress uniform is worn.

Any formal invitation should be answered within twenty-four hours, and good form decrees that replies to White House invitations should not be mailed, but should be delivered in person or by messenger. Since the invitation is worded in the third person, your acceptance or regrets also will be worded in the third person, precisely like the invitation. One does not reply to the Army and Navy reception invitation, since this is in the nature of a command. Dinners and musicales require an answer. Should you receive an invitation to lunch or dine at the White House, it amounts to a command, and takes precedence over any other engagement. Invitations to Army-Navy receptions do not include house guests.

The President is addressed as "Mr. President"; the First Lady as "Mrs. ...." A letter or note should be addressed:

To the President:
The President
  The White House

To the President's wife:
Mrs. ....
  The White House

To both:

The President and Mrs. ....
  The White House

You don't talk to the President unless addressed by him.

Junior officers and their wives are sometimes invited to White House teas or musicales. The latter are held after dinner at ten o'clock in the evening. To an afternoon musicale, an Army wife wears a daytime dress and hat, while her husband wears either uniform or a dark civilian suit. To an evening White House musicale, an officer may wear uniform or a tuxedo, and his wife is attired in a simple dinner dress.

PROTOCOL

"Precedence," and "who ranks whom," is the Nemesis of every Washington hostess, whether in official or social circles. You can play safe by submitting your guest list to the chief of protocol at the State Department, whose office knows all the answers.

In official circles there are a few points necessary for the Army hostess to know. The Secretary of War ranks the Secretary of the Navy, and the Chief of Staff of the Army ranks the Chief of Naval Operations (by one seat or file).

A major general, rear admiral and major general (commandant of the Marine Corps) rank equally but should be seated according to length of service. The reason for the War Department's ranking the Navy Department dates back to Revolutionary days. The Army was created before the Navy.

Equivalent Ranks of Officers of the Army and the Navy

General of the Army	Admiral of the Fleet
General	Admiral
Lieutenant general	Vice admiral
Major general	Rear admiral
Brigadier general	Rear admiral
Colonel	Captain
Lieutenant colonel	Commander
Major	Lieutenant commander
Captain	Lieutenant (senior grade)
First lieutenant	Lieutenant (junior grade)
Second lieutenant	Ensign

How to Distinguish the Rank of Army and Navy Officers

General of the Army	five stars
General	four stars
Lieutenant general	three stars
Major general	two stars
Brigadier General	one star
Colonel	silver eagle
Lieutenant colonel	silver leaf
Major	gold leaf
Captain	two silver bars
First lieutenant	one silver bar
Second lieutenant	one gold bar
Admiral of the Fleet	one 2-inch stripe with four ½-inch stripes above it
Admiral	one 2-inch stripe with three ½-inch stripes above it

Vice admiral . . . . .one 2-inch stripe with two ½-inch stripes above it

Rear admiral . . . . .one 2-inch stripe with one ½-inch stripe above it

Captain . . . . .four ½-inch stripes

Commander . . . . .three ½-inch stripes

Lieutenant commander . . . . .two ½-inch stripes with one ¼-inch stripe between them

Lieutenant (senior grade) . . .two ½-inch stripes

Lieutenant (junior grade) . .one ½-inch stripe with one ¼-inch stripe above it

Ensign . . . . .one ½-inch stripe

Air Force ranks and designations are the same as those in the Army.

The Marine Corps is part of the Navy, but the rank is the same as that of the Army.

Each arm and service has distinctive insignia and different colors. Enlisted men wear hat cords prescribed for their individual branch. Officers wear distinctive branch colors in uniforms and in cape linings.

Branch	Color	Insignia
General Staff Corps	Gold and black	Coat of arms on a star
Adjutant General's Dept.		Dark blue shield
Inspector General's Dept.	Dark blue and white	Crossed sword and fasces with wreath
Judge Advocate General's Dept.	Dark blue and light blue	Crossed sword and pen wreathed
Quartermaster Corps	Buff	Eagle surmounting wheel with crossed sword and key
Medical Dept.	Maroon and white	Caduceus
Engineer Corps	Scarlet and white	Castle
Ordnance Dept.	Crimson and yellow	Shell and flame
Finance Dept.	Gray and yellow	Diamond
Air Corps	Ultramarine and orange	Wings and propeller
Signal Corps	Orange and white	Crossed signal flags with flaming torch

Chemical Warfare Service	Blue and yellow	Benzol ring and crossed retorts
Chaplains	Black	Latin cross
Cavalry	Yellow	Crossed sabers
Field Artillery	Scarlet	Crossed cannon with red oval projector
Infantry	Light blue	Crossed rifle
Militia Bureau	Dark blue	Crossed fasces and eagle
Armored Command	Green and white	Tank
Tank Destroyer Forces	Golden orange and black	75 mm. gun
Transportation Corps	Brick red and yellow	Winged wheel

The newcomer into the Army may wonder about the Service medals and badges and decorations worn on state occasions by officers in uniform. These decorations are authorized by the government in recognition of an outstanding act of heroism or some especially noteworthy service rendered by individuals. Deeds of high valor on the field of battle have been rewarded in all wars. In case of posthumous awards, presentation of the decoration is made to the next of kin.

The *Medal of Honor* is the highest and most rarely awarded decoration conferred by the United States and was established by act of Congress in 1862. It is awarded for gallantry and intrepidity at the "Risk of Life Above and Beyond the Call of Duty." It entitles enlisted men to two dollars per month additional pay.

The medal is a five-pointed star, surrounded by a laurel wreath, suspended by a bronze star bearing the inscription "For Valor" and surrounded by an eagle. The ribbon on which it is suspended is light blue, with thirteen white stars. Whenever practicable the recipient of this decoration is ordered to Washington, and the presentation is made by the President of the United States.

The *Distinguished Service Cross* was instituted by Congress in 1918. It is awarded for "Extraordinary Heroism in

Military Operations Against an Armed Enemy." In rank of awards it is number two. It entitles an enlisted man to two dollars per month additional pay.

It is a cross of bronze with an eagle on the center. Below the eagle is a scroll bearing the inscription "For Valor." Its ribbon is a broad band of blue, bordered on both edges by narrow bands of red and white.

The *Distinguished Service Medal*, dating also from 1918, is awarded for "Extraordinary Heroism in Military Operations Against an Armed Enemy." It entitles an enlisted man to two dollars additional pay.

The coat of arms of the United States in bronze, surrounded by a circle of dark blue enamel, bears the inscription "For Distinguished Service" and the year of award. The ribbon is composed of bands of scarlet, a stripe of dark blue, a band of white, a stripe of dark blue and a band of scarlet.

The *Legion of Merit* is awarded for "Exceptionally Meritorious Conduct in the Performance of Outstanding Services." The design of the Legion of Merit, developed from the great seal of the United States, was approved by Congress in 1782 and established by George Washington. Awarded to members of foreign friendly nations.

The front of the badge is a five-pointed American star of heraldic form in red and white enamel, centered with a constellation of the thirteen original stars on a blue-enameled field breaking through a circle of clouds.

The *Silver Star* is given for gallantry in action and carries no additional pay for enlisted men.

The design is a silver star superimposed on a bronze star, the rays of the two coinciding.

The *Distinguished Flying Cross* is Awarded for "Heroism or Extraordinary Achievement while Participating in Aerial

Flight." It entitles enlisted men to two dollars per month additional pay.

On a bronze cross pattée is a four-bladed propeller. On the reverse side are engraved the grade, name, organization of the recipient with the date of the award.

The *Soldier's Medal* was instituted in 1926. This decoration is given for "Heroism Not Involving Conflict with an Enemy." It carries two dollars additional pay for enlisted men.

On a bronze octagon is displayed an eagle standing on a fasces between groups of stars and above a spray of leaves. On the reverse side is engraved, "Soldier's Medal, for Valor." The ribbon is composed of two outside stripes in blue, with the center containing thirteen white and red stripes of equal width.

The *Bronze Star Medal* was authorized February 4, 1944, by President Roosevelt. It is awarded for "Heroic Achievement against an Enemy not involving Aerial Flight." It carries no extra pay.

The bronze star has superimposed on it a smaller and raised bronze star, the center lines of all rays of both stars coinciding. On the reverse side is the inscription "Heroic Meritorious Achievement." The ribbon is of Old Glory red with a one-eighth inch vertical stripe of royal blue in the center.

The *Air Medal* is given for "Meritorious Achievement While Participating in Aerial Flight." It carries no extra pay. This medal is given in cases where the act of meritorious service does not warrant the award of the D.F.C.

This is a beautiful decoration. Pendant from a ribbon striped with the Air Corps blue and gold is a fleur-de-lis which surmounts a compass rose. In relief on the rose is a swooping American eagle with lightning bolts clutched in his talons.

The *Purple Heart* is given for "Wounds Received in Action Against an Enemy of the U.S." It carries no extra pay.

Originally established by George Washington, it was discontinued for many years but was re-established in 1932. On a purple heart of enamel within a bronze border is a profile head of Washington in relief in military uniform; above is his coat of arms between two sprays of leaves in green enamel. The ribbon is purple with white edges.

There are other badges and decorations, too numerous to mention, for the different branches of the Service. For instance, the Combat Infantryman Badge entitles enlisted men to ten dollars per month additional pay. The Expert Infantryman Badge entitles an enlisted man to five dollars per month additional pay. The Medical Corps has its own awards for courageous service for men on duty with Infantry units.

Medals go back to the Indian campaigns and to the Civil War. While few people know them all, it is quite a compliment if you recognize those of World War II. Certainly, you should be able to recognize those earned by your husband, and to know a bit of their history, also the order in which they are worn.

Undoubtedly there will come a time when you will have to serve as valet and you should know how to arrange your better half's insignia and decorations. It isn't easy, and what those sharp pins and rugged edges won't do to a manicure! Be sure to collect for your services: this one should rate a dinner at your favorite restaurant "come the *first* of the month." Don't become too expert at this valet service or you will have the job permanently!

Many wives are hard put to find a way or a place in which to display their husband's war decorations. Army men do not care for an ostentatious display, and seldom like them set under glass in coffee tables or on trays. Believe it or not, I have seen this done! The cleverest medals case I have seen was an old-fashioned spool case, the kind small department stores used to have for spools of thread. The drawers were relined with purple velvet, and the decorations and many beautiful awards of foreign countries were nothing short of regal in their smart setting. The case rested on a table in the library, the medals out of sight unless there was reason to display them.

Service medals worn indicate that the individual participated in the particular campaign, such as Spanish War Service Medal or Mexican Border Service Medal.

Badges worn on the uniform include aviation badges and badges for marksmanship, gunnery and swordsmanship.

Service ribbons and miniature replicas may be worn on prescribed uniforms on certain official occasions.

The Medal of Honor is worn pendant from the ribbon placed around the neck, outside the white collar and inside the coat collar. It is an honor to be authorized to wear decorations and medals, and under no circumstances should they be worn by anyone except the rightful owner.

INFORMATION IN REGARD TO WASHINGTON

As soon as your husband recieves his orders to Washington, remind him to write to the War College Commissary and apply for commissary privileges, also to the Fort Myer Laundry for laundry privileges, as they both have long waiting lists.

Clubs

There are many private clubs in Washington at which a great many Service people do their entertaining. Some of these are:

The Army and Navy Club: Officers find it convenient to lunch there. The cocktail lounge is smartly decorated. Aviation dioramas cover the walls, and the furniture is modernistic. Ladies are welcome to dine at the club, but the lobby, lounge, library and writing rooms are restricted to the use of officers. By far the most famous Army and Navy dish is curry. Always, on Mondays, a curry is featured at the club, though it can be ordered à la carte at any time. It is the same recipe presented by one Gil Allen, an Army officer returned from the Philippines in the early days of the empire. 'Tis wonderful! Try it, on your next visit to the club.

The Army and Navy Country Club: Located three miles from Washington. A popular club for Service people as it affords swimming, a good golf course, weekly dances and many social advantages.

The Columbia Club: Convenient for officers and their families residing in the residential sections of northwest Washington. Splendid golf course.

Kenwood Country Club: Has a popular golf course.

Washington Golf and Country Club.

Chevy Chase Country Club: Expensive, and has a long waiting list.

Chapter XIV

CAMP FOLLOWERS OF THE U. S. ARMY

Army life is like a three-ringed circus, and Army women must necessarily be versatile. Just being a good equestrienne isn't enough either in the Army or in the circus; in addition, the rider must learn to take the jumps. Sometimes they are easy little low barriers. At other times they are the five-foot-six variety with a blazing arch or a water hazard thrown in. This is when the Army woman shows her mettle, for which she will receive no silver trophy, no blue or red ribbon, but all in all she will gain a sense of satisfaction and achievement. If combined with a lot of fun, this adds up to that elusive thing everyone is seeking—happiness.

Army women laugh a lot, and they have a good deal of fun, believe it or not. Few of them would change places with their sisters who have permanent homes, definite systems and plans of schooling for their children, although it must be admitted that the "stable, well-ordered life" looks mighty attractive to the Army woman upon occasion. For instance, when you are expecting the colonel and his wife to dinner, and the maid walks out on the morning of the dinner party; the baby is teething; by some freak chance the water supply is turned off for the morning; the commissary order is late arriving; and friend husband unexpectedly brings home a visiting classmate and becomes so engrossed in his duties as host that he is worse than no help at all.

What does the Army wife do? Her first impulse may be "to go over the hill," but she doesn't. How she wishes she

374

could afford to take the entire party to the club! But she can't; so she hurriedly changes her plans and unsets the table that was planned for a seated dinner; and to include the "dear classmate" she switches to a buffet supper. By this time several of her friends have arrived at the scene of action, and things start happening.

All the girls pitch in . . . and are they expert at this sort of thing! One takes over the housecleaning, tactfully eliminating the husband and guest by inviting them over for lunch with her husband. Another offers to take care of the infant, and removes him from the scene of action. Others offer extra silver and linen, arrange the flowers and prepare the dinner. Thank goodness, the maid baked a ham the day before, and the aspic salad is made. The best culinary expert of the group prepares the potatoes au gratin and bakes a cake, the ice cream is sent in from town, and the hostess finds herself with absolutely nothing to do by noon but relax, take a siesta, a refreshing bath, and then, in her best evening outfit, greet her guests. The buffet supper goes off beautifully. The colonel and his wife compliment the young hostess, and a high mark goes on her unwritten efficiency report. Where could a situation like this be handled without this wonderful camaraderie and neighborly spirit?

The circus rider must take the jumps now and then, and must even jump through hoops and stand on her head. Just so must the Army wife take whatever comes and be able to adjust herself to rapid changes of environment and climate, meeting different peoples, leaving family and old friends, doing without accustomed luxuries; she must be able to "take it." All of this calls for courage, tact, self-control, philosophy, tolerance and, above all, a sense of humor. Without the last-mentioned trait, she is *sunk*.

It takes a very keen sense of humor and "youth" to live gracefully in a cantonment building at Fort Sill, Oklahoma,

ironically known as "The Love Nest." It may or may not
still be occupied today by struggling young lieutenants and
their brides, but on a sizzling summer day that I remember,
with the thermometer climbing to 115 degrees and an Army
range at full steam in the seven-by-nine boxlike kitchen, the
china doorknobs grew so hot that one had to use a homely
pot holder to open the kitchen door.

Older Army women love to get together and reminisce.
They tell about certain transport trips and rehash old stories
of former good times. Each storyteller is a story in herself.
One will relate tales of the old days in Mindanao, when
Army families lived in nipa shacks. Laughingly, this charming matriarch will tell you that the floors of rough planks
with wide cracks between them were very convenient—for
sweeping; that housekeeping, with native servants to wait
on one, was almost Edenlike. The modern conveniences in
the way of plumbing facilities were something else, however. Toilets were of the Chic Sale variety, and the bath-
rooms consisted of a cubicle with a sliding nipa door. A
square oilcan with nail holes punched in the bottom was
suspended by a rope, and after soaping oneself, the next
gesture was to leap under the water can, pull the rope and
let the homemade shower descend. The ablutions were
finally completed after several soapings, leapings and pull-
ings of cords. No need to worry about the water, since the
floor was a very flimsy affair of split bamboo widely enough
spaced for the water to run through.

The nipa houses bordering the jungle were built on stilts,
and at night the sentries made their inspections with lan-
terns, peering under the quarters and hoping not to find two
fiery eyes staring out at them. Unfriendly Moros were a
menace not to be taken lightly, either. Life was filled with
adventure. You may be assured that these thrilling stories
lose nothing in hair-raising quality by repetition. One well-

known story of the old days in the Philippines shows the dependence of enlisted men and the officers' families on each other.

There was the morning after a sleepless night caused by an abscessed tooth. What does a lieutenant's wife do about such things when no dentist is available? Why, she tells the lieutenant, of course, and he tells the sergeant, and the sergeant gets a corporal, five privates, four mules and an old escort wagon. A big wicker chair full of pillows is fastened in the wagon, and the lieutenant's wife, with her tiny baby, is lifted into the chair! The grinning corporal establishes himself on the ruthless edge of the wagon side in order that he may hold the paper Chinese umbrella over the Madonna in the chair. The men are all strapped about with 45's and plenty of ammunition. The whole company of soldiers turns out in the tiny quadrangle shouting "The Spirit of 49." So amidst cheers and laughter, off the "uncovered" wagon swings, jouncing its way up the trail to the base hospital twenty-five miles away.

The average Army women of thirty years' service at the side of her husband has lived an everchanging role: with or without servants, with or without social contacts, with or without conveniences, with or without her personal friends, and nearly always financially overburdened. She has lived in foreign countries, in small towns and in large cities, on tiny posts out in the great open spaces and on huge posts near metropolitan centers. She knows firsthand the rigors of an Alaskan winter, the humidity and heat of a Panamanian summer. She has been through disaster: fire, flood, tornado, typhoon and earthquake.

She prefers the luxury of an electric range, but she can manage about as well (with a few epithets) with green wood and a smoking G.I. stove or a campfire. She is equally at home in a general's quarters or a Quonset hut. Even in the Quonset she manages a feminine touch by making up a comfortable bed, and ten to one she will have thought to include a mosquito net, and will hang up a mirror and not forget to set the alarm clock.

She can play the Lady or Judy O'Grady . . . she can eat hamburgers from a counter at bus stops or Russian caviar with the general . . . she can entertain foreign diplomats as easily as intimate friends . . . she enjoys travel, whether by freighter or clipper, by bus or streamliner . . . she is at home eating bird's-nest soup in China or dancing the rumba in Rio. In other words, she is a cosmopolite.

Tension and nervous strain there are in this kaleidoscopic life, and much to discourage and dismay, but at least there aren't many dull moments. The Army woman learns that she must meet each new situation with philosophy, and that adaptability to change strengthens her fiber, stimulates her mentality and satisfies something in her soul. She remains young at heart, her life is well rounded by contacts with all types and kinds of people and she herself is interesting.

The Regular Army Wife*

There's a song for the General gray and grave,
    With his campaign successfully planned;
There's a song for the Colonel and Major brave
    And the Captains of their command;
For the young Lieutenant just starting in,
    For the Sergeant and Corporal, too,
For thousands of Regular Army men
    A-passing in grand review.
But there's never a song for the battles won
    Afar from war's red strife,
Nor a wreath of laurel for brave deeds done
    By the Regular Army Wife.

                    —Jane Comstock

* Reprinted by permission of the author.

APPENDIX

SOCIETY OF THE DAUGHTERS OF THE UNITED STATES ARMY

This organization was founded in January, 1928, at Fort Benning, Georgia, by Eugenia Bradford Roberts, wife of General George D. Roberts. Mrs. Roberts issued invitations to all of the Army daughters or granddaughters at Fort Benning, and at this informal tea the society was organized. There were twenty-two present at the first meeting, but from that small nucleus, chapters have been formed at various posts and the membership has grown to well over a thousand members.

The council meetings are now held at the homes of the different national officers.

Eligible for membership are daughters, granddaughters, stepdaughters and adopted daughters of commissioned officers of the Regular Army, upon reaching the age of sixteen years. The initiation fee is one dollar and the annual dues are seventy-five cents.

The objectives of the D.U.S.A. are: to carry on the ideals, traditions and customs of the Service; to support worthy causes and patriotic activities; to participate loyally in the social activities of the military communities in which the members are located; to renew old acquaintances and cement new friendships; and to preserve the identity of Regular Army officers' daughters who have married or who have lost touch with the Army on entering civil life.

Newly organized chapters often meet at first for purely social purposes, but after they are organized they carry out some very worth-while projects. Funds are raised by staging style shows, arranging bridge benefits, rummage sales and carnivals. This money is spent to the best advantage in assisting soldiers' families, in supplying milk for undernourished children on the posts, in furnishing layettes and in spreading Christmas cheer to the poor. The New York Harbor chapter recently furnished the Girl Scout house at Governor's Island. The Schofield Barracks chapter in Hawaii specializes in layettes and has recently raised sufficient money to buy an incubator for the post hospital. They are planning a D.U.S.A. room in the women's ward of the station hospital now.

THRIFT SHOPS

On many posts there is an independent local Army Woman's Guild. The guild is not an associated charity organization, nor is there any red tape connected with its loans and gifts. The needy persons simply come and ask for aid; and if and when they are able, they usually offer to pay back loans.

The commanding general's wife is the honorary president, and the board is composed of the wives of the senior officers of the command. One of their activities is the Thrift Shop, and by this means a great portion of their working fund is raised.

Many of the larger posts, such as Fort Benning, Fort Leavenworth and Fort Sam Houston, have active and profitable Thrift Shops, but Schofield Barracks in Hawaii maintains the largest one of all. It is a glorified Woman's Exchange, the only difference being that you will see bachelors shopping for used furniture, and departing officers bringing in anything from a mouse trap to a kiddie coop. Truly, the Thrift Shop handles everything from boots, uniforms, civilian clothes, automobile tires, kitchen utensils, dishes, glassware, all sorts of electrical appliances, rugs, dresses, children's apparel, to all kinds and types of furniture. Some of the loveliest merchandise is brought in by brides.

Young brides often prefer modernistic bedroom furniture to the lovely old four-poster from home. So they trade what is a "white elephant" to them, along with other wedding presents they consider useless. Consequently some truly lovely buys in the way of antiques are to be found in the Thrift Shop.

Each article is taken in on consignment, and when sold at the owner's price 10 per cent is claimed by the Thrift Shop, and this sum is turned over to the Woman's Guild for charity.

ARMY RELIEF SOCIETY

The Army Relief Society's headquarters are located at 140 West 57th Street, New York City, but there is usually a local chapter at each post. The aid it gives is limited to dependent widows and minor orphan children of deceased officers and enlisted men of the Regular Army.

The funds are raised by various kinds of benefits, or if preferred, officers and enlisted men contribute a certain portion of their pay (often a day's pay, if they can afford it) to this worthy cause.

AMERICAN RED CROSS

Everyone is familiar with the great work of the Red Cross both in peacetime and in times of war and distress. The Red Cross "looks beyond race, creed and cause, and sees in the wounded, only a sufferer to be made less miserable."

Army women are particularly active in this national organization, and give of their talents and services willingly wherever they are stationed. Also, Army officers and their families feel a moral obligation to help the Red Cross by donations of money and service to the best of their ability.

In the chapter house in Washington, D.C., one sees Army women working industriously in the Production Corps. Some knit, sew or make surgical dressings; others of unusual talent serve as linguists in the Translation Division, while those experienced in Braille transcribe material for the blind. The Administrative, Canteen, Motor Corps, and Staff Assistance Corps also have diligent workers among Army women. Practically every Army post has its own Red Cross unit or branch, depending on the size of the post.

ARMY AIR FORCES AID SOCIETY

"In March, 1942, the Army Air Forces Aid Society was incorporated in the District of Columbia, to collect and hold funds and to relieve distress of personnel of the Army Air Forces and their dependents, including dependents of honorably retired or discharged or deceased personnel thereof, to provide for their education, and to secure employment for honorably retired or discharged personnel and their dependents and the dependents of deceased personnel."—Captain Benjamin J. Grant, in an article from *Air Force*

Civilians as well as military personnel are eligible for membership. The director of the society, General Howard C. Davidson, is active in establishing an Air Forces Aid chapter on each military airfield. On March 1, 1946, it was designated by the War Department as the official relief agency of the Army Air Forces.

There is a Memorial Division of the A.A.F. Aid Society, and on the Memorial Roll hundreds of names have been written in loving memory. The gifts that established these memorials came from families and friends, from bombardment groups and squadrons overseas, from officers' wives' clubs and from officers and men at Army air bases in this country. All of these individuals and organizations wanted to pay a more lasting tribute than a gift of flowers to the bereaved family. They wished to establish a memorial that would live throughout the years in the work of the Army Air Forces Aid Society.

THE ARMY AND NAVY MEMORIAL AID SOCIETY

This society furnishes relief or assistance in the form of loans or donations of funds to honorably discharged enlisted men and their families, to retired officers and enlisted men and their families and to the dependents of deceased officers and enlisted men of the Army, the Navy and the Marine Corps. Its rules are much more liberal than those of the other Army and Navy relief organizations, and thus it extends to many cases that cannot be reached by other societies.

The Army and Navy Memorial Aid is supported by voluntary contributions, which may be in the form of dues of one dollar a year or more, or in the form of memorial gifts. Such gifts are often made instead of sending flowers to a funeral.

When a memorial gift is made, a card announcing that fact,

with the name of the donor, is sent by the secretary to the family of the deceased, and the name of the person so commemorated is entered in the Memorial Roll which the society keeps as a permanent record. The present secretary is Miss Julia Fiebeger, 2318 19th Street, N.W., Washington, D.C.

BIBLIOGRAPHY

Boots and Saddles, Elizabeth Custer, *Harper & Brothers,* New York, 1885

Reminiscences of a Soldier's Wife, Ellen McGown Biddle, J. B. Lippincott Co., Philadelphia, 1907.

Vanished Arizona, Martha Summerhayes, Salem Press Co., Salem, Mass., 1911.

Tenting on the Plains, Elizabeth A. Custer, Harper & Brothers, New York, 1895.

With Custer's Cavalry, Katherine Gibson Fougera, Caxton Printers, Ltd., Caldwell, Idaho, 1940.

Old Days in the Old Army, Lydia Spencer Lane.

Following the Guidon, Elizabeth Custer.

Following the Flag, Alice Sargent, P. N. Barnett, Sidney, N.S.W., 1920.

History of the United States Army, William Addleman Ganoe, D. Appleton and Co., New York, 1924.

Army Letters from an Officer's Wife, Frances Roe, D. Appleton and Co., New York, 1909.

The Officers' Guide (no author), Military Service Publishing Co., Harrisburg, Pa., 1st edition, 1930, and 4th edition, 1941.

Officers' Manual, Col. James A. Moss, George Banta Publishing Co., Menasha, Wisconsin (1917?).

Customs of the Service, Col. James W. Powell, The Franklin Hudson Publishing Co., Kansas City, Missouri, 1905.

Army Posts and Towns, Charles J. Sullivan, Free Press Interstate Publishing Co., Fort Thomas, Kentucky, 1926-1935.

West Point Today, Kendall Banning, Funk and Wagnalls Co., New York and London, 1937.

The Fleet Today, Kendall Banning, Funk and Wagnalls Co., New York and London, 1940.

Annapolis Today, Kendall Banning, Funk and Wagnalls Co., New York and London, 1938.

Ups and Downs of an Army Officer, George A. Armes, Washington, D.C., 1900.

Who's Who in the Regular Army, John McDonald Thompson, San Antonio Printing Co., San Antonio, Texas, 1925.

Etiquette, Emily Post, Funk and Wagnalls Co., New York and London, 1937.

Let's Set the Table, Elizabeth Lounsberry, Funk & Wagnalls Co., New York and London, 1938.

Social Washington, Anne Squire, Washington, D.C., 1929.

Naval Customs, Lt. Commander Leland P. Lovette, George Banta Publishing Co., Menasha, Wisconsin, 1934.

Maid Craft, Lita Price and Harriet Bonnet, Bobbs-Merrill Co., Indianapolis and New York, 1937.

Someone to Dinner, Winifred Hope Thomson, Cobden-Sanderson Co., London, 1935.

Etiquette, Lillian Eichler, Garden City Publishing Co., New York, 1939.

Good Manners and Bad, Hugh Scott, Ernest Benn, Ltd., London, 1930.

Profits from Courtesy, Mary Alden Hopkins, Doubleday, Doran and Co., Garden City, New York, 1937.

The Young Hostess, Beatrice Pierce, Farrar, New York, 1938.

Business of the Household, C. W. Taber, J. B. Lippincott Co., Philadelphia, 1926.

To Market, to Market, Margaret Turner Gamble and Margaret Porter, Bobbs-Merrill Co., Indianapolis and New York, 1940.

So You're Going to Get Married, Bell Wiley, J. B. Lippincott Co., Philadelphia, 1938.

Housewifery, Lydia Ray Balderston, J. B. Lippincott Co., Philadelphia, 1936.

The Shopping Guide, E. B. Weiss, Whittlesey House, McGraw-Hill Book Co., New York, 1937.

Three Years Old, Frances W. Danielson and Jessie E. Moore, The Pilgrim Press, Boston, 1935.

The Curriculum Records of the Children's School, Bureau of

Publications, National College of Education, Evanston, Illinois, 1932.

Child Training, V. M. Hillyer (Head Master of the Calvert School), D. Appleton and Co., New York, 1915.

How to Be an Army Officer, William H. Baumer, Jr., Robert M. McBride and Co., New York, 1940.

Adventures in Alaska, S. Hall Young, Fleming H. Revell Co., New York and Chicago, 1919.

Travels in Alaska, John Muir, Houghton Mifflin Co., Boston, 1915.

Public Education in the Territories and Outlying Possessions, Pamphlet No. 16, Advisory Committee on Education, U. S. Government Printing Office, Washington, D.C., 1939.

Songs of the Army Flyers, courtesy of the Order of Daedalians.

The Book of Navy Songs, The Trident Society, Doubleday, Page and Co., Garden City and New York, 1926.

Songs of the U.S.M.A., Lt. Philipps Egner and Fred C. Mayer, Egner & Mayer, West Point.

The Blood of the Shark, Beatrice Ayer Patton, Paradise of the Pacific Press, Honolulu, 1936.

Soldiers in the Sun, William Thaddeus Sexton, Military Service Publishing Co., Harrisburg, Pa., 1939.

When You Go to Hawaii, Townsend Griffiths, Riverside Press, Cambridge, Mass., 1930.

The Bum Bugler, Jane Comstock, The Mellen Associates, Honolulu, 1926.

Army Directory (published semiannually), War Department, Washington, D.C.

Thomason Act, regulations quoted from *Army Regulations*, and regulations quoted from special pamphlets printed by the Adjutant General's Department, U.S. Army, Washington, D.C.

Army Register and *Army & Navy Journal*.

Various fashion and travel articles appearing in *Vogue, Harper's Bazaar, House and Garden, House Beautiful, Fortune, Mademoiselle, Seventeen, The Bride*.

Traveler from Tokyo, John Morris, Sheridan House, New York, 1942.

Carribbean Cruise, John Vandercook, Reynal & Hitchcock, New York, 1938.

The Immortal Wife, Irving Stone, Doubleday & Co., New York, 1943.

Your Child, Frances Bruce Strain, D. Appleton-Century Co., New York, 1943.

Hold Your Man, Veronica Dengel, Coward-McCann, New York, 1945.

Personality Unlimited, Veronica Dengel, John C. Winston, Philadelphia, 1943.

Entertaining Is Fun, Dorothy Draper, Doubleday & Co., New York, 1944.

INDEX